The 33rd

DREXEL UNIVERSITY
College of
Arts and Sciences

Managing Editor	Gail D. Rosen
Senior Editor	Kathleen Volk Miller
Layout Editor	William Rees
Graphic Design	Courtney Mattson
Editorial Assistant	Frances Canupp
Editorial Co-op	Brittany O'Gilvie
	Ali Ziabakhsh-Tabari
Student Interns	Taya Stevens-Allen
	Jorge Fortin Mejia
	Sarah Goldberg
	Madena Kusi
	Bryce Mick
	Sarah Miller
	Fernando Lopez-Pabon
	Brittany O'Gilvie
	Halle Porter
	Caroline Rabuano
	Tamia Santiago
	Ali Ziabakhsh-Tabari

Sponsors

Drexel University
The College of Arts and Sciences at Drexel University
The Department of English and Philosophy at Drexel University

Dr. Maria T. Schultheis, Interim Dean, College of Arts and Sciences, Drexel University
Dr. J. Roger Kurtz, Department Head, English and Philosophy, Drexel University

The 33rd Volume 12
Drexel University
Department of English and Philosophy
3141 Chestnut Street
Philadelphia, PA 19104
www.5027mac.org

Cover photo (front) by Jordan Franklin
Cover photo (back) by Kyle Prekeris

The 33rd is published once a year.

Submissions are open in the spring, winter, and fall terms of each academic year. Manuscripts must be submitted as an e-mail attachment (MS Word). Look to www.5027mac.org for submission guidelines.

ISBN 978-1-7324500-1-1

Deepest thanks to: Dr. Maria T. Schultheis; Dr. J. Roger Kurtz; Dr. Ira Taffer; all the judges from the Drexel Publishing Group Creative Writing Contest (Benjamin Barnett, Ken Bingham, Lisa DiMaio, Gabriella Ibieta, Henry Israeli, Elizabeth Kimball, Rachel Kolman, Deirdre McMahon, Harriet Millan, Jill Moses, Don Riggs, Donna Rondolone, Doreen Saar, Fred Siegel, Robert Wetherill); the Drexel Publishing Group Essay Contest (Stacey Ake, Valerie Booth, Meghan Butry, Zoltan Buzas, Evangelia Chrysikou, Tim Fitts, Cassandra Hirsch, Craig McClure, Karen Nulton, Sheila Sandapen, Fred Siegel, Scott Stein, Fengqing Zhang); the Literature Essay Contest (Gabriella Ibieta, Miriam Kotzin, Scott Stein): the First-Year Writing Contest (Jan Armon, Benjamin Barnett, Valerie Booth, Daniel Boulos, Judy Curlee, Lisa DiMaio, Anne Erickson, Timothy Fitts, Lea Jacobson, Jen Jolles, Jacqueline Landau, Deidre McMahon, Errol Sull, Margene Petersen, Donald Riggs, Gail Rosen, Sheila Sandapen, Fred Siegel, Maria Volynsky, Vincent Williams); the Department of English and Philosophy, especially Mary Beth Beyer and Eileen Brennen; contest participants; and the Drexel Publishing Group staff.

The fonts used within this publication are Archer and Avenir.

Credits

Fitts, Tim. "Grasshoppers" was previously published in *Fugue* (Fall 2018). "Zero" will be published in *New South.*

Fox, Valerie. "Andy Warhol Sightings" appeared in *Juked* (May 2019).

Katerinakis, Theodoros. "Philotimo": The Concept and Semantics of a Unique Greek Term in an Era of Crisis" was previously published in Valeontis K. (Eds) *Proceedings of Hellenic Language and Terminology, Hellenic Society for Terminology,* Athens, Greece, 2017.

Kotzin, Miriam. "Lists" was previously published in the *Goliad Review,* Fall 2018.
"The Red Tiger" was prevously published in *Country Music,* Spuyten Duyvil Press, New York, 2017.

Levin Millan, Harriet. "Bumming a Cigarette" originally appeared in *The Chiron Review.* "Crush" originally appeared in *H_NGM_N.* "My Oceanography" originally appeared in *Plume.* "Waterfall" originally appeared in *My Oceanography* (CavanKerry, 2018).

Levin, Lynn. "Insecurity Questions" and "To My Teens" were previously published in *Nerve Cowboy* (Spring 2018). "Six Riddles" was previously published as: Riddles I, II, III, and IV: The *Feathertale Review* (Spring 2019) and Riddles V and VI: *Lighten Up Online* (June 2018).

Miller, Jonson. "Samuel Spangler's Handmade Table" was published in the Fall 2018 issue of *The Schuylkill Valley Journal.*

Riggs, Don. Review of Labarre, Nicolas' *Heavy Metal, l'autre Metal Hurlant* [Heavy Metal, and Other Metal Hurlant] was previously published in *Journal of the Fantastic in the Arts* 29.2, 2018.

Santucci, Jack. "Why Adopting Proportional Voting May Bring Back the Big-Ten Political Party" was previously published on November 5, 2018 on the *United States Politics and Policy Blog, London School of Economics.*

Seltzer, David. "Taking Back Philosophy – Through Reform, not Revolution" was published in *Expositions,* Vol 12 N.2 (2018) pp 1-14.

Stein, Scott. *The Great American Deception* is to be published by Tiny Fox Press in 2020.

Volk Miller, Kathleen. "At Harleigh Cemetery" was published in *LitHub,* in May, 2019.

Warnock, Scott. "Can We, Should We, Introduce Adversity, Even Pain?" was previously published on October 29, 2018 on the website *When Falls the Coliseum.*

Welcome

The 33rd anthology was first produced by the College of Arts and Sciences over 10 years ago to celebrate the diverse scholarship and voices of Drexel University – and, in particular, to showcase the power of communication. That mission has never wavered.

No matter our age, experience or field of study, the tools of communication empower all of us to share our unique perspectives with the world and to work across boundaries to affect change in distinct and valuable ways. Whether in poetry or scholarly text, fiction or essay, the pieces in this work embody the spirit of Drexel: the drive to embed ourselves in the world, to observe and reflect, to ask critical questions, to research and innovate, and to take others with us on the journey – our peers and colleagues, our local and global communities.

In this volume, undergraduates, graduate students and faculty from biology to public health to playwriting are published alongside each other, just as they work alongside each other in our classrooms and labs – a reminder that we all have something valuable to contribute.

As you read through these pages and reflect on your own communication, remember: Your unique perspective of the world is what makes you powerful; its potential is only limited by your willingness to share it. And in sharing, the sum of our unique perspectives transcends our individual disciplines.

Sincerely,
Maria T. Schultheis, Ph.D.
Interim Dean, College of Arts and Sciences
Drexel University

Preface

In your hands is the twelfth annual edition of *The 33rd,* a unique anthology of writing from the Drexel Publishing Group. This is just one of many creative writing initiatives housed in the Department of English and Philosophy.

Cultivating curiosity and creativity in a supportive environment is the hallmark of the Department of English and Philosophy. We are a place where all Drexel University students hone their skills of effective writing in real-world contexts. Through our department, students collaborate with young patients at the Children's Hospital of Philadelphia to write, plan and produce short vignettes that are broadcast through the hospital. Through our department, students sit with hospice patients to hear, write, and shape their life stories through a memoir-writing class. Through our department, students partner with our neighbors in the Mantua and Powelton communities to craft personal stories and record the experience of urban neighborhoods in transition. Through *The 33rd* and other DPG projects, our students find multiple outlets for their writing to reach the world.

The 33rd contains student and faculty writing from all disciplines, adjudicated through a competitive process, and we use it as a textbook in many of our writing classes. It's different every year, with new and creative surprises each time. What remains constant is the way that *The 33rd* embodies our mission of promoting imaginative and effective writing, starting right here on the street that gives the publication its name, and reaching out into a world that is limited only by our creative imagination.

J. Roger Kurtz, Ph.D.
Professor and Department Head
Department of English and Philosophy

Table of Contents

First-Year Writing Contest
Erika Guenther and Gertrud Daemmrich Memorial Prizes

Drexel Publishing Group Essays

Contributors

Writings Arranged by Context

Literary Criticism

Memoir/Personal Narrative

Poetry

Politics

Popular Culture

Profile

First-Year
Writing

First-Year Writing Nominees

The following students were nominated for the First-Year Writing Contest.
Congratulations to all!

Farah Abdel-Jawad

Madeline Ballard

Olivia Casabianca

Jack Cloutier

Catherine D'Jay

Holly Edwards

Kealy Faughnan

Max Gallagher

Brendan Habeeb

Audrey Houck

Kyla S. Jackson

Jahnavi Kalyan

Anna Kretzer

Crystal Lim

Kathleen Marsili

Long May

Aliya McDonald

Xiang Merry

Afrah Morshed

Jake Naccarella

Khanh Chi Thi Nguyen

Kelly Oduro

Alexandra Pachkowski

Isabella M. Pedreira

Bibhav Pradhan

Micah Quillen

Nicole Robinson

Mackenzie Sadlon

Daniel Scerbo

Dhruv Shah

Annika Surapaneni

Mallory Toci

Lauren Viola

Sophia Watkinson

Lucas Williams

Alaina Zaki

Emmanuel Abeye

Klye Bloom

Akilah Chatman

Sophia Desko

Hannah Dolen

Daniel Erbynn

Troy Fluks

Nicole Geris

Lauren Herman

Melissa Hoxha

Emily Johns

Leanne Khov

Harshita Kumbham

Richard A. Mantellino

Michael J. Martin

Zak McConnell

Grace McInnis

Kartik Mohan

Jhannae B. Mundell

Nicole Nemzer

Jessica Niebuhr

Omololu Omoteso

Nina Pagano

Anastasia Perry

Molly Pratzner

Diana Radu

Tony Rowe

Christian Sanchez

Sydney Schoenholtz

Junhan (Tony) Shin

Alison Tang

Tommi Traister

Rosalie Vitale

Anastasia Weggel

Kenan Wursthorn

Andrew Zheng

Yaseen Ahmid

Timothy Carey

Kyle Chen

Spoorthi Dingari

Maximillon Dombrowski

Ayomide Falae

Prachi Gaddam

Sofia Gomez

Ethan Hermann

Jack Hoye

Charlotte Kalilec

Dokyeong Kim

Daniel Lee

Tracy Marcelis

Kristhine Martinez

Mary McCoy

Jarod Mellus

Delilah Morales

Uswa Mutaal

Tracy Ng

Aaron Ocampo

Ivan Orlov

Rani Patel

Jhosbel Polanco-Rodriguez

Ryan Pumo

Jacob T. Roberts

Julianna Rudnick

William Scales

Andrew Senin

Alexa L. Stephens

Charlene Tang

Christy Tran

Andrew Viveiros

Lola Weinstein

Grace Zaborski

Introduction

As the Director of the First-Year Writing Program, I work with over 60 dedicated instructors who coach, cajole, and mentor close to 3,000 incoming students who produce tens of thousands of pages of writing. One of the best parts of my job is working with Sheila Sandapen, our Assistant Director, on the First-Year Writing Contest.

This section of *The 33rd* includes essays written by the winners, runners-up, and honorable mentions from the contest that ran in the 2018-2019 academic year. Here is how the essays get from the classroom into this book:

• Students work very hard in their classes to produce lively, engaging writing about themselves and the world around them. Their instructors work hard, too, giving advice and encouragement throughout the writing process.

• Towards the end of the fall term and again in the middle of the spring term, we ask instructors to invite no more than two students from each of their sections to submit their best work to the First-Year Writing Contest. Last year, we got 120 excellent entries.

• With the help of 15-20 faculty members, we go through a two-step judging process. After much deliberation, the judges come up with a winner, a first runner-up, a second runner-up, and ten honorable mentions.

• During the spring term, the winners, runners-up, and honorable mentions are announced at the English Awards Ceremony, along with the winners of various other contests. Furthermore, our winners receive prizes supported by a very generous endowment from the Erika Guenther and Gertrud Daemmrich Memorial Prizes.

• Finally, the editors of *The 33rd* step in to get permissions, to edit, and to create the book you are holding.

So, here is *The 33rd*. Your instructors in the First-Year Writing Program will ask you to read essays that won prizes last year so you can discuss them, debate them, and learn from them.

Are you interested in writing? Will you be in this book next year? On behalf of the First-Year Writing Program, we look forward to reading your work.

Fred Siegel, Ph.D.
Director of the First-Year Writing Program

Write a literacy narrative or a memoir.

—Dr. Jan Armon

Mary Kilgallon

Protector: A Story About Family

AS FAR BACK AS I CAN REMEMBER, I'VE HAD MY SISTER RACHEL.

FOR THE PAST SIXTEEN YEARS,

SHE'S BEEN MY PLAYMATE,

MY CO-STAR,

MY STUDY BUDDY,

AND MY LIFELONG FRIEND.

I CAN'T IMAGINE WHAT MY LIFE WOULD BE LIKE WITHOUT HER.

I WOULD BE LYING IF I SAID I NEVER RESENTED HER.

WITHOUT RACHEL, I NEVER WOULD HAVE LEARNED HOW TO SHARE.

IF I WAS SLIGHTLY WISER THAN HER DUE TO MY AGE,
THEN RACHEL WAS BRAVER THAN ME BY CENTURIES.

RAY WAS
ALWAYS
ENCOURAGING
ME TO CLIMB
OUT OF MY
SHELL.

SHE WAS THE KIND OF PERSON WHO COULDN'T STAND
BY AND WATCH IF SOMEONE NEEDED HELP.

UNFORTUNATELY, THIS MADE
HER THE PERFECT TARGET
FOR BULLIES.

SHE WOULD NEVER ADMIT TO IT, BUT I COULD TELL IT REALLY HURT
HER. RACHEL WAS BRAVE, BUT SHE WAS STILL JUST A KID. MORE
THAN ANYTHING, SHE WANTED SOMEONE TO FIGHT FOR HER.

FRESHMAN YEAR OF HIGH SCHOOL WAS ESPECIALLY HARD FOR RACHEL.

AS ALL TEENAGERS DO, SHE STARTED HAVING FIGHTS WITH OUR PARENTS.

WITH THAT, PLUS A NEW SCHOOL, HARDER CLASSES, AND ALMOST NO FRIENDS, SHE WAS UNDER CONSTANT STRESS. I WANTED TO HELP, BUT...

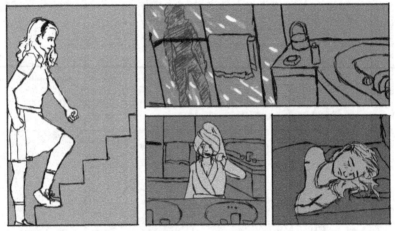

I HAD BEEN THROUGH IT ALL BEFORE. I KNEW IT WAS IMPORTANT TO GIVE MY SISTER SPACE TO GROW AND LEARN. SHE COULD TAKE CARE OF HERSELF.

7:30 AM, MONDAY
DECEMBER 2ND, 2017

FIFTEEN MINUTES LATER...

WHAT I REMEMBER MOST VIVIDLY ABOUT THAT WEEK WAS THE SENSATION OF BEING ALONE.

SINCE MY PARENTS WERE GONE ALL THE TIME TO VISIT RACHEL IN THE HOSPITAL, I HAD A LOT OF TIME TO THINK.

YOU PEOPLE MAKE ME WANT TO KILL MYSELF!!

ABOUT HOW ALL THE WARNING SIGNS WERE THERE.

ABOUT HOW I ASSUMED SHE WOULD JUST GET BETTER ON HER OWN.

THIS HAS TO STOP NOW, RACHEL.

I HATE YOU!!

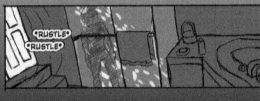

RUSTLE
RUSTLE

ABOUT HOW IF I HADN'T LOCKED THE DOOR WHILE I WAS SHOWERING, THEN SHE WOULD HAVE GOTTEN INTO THE MEDICINE CABINET,

AND THEN...

SHE WOULD'VE...

I TRIED NOT TO THINK ABOUT THAT PART TOO MUCH.

THE FIRST TIME I VISITED HER, I WAS SCARED. NOT FOR HER - I WAS TOLD SHE WAS MAKING GREAT PROGRESS IN THE PSYCHIATRIC CLINIC. I WAS SCARED SHE WOULD HATE ME FOR FAILING TO PROTECT HER.

WE TALKED A LOT THAT NIGHT. I HADN'T FORFEITED MY ROLE IN HER LIFE. I COULD STILL HELP HER THROUGH THIS.

CHRISTMAS BREAK, DECEMBER 14, 2018

ME, AGE 18

I'M HOME!

MARY! WE'VE MISSED YOU. HOW'S COLLEGE?

IT'S GOOD. WHERE'S RACHEL?

RACHEL, YOUR SISTER'S HOME!

I'LL JUST GO UP TO HER ROOM.

HI, RAY.

HEY, MARY. NICE HAIRCUT.

WHATCHA DOIN'?

I'M TEXTING MEGAN! SHE'S THE FRIEND I WAS TELLING YOU ABOUT FROM THE SCHOOL PLAY. ACTUALLY WE WERE HANGING OUT THE

UH, WHY ARE YOU LOOKING AT ME LIKE THAT?

I'M JUST SO HAPPY TO SEE YOU AGAIN.

Write a literacy narrative or a memoir.

— Dr. Patricia Egbert

Alexandra Schneeman

Last Words

March 15th, 2010, was the day everything changed. I wouldn't say it was the worst day of my life, considering the ones that followed were no better for a while. However, it was the day my aunt picked me up early from school so that I could say goodbye. It was the day my sister and I spent the night at a distant relative's house in order to avoid going home. It was the day my family was changed forever. It was the day my mother lost her devoted husband. It was the day my sister and I lost our loving father.

The following days consisted of being visited by family and friends as the number of flower arrangements on our kitchen table piled up. My mother was focusing most of her energy on planning the service, and my sister and I focused on sticking together through all the chaos around us. My mom told me that at the funeral, some people were going to get up and speak about my dad. Just to make sure she provided me with the opportunity in case, she asked me if I wanted to say something at the service. I do not think she was expecting me to say yes considering I was only ten. However, to her surprise, I said that it would mean a lot to me if I could say something. I decided I wanted to write a speech that I would give in front of my family and everyone else that my dad had touched in his life. I was going to deliver final words to the many people that did not get to say goodbye to my dad.

Writing has always been a big passion of mine, although, writing that particular speech was not very enjoyable. While it was nice to put my feelings on paper, I had to let myself think about everything that had just happened in great detail. I sat at my kitchen table trying to find the words to explain my feelings and the impact that my dad had on my life. My mom sat by my side, answering any questions I had as the cycle of typing and backspacing continued for hours. I don't remember the speech very well now and I have never had the desire to read it to revisit the thoughts that my ten-year-old brain had in the days following my dad's passing. I do, however, distinctly remember the experience of reading it at the funeral.

After many prayers, speeches, and songs, the priest looked at me, giving me my cue to rise from the pew and walk to the altar. As I approached the microphone, I walked past the only spot of color in the whole church, which consisted of all the girls in my fourth-grade class, sitting there in their bright blue jumper uniforms. Once I made my way up to the front, I looked out and saw the sea of black suits and dresses accompanied by the heartbroken expressions on everyone's faces. Ever since I was young, music has been a huge part of my life. My mom requested that I sing a short song at the service before I gave my speech. I learned to sing the song "Live Like We're Dying" by Kris Allen. The accompanist started playing and I sang the song.

Toward the end of my father's life, I was participating in a singing competition. One night, he decided that he did not want to go to my performance because he was not feeling well and wanted to be alone and stay home. His absence at my performance was something that really upset me, so singing at his funeral made it feel like I had been given another chance to sing to him and he had been given one last chance to listen. For this reason, singing at the service was the easy part for me. However, as I sang my final note, I realized that the speech I was about to give after was not going to be so easy.

I started to feel very nervous, scared that I would not be able to deliver the words without breaking down in front of everyone. These were my words for my dad and my family that I had worked so hard on. Sharing them with all these people that I barely knew felt wrong. On the other hand, this was my opportunity to give honor to my father and his life in front of everyone that devoted their day to celebrating it with us. These thoughts came to mind as I was about to start, and I felt a sense of calm. I recited the paragraphs that were printed on the paper in front of me. I got through the speech without any major problems. Without looking up at the congregation before me, I headed back to my seat next to my family. Eventually, the service concluded, and we made our way to the back of the church to thank people for coming as they exited.

As we said goodbye to everyone, I was approached many times and complimented on my song and speech. People kept emphasizing the strength that it must have taken to get up there and do that. I was puzzled by those comments though because I didn't see it like that. Sure, it was hard to find the right words and it wasn't easy to work through the nerves, but I wasn't able to do it because of strength. I was able to do it because I saw it for what it was, and I found inspiration in the unique opportunity. I was able to do it because I was given the opportunity to speak to my dad and tell him what he meant to me and my family while also giving people at the funeral a better understanding of just how great a person my dad was. Regardless of anything else, it was an opportunity to have the final words about my dad. Writing and giving that speech was absolutely not a burden. It was a privilege.

For this assignment, you will research a problematic issue, propose one or more solutions to the problem, and present an argument supporting your solution.

—Professor Robert Finegan

Sanjana Ramanathan
An End to Sexism in Gaming Communities

On June 18, 2016, 16-year-old Kim Se-Hyeon (competing under the gamer tag "Geguri") entered an amateur *Overwatch* esports tournament from her home in Seoul. Within 24 hours of her team's victory, rumors began circulating online that Geguri, who was the only female player in the tournament, had been cheating. Players "ELTA" and "Strobe" said her performance and mouse precision were too good and accused the teenager of using automated aim-assist software. Many people took the accusations seriously despite the lack of proof, and began harassing Geguri, hurling gendered slurs and vulgar, often-sexual insults. Strobe even resorted to death threats, saying "if there is a problem with our sponsors and such, I may visit Geguri's house with a knife in hand. I am not joking" (Preston).

To any woman who plays video games, these remarks may seem uncomfortably familiar. Sexism appears among every level of the gaming community, from casual players to professionals. A female player who turns on her microphone to communicate with her male teammates may find herself instantly harassed because her voice gives away her gender. She may be accused of playing to attract men's attention. If she has skill, it is likely that she will be accused of cheating far more often than any male player. Reasonably, many women choose to use gender-neutral gamer tags and voice modifiers to hide that they are female (Easpaig, Humphrey).

Although blatant sexism has been present in gaming communities for decades, the most famous controversy occurred in 2014. "Gamergate" started with a harassment campaign targeting women in the gaming industry and feminist critics of video games. These women were subjected to months of harassment, including death and rape threats (Parkin). The campaign shed a light on the rampant and often violent sexism surrounding video games: in the industry, the communities of players, and the content of the games themselves. But even after the controversy died down, little change was made to solve the problem; two years later it made the media once again when 16-year-old Geguri was subjected to the same harassment.

As the online threats and abuse mounted, Geguri was invited by tournament casters to stage a demonstration proving her skill level. When she arrived at the studio, caster Kim Young-Il noted that the high school girl "wasn't mentally ready" to face the public; she wore a white mask to hide her face and spoke very little during her introduction (Kimes). Geguri's demonstration proved once and for all that the accusations hurled at her were baseless. However, the scandal had shattered her self-confidence. "Because [my opponents] attacked me publicly, everyone in the community was attacking me, calling me a crazy bitch. I was scared," Geguri admitted in an interview with ESPN's Mina Kimes. For a year after clearing her name, Geguri disappeared almost entirely from esports.

Gender-based threats and stereotypes keep women from succeeding in professional esports, despite women accounting for 45% of today's gamers (Pugh). Although "female gamers don't have the same physical disadvantages against males as, say, female basketball players, very few have thrived on a professional level" due to harassment from male players and an unwillingness from professional teams to recruit them (Kimes). This toxic environment prevents women from succeeding in-game and engaging with other players.

The video game industry itself is where we must look to solve the problem. Despite more and more girls playing video games, there is a huge underrepresentation of women involved in making them. This "anomaly does not restrict itself to just one area of the industry, but affects the industry as a whole," causing casual gamers and esports to become affected as well (Pugh). Because the industry is dominated by men, a majority of games are marketed to men and serve their perspective. Themes of misogyny and mistreated female characters are ever-present in today's video games, ones that are often picked off the shelf by teenage boys who pocket the harmful messages.

Involving more women in the gaming industry means creating a safe and fair environment for them to work. Women are discouraged from even entering the "games industry because the nature of the industry is particularly restrictive to females," and those in the industry are restricted from higher-level jobs because it is assumed women will not be able work the long hours needed (Elliot, Prescott). In addition, Gamasutra's Game Developer Salary Survey revealed that on average, women who work in the field make 86% of what men make in the gaming industry. By eradicating this wage gap, game companies can create a more welcoming workplace for women interested in entering the field.

Many have argued that because the game industry requires long hours and a flexible schedule to meet deadlines, women will be unable to dedicate the needed time because they will be busy raising children (Elliot, Prescott). This is an antiquated notion, and there is no reason men should not spend as much time with their families as women. Others object that there are enough women in the industry, but "the few females that are employed in this workplace are typically working in non-developmental roles such as administration," so they have little influence on the actual content of the games (Elliot, Prescott). It could be said that women who enter the industry may choose not to combat the sexism at all. Fortunately, female gaming students interviewed for University of Bolton's study already expressed a desire to de-sexualize female characters and change how video games are marketed towards girls.

By bringing more women into the industry, companies will invite a new perspective of a game's script, character design, and marketing. The industry itself will benefit by having more diversity, as women will market to the untapped female player base. Gaming companies can encourage more women to enter the field by removing the deterrents. 2014's Gamergate controversy revealed that the game industry was unsafe place for women; it is up to companies to change their male-dominated workplaces and prove that change from the current mindset is possible.

Already, the future is getting brighter for female players. Early this year, Geguri decided to rejoin the esports scene, and was recruited by the Shanghai Dragons, making her the first and only female player in the international Overwatch League. However, she is still one of the few women competing professionally in esports at an international level (Breslau). Big changes to end sexism in the industry itself may be enough to change the attitudes of the player base, and the attitudes of professional teams. If game companies take steps to solve the problem of sexism within their own walls, other female players may be able to follow Geguri's success without the brutal struggle that came before.

Works Cited

Breslau, Rod. "Sources: Geguri Set to Join Shanghai Dragons, Become Overwatch League's First Female Player." *ESPN*, ESPN Internet Ventures, 14 Feb. 2018, www.espn.com/esports/story/_/id/22348024/geguri-set-join-shanghai-dragons-become-overwatch-league-first-female-player.

Easpaig, Nic Giolla & Rhi Humphrey. "'Pitching a virtual woo': Analysing discussion of sexism in online gaming." *Feminism & Psychology*, 553–561, 2016. http://journals.sagepub.com.ezproxy2.library.drexel.edu/doi/full/10.1177/095935351666

Elliot, Lauren, and Julie Prescott. "The Only Girl in the Class! Female Students' Experiences of Gaming Courses and Views of the Industry." *IGI Global*, University of Bolton, 2014, www-igi-global-com.ezproxy2.library.drexel.edu/gateway/chapter/full-text-html/110630.

Graft, Kris. "Gender Wage Gap: How the Game Industry Compares to the U.S. Average." *Gamasutra*, 22 July 2014, www.gamasutra.com/view/news/221586/Gender_wage_gap_How_the_game_industry_compares_to_the_US_average.php.

Kimes, Mina. "Esports Is Dominated by Men. Can a 17-Year-Old Korean Girl Change That?" *ESPN*, ESPN Internet Ventures, 15 Sept. 2017, www.espn.com/espn/feature/story/_/id/20692051/how-teenage-gamer-became-reluctant-icon-south-korea-feminist-movement.

Parkin, Simon. "Gamergate: A Scandal Erupts in the Video-Game Community." *The New Yorker*, 6 Apr. 2018, www.newyorker.com/tech/annals-of-technology/gamergate-scandal-erupts-video-game-community.

Tang, Wai Yen, and Jesse Fox. "Men's Harassment Behavior in Online Video Games: Personality Traits and Game Factors." *Wiley Periodicals, Inc.*, 14 Oct. 2016, onlinelibrary-wiley-com.ezproxy2.library.drexel.edu/doi/full/10.1002/ab.21646.

The purpose of this assignment is to write a paper built around your own primary research. Choose a topic that interests you and figure out a way to use primary research to explore it. Remember that you can generate primary research in many ways, such as:
interviews
surveys
personal observations
experiments

—Professor Henry Israeli

Michael Bash

My Experience with the World's Most Popular Drug

Here's a fun fact. The world population consumes over 100,000 metric tons of caffeine every year (Caballero 560). That's not including the weight of the coffee, soda, or tea; only the caffeine itself which makes up about 0.04% the weight of a cup of coffee. To put that into perspective, 100,000 metric tons is about the weight of 490 Statues of Liberty. This rank's caffeine as the most highly used drug in the world (Weinberg 10). In fact, nearly 87 percent of Americans consume caffeine on a daily basis (Frary). Amongst that 87 percent is myself.

All throughout high school I would start my day with a single cup of coffee, and that was it. It wasn't until I joined the United States Coast Guard that I began to consume multiple cups of coffee throughout the day. As an engineer on a ship, many of the days were long and demanding. Some days our crew would be tasked to perform a search and rescue mission for a vessel in distress hundreds of miles off the coast. Other days, we would be involved in a pursuit with drug smugglers transporting multiple tons of narcotics amongst the high seas. On these high-activity days, I would often find myself awake for more than 24 hours, so I would consume well over ten cups of coffee just to maintained the ability to perform my duties. Ever since then, I drink about five cups of coffee throughout the day as a normal routine. The fact that I consume so much coffee had me wondering; what exactly is caffeine, why does it make me alert, and what would happen if I just stopped using it? As I explore these questions, I've decided to completely discontinue my intake of caffeine. For the duration of my caffeine-free experiment, I took day-by-day notes on my overall alertness, mood, and cravings to understand first hand exactly what is going on within my body.

Ironically enough, I came to the decision to stop consuming caffeine while sipping on the last few ounces of a hot brewed, caffeine packed, Wawa coffee. That would be my last jolt of 'energy' for the next three weeks. I emphasize 'energy' because contrary to popular belief, caffeine doesn't actually give you energy. Rather it prevents the body from feeling tired. It sounds redundant, but it makes sense when we zoom in and take a look at what is going on at the molecular level.

One of the human body's primary sources of energy is adenosine triphosphate (ATP). A bi-product from the result of ATP being broken down for energy is adenosine (Caballero 574). Adenosine, is a molecule that attaches to specific neurons in the brain called A1 and A2A adenosine receptors. A1 neurons make the body alert, while A2A neurons promote the body to feel tired (Caballero 575). Adenosine performs double duty since it deactivates the A1 neurons and activates the A2A neurons when it attaches to the receptors. As the body consumes more energy, more adenosine is produced which is why we feel progressively tired as the day goes on. This is a natural safety mechanism to promote sleep so that the we can enter a state of rest to refresh the mind and body.

Now that we have a basic understanding of what makes us feel tired, let's go back to the original question; how does caffeine gives us 'energy'? Caffeine is considered an adenosine antagonist (Caballero 575). Essentially, it's an imposture that takes the place of adenosine in the body. Take a look and notice how similar the structure of the two molecules are. Caffeine has such a similar structure to adenosine, that it has the ability to attach to the adenosine receptors. However, since there is a variation in the molecular structure, caffeine does not actually activate any of the receptors, rather it just takes up space and prevents adenosine from attaching to the receptors (James 18). This is why it feels like caffeine gives us energy; it just prevents adenosine from promoting a sense of tiredness.

So how did I become such a heavy caffeine user? Why did it seem like I needed more and more cups of coffee to achieve the same sense of alertness? It just so happens that a tolerance for caffeine can be formed just as a tolerance for many other drugs can be formed. When caffeine is consistently consumed to prevent feeling tiredness, caffeine is perpetually bonded to the adenosine receptors. Since adenosine can't perform its normal duties with too much caffeine in the way, the body must come up with plan "B." Plan "B" is the production of more adenosine receptors. This provides more receptors so that adenosine does not have to compete as much with the caffeine (James 29). However, this can create a vicious cycle of consuming more caffeine to block the additional adenosine receptors, which in turn prompts the body to create even more receptors. Before you know it, you end up like myself, drinking five cups of coffee a day just to feel normal.

The first couple of days without caffeine was pretty brutal. I found myself extremely tired throughout the day, and my concentration was sub-par. I was craving everything and anything that contained caffeine. I rarely drink soda, yet I saw a Coca-Cola that looked more inviting than ever just a few days into my experiment. I'm aware of the fact that I am considered a heavy caffeine user and had formed a tolerance, but why did discontinuing the use of caffeine affect me so severely? What was different about me as opposed to someone that may have a few cups of coffee a week? Why didn't they feel as incapacitated as me on the days they didn't consume caffeine? This traces back to the tolerance I had formed. With my five cups of coffee a day, I had found a balance of caffeine vs. the number of adenosine receptors that I had. Since I abruptly stopped the consumption of caffeine, I now had a plethora of wide-open adenosine receptors in my brain. With no caffeine to compete for the receptors, adenosine molecules readily filled the excess amount of adenosine receptors. I had formed an over-stimulated sense of tiredness as opposed to a normal caffeine user who has far fewer adenosine receptors to fill (James 31). What I was going through was withdrawal, and it was brutally noticeable.

About a week into my experiment, I noticed the feeling of withdrawal begin to fade. My energy levels were not as high as they were when I would drink coffee, but they were much steadier throughout the day. I didn't feel the need to consume a mid-day cup of coffee to counter the mid-day energy crash that I would typically feel prior to the start of this experiment. I felt more relaxed and actually began to feel fairly refreshed and alert when I would wake up. I did some more research and found that the body eliminates the excess adenosine receptors after about a week of no caffeine consumption (James 31). This would mean less receptors to promote a sense of tiredness.

After about three weeks of no caffeine, I had essentially gone back to the state I was in prior to the high-demand days of the Coast Guard. I had given my body more than enough time to re-adjust back to a normal amount of adenosine receptors. The experiment doesn't end here though. I had formed a love affair with the taste of coffee, and not just its stimulating properties. I refuse to give up coffee regardless of whether the effects of this experiment were negative or positive. Aware of the fact that I had a significantly reduced number of adenosine receptors, I still decided to consume my normal dose of coffee for my first day just to see how different it feels. Just as I didn't ween myself off caffeine, I jumped right back into it by waking up and consuming my standard two oversized mugs of coffee to start my day. The best way I could describe the sensation, about thirty minutes after my two cups of coffee, is that it felt like I had ants marching under my skin. It was an incredibly uncomfortable feeling that stuck with me for a few hours to follow. Two cups were it for the day; I never even considered the other three after that.

With the experiment behind me, I now find comfort with just a single cup of coffee to start the day. It gives me that initial boost to get the day started, and I get the satisfaction of the taste of coffee that I enjoy so much. My energy seems to be much more consistent throughout the day as well. The biggest take away from this experience is the fact that more caffeine is not a long-term solution. It works in a pinch to get you through that one late night, but it is important to not make it a habit. The body's need to rest will surpass any attempts to deny that. Once a tolerance is formed, the effects of caffeine become diluted which in turn starts the domino effect that makes you into a five-cups-a-day kind of person like I was. Aware of the mechanics involved with adenosine and caffeine, I can now enjoy a more effective boost of caffeine when I need it, I can notice when a tolerance it being formed, and I keep more cash in my wallet and not in the café register.

Works Cited

Caballero, Benjamin. *Encyclopedia of Food and Health.* Academic Press, 2016.

Frary, et al. "Food Sources and Intakes of Caffeine in the Diets of Persons in the United States." *Journal of the American Dietetic Association*, vol. 105, no. 1, Jan. 2005, pp. 110–113., doi:https://doi.org/10.1016/j.jada.2008.02.005.

James, Jack E. *Understanding Caffeine: a Biobehavioral Analysis.* SAGE, 1997.

Medicurio, director. *Caffeine and Adenosine Receptors.* YouTube, Medicurio, 6 Apr. 2017, www.youtube.com/watch?v=jOfquPE1cnU&t=256s.

Weinberg, Bennett Alan., and Bonnie K. Bealer. *The World of Caffeine: the Science and Culture of the World's Most Popular Drug. Routledge.*

Write a profile on a person or place.

— Dr. Elizabeth Kimball

Marisa Browne
The Social and Liminal Aspects of Highway Rest Stops

Off the exit ramp, pandemonium reigned in the parking lot. Paths were trampled by cars and people crisscrossing to get to where they needed to go. Gas, bathroom, coffee, and food appear to be the most important commodities in that order, as one woman called them the rest stop "trifecta." As I reached the door, a man remarked to his wife, "Let's get out of this hole." No one looked at each other. No one talked to each other. Their eyes faced upward, searching, scanning. They discovered the sign for the bathroom, marched in, and marched back out. If they did not immediately depart, they paused and purchased refreshments. Across from the mini mart and the bathrooms was a Starbucks. In between was a food court with Roy Rogers, Quiznos, and Pizza Hut. Young adults were quiet and businesslike, traveling alone. Older people traveled in groups or with their husband or wife and laughed or ate quietly. Families were most easily spotted, especially the ones with young children. The children wandered carefree and the parents kept watch, lackadaisically vigilant. All of the people, brands, and movement construct this place, this disjointed rest stop. However, amongst it all, can a rest stop such as this be considered a place as defined by social constructs?

Travelers—people of all categories of ages, races, genders, shapes, sizes—quell their journeys on the highway alone or with their friends, family, or otherwise fellow travelers to stop at a rest stop. This is not, of course, for leisure (one would assume). They delay to meet tangible needs. If their car requires gas, if they need to use the restroom, get coffee, stretch their limbs, eat food, or take care of any other ailment, they stop at the rest stop. One woman described rest stops as the kind of place one "comes to out of necessity" and "never again." In this sense, it is perhaps appropriate to informally nominate rest stops the "field hospitals of the highway." It is a place for people to patch up and move on, notwithstanding the chaos of hundreds of other people trying to "patch up and move on" at the same time.

The rest stop I observed was along the New Jersey Turnpike, which cuts diagonally across the state for approximately 122 miles, running roughly between the states of Delaware and New York. The state has become the butt of many jokes because of the industrial view of it provided by this highway, which can also create a relatively boring and mind-numbing ride. To break up the monotony, there are 12 rest stops along that way, all of which are named after deceased individuals with some sort of connection to the state. My rest stop's namesake was Woodrow Wilson, a New Jersey native, and former U.S. president, governor of New Jersey, and president of Princeton University. The Woodrow Wilson Service Plaza, along with all other rest stops along the turnpike, are run by a company called HMSHost. This is the same company that operates the food and retail concessions in many airports. They call themselves a "global restaurateur" and call the rest stops that they operate "motorway travel plazas," which adds a level of sophistication beyond a mere rest stop to "create culinary experiences to ensure you're feeling good on the move." The goal of my observations was to explore people's feelings about rest stops, assess if they conform to the definition of space, and by extension determine of HMSHost delivers on their promise.

I visited the Woodrow Wilson Service Plaza twice. Much of the description thus far is from the first time I visited during mid-day on November 24th, the Saturday after Thanksgiving. Everyone who stayed with their relatives during Thanksgiving break seemed to be driving back home. Although I did talk to a few people, I mainly observed. It was crowded and very busy. Many people had been in the car for hours, and everyone went about their own business, navigating around their fellow travelers. Striking up conversation with strangers at rest stops is often inefficient and unusual, especially if the individual is traveling in a group that he or she could talk amongst. However, I tried talking to people who were waiting to receive their Starbucks drinks or who were done eating and sitting at a table. In my experiences, travelers are not usually opposed to conversation if they have time or energy to spare. With the stress and exhaustion that so often follows holidays perhaps, many people did not want to bother talking to a stranger such as me. Although some agreed to talk, several simply refused.

The second time I visited the Woodrow Wilson Service Plaza was mid-day on the following Saturday, December 1st. By then, the rest stop was relatively calm, and travelers were not in as much of a hurry. Not one of the travelers I approached denied a quick conversation. I asked them how long their trip was, why they stopped, and different questions about the overall feel of this particular rest stop and the category of rest stops as a whole. The individuals being questioned used words like "basic," "fine," "average" to describe the rest stop in general. A few people said it was one of the better rest stops they had been to. I heard a man walking in with his wife remark, "Oooh Quiznos! This is a good one." It was pretty clean and had a good variety of accommodations, including gas, coffee, and a few fast food chains. However, this was starkly contrasted by the previous week. I witnessed a mother scold her children, "Don't touch it!" and kick the door open to exit. Similarly, another mother told her husband, "Don't sit there. It's filthy." These negative comments are most likely due to the rest stop's crowded status and the difficulty of cleaning in the midst of so many people using various facilities. Reviews online of New Jersey rest stops generally rank Woodrow Wilson as one of the top rest stops. The opinions of people on my second visit seemed to concur with this notion, and I would have to agree as well.

I have had the privilege of being on the road frequently. I have driven in 20 states, and I enjoy being in the car a lot. Although I am no expert, I have seen my fair share of rest stops, and Woodrow Wilson is definitely not a bad rest stop. Those in the northeast and more urban areas are generally similar to this one. In other parts of the U.S., however, this is not always the case. Rest stops can be characterized on a spectrum. On one end are the ones that are housed in large buildings and have been commercialized with convenience stores, food chains, Sunoco gas, and renovated bathrooms. They are like watering holes. A young woman I spoke to described the atmosphere as, "get in and get out." Especially when they are busy, they have a similar sense of place to stores on Black Friday; everyone goes about their business before they get back on the road. This is the overall feel I perceived when the first time I observed, ironically, on the day after Black Friday. The second time I observed did not have the same sense of place. When the rest stop was not as busy, it felt akin to a food court, fast food chain, or coffee shop without some of its usual charm. As before, people initially kept to themselves and went about their business, but they were more open to talking with a stranger. These fluctuations in the sense of place are natural and occur often.

According to Oxford Reference, "People constitute their surroundings, *placing* themselves and others as well as the physical objects, meanings, and actions which, taken all together, make up a place that is shared, negotiated, and contested." In other words, places are social constructs. People define them. First, they surmise, deliberately or subconsciously, the boundaries, culture, and conventions that characterize a place. Second, their characterizations of a place contests with the perceptions of all of the other people at or a part of that place. At rest stops, the travelers have removed themselves from the usual context of their lives to embark on their journey, whether business or leisure. There is a sense of temporary equality as they go about the business of meeting their needs within a socially acceptable way. They experience a temporary equality and absence of rank.

When asking one gentleman what he thought of the Woodrow Wilson rest stop, he responded that he thought it was pretty good, especially compared to some of the rest stops in North Carolina. Having stopped at some of these rest stops when travelling to softball tournaments, I understand his comment completely. These rest stops are on the other end of the rest stop spectrum from Woodrow Wilson, and consisted of small, old, concrete building with small restrooms, a vending machine, and a few picnic tables. These rest stops were far apart and in sparsely populated areas. When I stopped at them at night sometimes, they felt dangerous, surreal, eerily ambiguous. These types of rest stops lack the "sense of place" that their more developed sisters have, and can be considered a liminal space.

Anthropologist Arnold Van Gertz first introduced the idea of liminality in his book *Rites of Passage*. Liminality describes the ritual involved in any transition. This concept is most commonly applied to transitions in life such as getting married, getting a new job, having children, or growing up. Someone who is involved in a liminal transition enters into the process of letting go of their previous perspectives or beliefs, struggling in accepting newly discovered perspectives or beliefs, and integrating them into a part of their identity. In this case, however, liminality is being applied to physical places and referred to as "liminal space." Liminal spaces are impermanent, non-destination, transitionary places, examples of which include train stations, airports, waiting rooms, and rest stops. One woman I mentioned earlier even noted the impermanent nature of rest stops, remarking that rest stops are the kind of place that no one revisits.

Another characteristic of liminal space is they frequently lack clear context because of their nature as a non-destination. This feature is especially pronounced at small non-commercial rest stops. Without the name brand food chains and crowds of people, its impermanence and remoteness tend to subconsciously trigger red flags in people's minds. Any number of terrible things could happen out in the middle of nowhere, away from society. Especially at night, employees and other travelers can often seem strange and intimidating. Even if logic denies the possibility of danger, this subconscious fear lingers as uneasiness or mild apprehension. Without the definitive characteristics that true destinations hold, non-commercial rest stop's eerie, surreal quality is only amplified.

There are some scholarly articles on the topic of travel and liminality. In *Airports as Liminal Space*, the authors explore the nature of international airports as liminal spaces and assert that passengers may experience a wide range of emotions, such as the thrill of travel, anxiety and fear of flying, and the joy and sorrow of hellos and goodbyes. The experiences of travelers were viewed within the overall context of them going through a "ritual process of spatial and social separation" from their social structure to a state of liminality, and ultimately reintegration. In addition, in *Hotel Babylon? Exploring Hotels as Liminal Sites of Transition and Transgression,* the authors explore the concept of hotels as liminal spaces that present dual opportunities that may offer "freedom for some, but unease, constraint or even threat for others." They acknowledge that liminal spaces can be places of anxiety, threat, and danger.

Based on my observations and experience, I believe that rest stops can qualify as both a socially constructed place as well as a liminal space. The degree to which a particular rest stop is viewed as more socially constructed versus liminal generally depends on the number of amenities and the amount of traffic. Those rest stops that are located in more high traffic areas such as the NJ Turnpike, and that have more amenities that may include convenience store, name brand fast food and quick service restaurants, and name brand coffee shops, will generally meet the Oxford definition of place. Though people are there only briefly, or liminally, they negotiate the space in a socially acceptable way to meet their travel needs. Conversely, those rest stops that are located in more remote areas, and that have less amenities that may include only picnic tables, restrooms, and a vending machine, may rarely meet the Oxford definition of place. There is less of a social construct to the location, and people may generally experience strange and uneasy feelings and emotions that can be associated with liminal spaces.

Citations

Huang, Wei-Jue, et al. "Airports as Liminal Space." *Annals of Tourism Research*, vol. 70, 2 Feb. 2018, pp. 1–13., doi:10.1016/j.annals.2018.02.003.

Pritchard, Annette, and Nigel Morgan. "Hotel Babylon? Exploring Hotels as Liminal Sites of Transition and Transgression." *Tourism Management*, vol. 27, no. 5, 11 May 2005, pp. 762–772., doi:10.1016/j.tourman.2005.05.015.

First, review the *Norton* chapter on, "Summarizing and Responding: Where Reading Meets Writing" and the chapter on "Analyzing Texts." Next, using the databases on the Hagerty Library web site, find a reliable article that makes reference to a specific idea that emerged for you in your literacy narrative or memoir. Then, using the guidelines in the chapters, write either a summary/response or a textual analysis.

—Dr. Donna Rondolone

Amy Carson

Donald Trump and the Complicated History of the Rust Belt

In his paper "The Revolt of the Rust Belt: Place and Politics in the Age of Anger," Michael McQuarrie, a professor of sociology at The London School of Economics and Political Science, investigated the atypical voting behavior of Rust Belt residents during the 2016 US presidential election. McQuarrie sees the Rust Belt's strong support for Donald Trump not entirely built on Trump himself, but as the natural culmination of a variety of complex issues and events that have affected the Upper Midwest beginning in the 1970s. These issues include the deindustrialization of the Rust Belt, the Democratic Party's gradual shift on economic policy, and the general peripheralization of the region in respect to national importance, which Trump was then able to take advantage of during the election.

Concerning the economic downturn that transformed the prosperous Upper Midwest into what is today known as the Rust Belt, McQuarrie begins by investigating the overall economic history of the region. For much of the 20th century, the Upper Midwest was the center of American industry, making it the primary economic source for the national economy. As a result of this economic strength, the workers and residents of the region were also an incredibly valuable group within American politics. The population of the area was mostly made up of working class laborers who held a voice in the national political through the power of their unions. For many decades, the area was a strong source of Democratic Party votes, due in large part to the Democratic Party's historically strong association and interest in labor unions.

However, starting in the '70s, major manufacturing companies began to move their factories out of the area due to lowered transportation costs and cheaper, unregulated labor overseas. This began the very long and painful process of deindustrialization in the Upper Midwest. The region began losing industry, its most important resource, as well as the population that comes with it. The loss of factory jobs led to many laborers leaving the area in search of work, weakening the area's unions in membership, and in turn, political power. Beginning in the 80s, the US economy also began the major shift from an industrial economy, built on unskilled labor and centralized in the Midwest, to a service economy, built on skilled and knowledge-based work and based out of US Coastal Regions. By the '90s, the Democratic Party also shifted their focus away from the working class towards a Neoliberal economic stance that supported this "New Economy" by way of policy that supported globalization and drove the economies of the US coast, like finance and technology. These policies, though stimulating for the US economy as a whole, further hurt the regions in the Upper Midwest.

McQuarrie argues that the Democratic support of the New Economy felt like a betrayal to many residents of what was now becoming the Rust Belt. The party that historically fought for laborers and the working class of the region had seemingly abandoned them. The region's loss of population, union membership, and economic significance was beginning to push residents of the Upper Midwest from being one of the most important groups within the sphere of national economics and politics, to the peripheries of those spheres. The issue of deindustrialization was one that was recognized while it was happening, but the prosperity of America on the national level kept the issue from being addressed in any significant way outside of local politics of the areas that experienced it. The issues and people of the Rust Belt were now seen as a special interest group within national politics, a far cry from their prominence only a few decades prior.

When the housing crisis of 2007 occurred, the deindustrialized areas of the Rust Belt were hit particularly hard, because the crisis drank up the last remaining pieces of equity the area had. As put by McQuarrie, "In much of the Midwest the foreclosure crisis was not a 'banking problem' but the culmination of a decades-long devaluation of the human and physical capital of the region" (S134). McQuarrie then goes on to discuss how the region was even further, literally stripped of its equity. During the Recession, scrap resale became a very lucrative business in the Rust Belt. Scrap dealers would buy, but most often steal, metal off and out of foreclosed homes and empty factories, which would then be sold to companies in China to be processed and reused. This physical destruction to the infrastructure of post-industrial regions is both part of where the name "Rust Belt" for the region originates, as well as a sadly fitting metaphor for what globalization did to the Rust Belt.

By the time of the 2016 presidential election, the Rust Belt had endured near catastrophic economic disruption, its people felt that their voice in national policy and politics had been taken away from them, and the

Democratic party lost its stronghold on the region. McQuarrie sees that these circumstances, when put together, created an environment that was prime for a candidate like Trump. Donald Trump went directly against the globalization-based economic strategies supported by both political parties, gave special and focused attention to the people of the Rust Belt, and ran as a Republican, which people of the Rust Belt did not hold feelings of abandonment with. Trump's racial rhetoric also hit a nerve amongst many white, working-class voters of the Rust Belt. As explained by McQuarrie, the beginning stages of deindustrialization in the 70s and 80s, when the Upper Midwest began to lose immense amounts of capital and power on the national level, was happening concurrently with racial minorities gaining more access and privileges within society. This included many institutions that were built to support white, working class people, like unions and federal welfare systems. As racial minorities gained privileges within society, and the white working class of the Midwest became peripheralized, the white working class of the region came to "…interpret their plight as an effect of government policy that privileges people of colour and their communities" (S131).

I, myself, experienced living in the Rust Belt during the 2016 election, and I widely agree with McQuarrie's explanations as to why Trump was so extremely popular in the region. It's hard to express just how enthusiastic Trump supporters in my area were, and still are. I know of multiple businesses that were plastered with Trump quotes and signs, as well as both a vehicle and a barn painted with Trump's "Make America Great Again" poster design. I saw firsthand Trump's popularity within members of the local Democratic Party, with people I knew as lifelong Democrats advocating for Trump, as well as phone calls from local Democratic leaders urging party members to vote for Trump. Even today, two years into his presidency, many of the Trump supporters in my hometown are still as enthusiastic and supportive of Trump as they were during the 2016 election cycle.

However, I can tell that those who support Trump in my area are not doing so just because they agree with his policy or style. There was a strong emotional component, and many of the analyses made by McQuarrie help explain that emotional aspect. Trump made the people in my area feel important again, and much of his campaign rhetoric within the region harkened back to the days when the area was prosperous and labor was an integral part of. Even his campaign slogan, "Make America Great Again," further promised, when interpreted in the context of the Rust Belt, to bring back the days when the white working class of the region held power within society.

People from the Rust Belt are also proud of the area's past, which Trump would also exploit. I explicitly remember when Trump made a campaign stop in Youngstown, the nearest city to my hometown, and was making promises to bring the steel companies back to the city. So many people in my area latched on to the notion that Donald Trump was going to bring back the steel industry and bring us back to our days of prosperity. People were so enamored by the idea of returning to our economic heyday, that they failed to consider the practicality of that promise. Most of the people who had experience working in a steel mill had aged out of working. The steel mill buildings themselves were all razed and built over by the 80s. Bringing a steel mill back to Youngstown would be so expensive that it does not make sense for any company to take that risk. Nonetheless, people were so emotionally invested in that promise, in combination with a national politician concerned about both their real and falsely perceived grievances, that white, working class people across the political spectrum, supported Donald Trump.

Work Cited

McQuarrie, Michael, "The Revolt of the Rust Belt: Place and Politics in the Age of Anger." *The British Journal of Sociology,* vol.68, no. S1, Nov. 2017, S120-S152. doi:10.1111/1468-4446.12328. Accessed 28 Oct. 2018.

One of the goals of this course is for us to begin doing primary research. Using the guidelines in the "Profiles" chapter in The Norton Field Guide, write a profile of an interesting person, place, or event.

—Dr. Fred Siegel

Humna Chaudhry
A Blue Dot in a Red Sea

It was any ordinary middle school day for Usma Baban — classes were in session, lockers were being slammed out of either misery for failing an exam or being late to class, and everyone was simply trudging through the day, eagerly awaiting the dismissal bell at 3:00 PM. It was during the changing of class periods, Usma recalls, where she noticed the sign. A fellow classmate, standing by the lockers a few feet across from her, had been wearing a black t-shirt with white text reading, "Islam is of the devil." Shock covered Usma's face as she described encountering the t-shirt, as though she were back in that dimly lit hallway of middle school.

Usma was on her way home from school when she heard the news from her mother, and suddenly, her questions were answered. Terry Jones, a pastor for the Dove World Outreach Center, had called for an "International Burn a Koran Day." Both Jones and Usma lived in the small university town of Gainesville, Florida. "It is a blue dot in a red sea," Usma states, a small hint of pride glistening in her eyes as she describes her hometown. "It is quite liberal, but once you are out of the city limits it is extremely country."

Both Usma and her family were unable to comprehend the hate being spurred from their fellow community member. Usma's grandmother had immigrated from India to the United States during her teenage years for the very purpose of religious freedom. For three generations, her family has lived in the U.S., growing up and pursuing different paths of the "American Dream"— whether it be in medicine, engineering, business, and more. And while living here for so long, the Baban family had never witnessed such violence against their religion — or any religion for that matter.

"My family was honestly shocked," Usma recalls. "We knew something needed to be done, especially because the school that all the kids were wearing the shirt was the school that me and all my cousins were at." As such, Usma and her family decided to take on the media. The Baban family became the "go-to" family covering the event, talking about the impact Jones' remarks had on them, their community, and the country overall. Usma even remembers reciting the Qur'an — the Islamic holy text — for BBC Canada, recalling it being one of the coolest moments of her teenage years.

Soon, the whole world had come to know of "International Burn a Koran Day." The local law enforcement and the FBI had come to the university town to investigate Jones' actions, and both national and international news outlets covered the event. Political, religious, and public figures condemned the act as a means of provoking hate and separation. Even in the Middle East, a riot had taken place against Jones, and the terrorist group, Al-Qaeda, had put him on their "most wanted" list.

As is the norm with the news, Gainesville received attention for a few days before everyone forgot about Jones' Islamophobic remarks, and focused on the next big story. The investigation had closed, and the pastor was arrested right before he planned to burn over 2,000 copies of the Islamic holy text. Law enforcement, community members, and all of Gainesville had come together against his ignorance. Usma recalls, "As a community, Gainesville joined together. Lots of interfaith dialogue was started that still goes on to this day," the pride for her hometown once again showing through her eyes. "We all joined together, but we didn't give the Dove church any attention; we didn't protest outside of it or anything. We all just came together, and understood each other. It was beautiful honestly."

Today, after giving up his position at the church and losing a family fast-food business, Jones works as an Uber driver. As for Usma, she is currently a junior at the University of Florida, and also works as part of start-up production company. She hopes to one day become a therapist, as a means a of bringing psychiatry and Islam together. "I think it made me realize how much the Muslim community can be lonesome, and not necessarily always place importance on mental health. I think bringing the two (Islam and mental health) together is something we need in order to keep our community thriving and healthy."

Usma explains how even after eight years, Jones' actions leave her questioning why people would hate her even though they do not know her. "But the overwhelming amount of love and support I received then proved to me that hating a group so blindly is wrong," she states. "I think it affects me in the sense that I know there are people out there who don't understand Islam and don't want to. As a third-generation family, we place very little value on the culture of our Indian heritage. The most important things I've been taught growing up is to be a good Muslim and to be an American."

Write a profile on a person or place.

—Dr. Sheila Sandapen

Nishat Fariha

The Writer

In Trishal, Bangladesh, a young boy sits at his small desk. The pencil in his hand scratches the paper as the lights flickered above. The boy hears a small *click*. The lights go out and the little fan in the room stops its low humming. The power goes out. Again.

He grabs his papers and walks out of the room to the porch. There, he finds his mother sitting on a rickety chair as she watches the young boys and girls run barefoot across the mud. He sits down once again and begins to write.

"Saiful," his mother says softly, "Tell me what are you writing today."

And he does. He writes about the hot air, the clear sky, the kids running around without a care in the world. He thinks about a life outside his own. A place where a man could work hard and gain the opportunity to better his life. A place he would be proud to call his home. A place that is nothing like the little village he lives in now.

In 1997, the boy, now a young man, finds that the land of opportunity is only an expensive flight away. He and his bright-eyed wife leave their entire world behind as they board a plane for the first time. They wave goodbye to the only people they have ever known. At 30,000 feet in the air, the man looks out the window. He sees his country disappearing beneath fluffy clouds and he's unsure of whether or not he has made the right decision. His wife gently hands him a small notebook. He writes about his wife's black hair and brown skin, the endless clouds, and the beginning of a new life.

In 1999 and again in 2002, the man finds himself crying. He holds his children for the first time, a girl and a boy, in his arms and promises himself that no harm will ever come to them. These days he finds that he can't find the time to write. He works until he can't work anymore. Every day ages him. His once youthful features and full head of hair slowly but surely fade away. But his kids keep him happy. He sits at the dinner table watches his little girl write on the back on an envelope. He finds her a notebook, and they begin to write together. They write about the apples sitting on the counter, the garden growing in the backyard, and the smell of *biryani* cooking.

In 2018, the man —my father— sits at the dinner table and thinks. His back hurts today, so he decides to stay home. He pulls out an old notebook and his wife —my mother— places a pot on the stove. The smell of spiced milk tea fills the kitchen as my father's deep voice reads aloud. The piece is entitled "The Letters in The Lake." He reads the story of a young woman falling in love with the words in a letter from a man she once knew. My father's glasses slip slowly and slowly down his nose as he reads.

"The young woman sits by the lake and holds the letter close to her heart. 'My love, I've written you a thousand letters but only this lake knows all the secrets I've kept from you,' she thinks to herself. 'Will you still love me, even from above?'"

We wonder about the wistful woman as my mother places the cups of tea in front of us. My father asks her to bring her favorite book. She walks to the living room and heads to a small bookshelf. She runs her hands over the spines. Every book on the shelf is special, each with their own memories attached. My father's books, the ones he's endlessly inspired by and the ones he recently published are front and center. My mother brings back a purple covered book and opens it up. My father smiles as she reads the title proudly, *"New Beginnings by Saiful Islam"*.

Write a literacy narrative or a memoir.

—Dr. Patricia Egbert

Isabella Kaiser

A Stranger's Shower

I'm standing drunk and alone in a shower which isn't my own. The drunken fuzz of foolishness and confusion coats my entire body. I'm trying to sober up but it's something I can't shake. The heavy sweet alcohol splashing around my stomach and up to my throat eventually makes its way into the toilet bowl. I drag my weak and dripping body back into the shower and try again, unsuccessfully, to nurse myself back to sobriety. It isn't working.

I hear the door open a creak. An intentionally slow creak. I hear the creak and I pray to god it's a friend coming to help me. But the creak does not reveal a friend. Not even close. I peak out of the shower mascara running down my face. My red splotchy arms stung from the hot water push back the curtain and it isn't a friend. Even in my drunken, unsettled state I know he's not a friend and I know he did not come in to help me.

He starts to take off his clothes and I realize more rapidly that he has no intention of saving me. He kicks off his massive shoes and they clunk against the cold tile. He unzips his pants. The sharp and shrill noise sends shivers down my spine. I am frozen. I try to ask what he's doing but nothing comes out. He takes off his socks. One at a time. I watch them as they hit the floor. Why would he be getting in the shower with me? He peels off his Patagonia shirt and it hits the floor. Where are my friends? His boxers drop and I black out.

I say stop. I know it. I scream it. But he covers my mouth. What did I say when I blacked out? Did I ask for this? Why would I ask for something like this? I try to push him away but his weight forces me into the shower wall. The cartilage in my nose bends from his forceful thrusts and my face continues to flatten into the wall. My nose ring drops and I can hear the clank echoing down the drain. My mind wanders and the only thing I can focus on is the steam from the shower burning my back. I am helpless.

I hear noises outside the door. People laughing, drinking, completely unaware of what is going on behind the cracked door in the stranger's shower. I hear another noise. A package tears open and I know what it is. I silently thank the Lord that he's at least using a condom. A tiny victory. With my legs growing weaker and my mind shutting down I try again to get him off. I kick and flail and as much as I can. I try but my weakness overtakes me and I fail. Blacked out for the rest of the night. Unaware of what he did to me, what he said to me, and what was just my imagination.

The sun peeks through the crisp winter sky. Not in a beautiful way. But in a way that is sad and cold. I'm awake. After the night I've had I shouldn't be awake before the sun but I'm crawling in my skin. I boil with embarrassment and anger and throw myself out of a bed which is not my own. I grab my damp and sickening clothes and try to tie back my still wet hair. Tripping over beer cans and slumped teenagers I flee for the door.

The door flies open and the frosty wind of February is assaulting. Grappling up the icy sheet, which dropped the night before proved more difficult than I thought it to be. Slipping and sliding up the tundra to my car all I could think about was the pain between my legs. I looked for my friends' cars but they were gone. They hadn't come to help me the night before because they left. Left me alone in a strange house, drunk and vulnerable. The tears began flowing down my cheeks but froze before they could fall.

The penetrating questions began to circle in and out of my mind but I knew I had to leave. As I turned the key in the ignition I thought about my mom. What do I tell her? Do I tell her anything? I pulled away from the driveway and sped down the impressively manicured side streets. Why did I let this happen? Drive. Why am I such an idiot? Just keep driving. The tears started flowing again, this time harder. My body shook with each sob, and my eyes flooded with tears. The lines on the road blurred and the empty shops became swirled watercolor versions of themselves. The rest of the way home was muscle memory. Left, right, merge, exit 10, right, left home.

By the time I pulled into the driveway I was out of tears. Still crying but no more saline trickled down my puffy face. My feet crunched on the chipped ice but I didn't bother being quiet. The noise wouldn't wake my family. I pushed my key in the lock and forced the door open. Unloading my damp clothes and stealing my dad's sweatshirt warm from the dryer, I settled for the spot on the couch next to my dog. Through her snores I tried to convince myself it didn't happen. Just a dream. Completely made up and the product of watching too many *Law and Order SVU's*. The more I thought about it, the more I started to remember. I didn't want to remember. The events of the previous night wouldn't stop swirling in my mind. The warmth from the sweatshirt and the soft rise and fall of my dog's frail body brought me back down. I knew I couldn't do anything to change last night. I would just have to move on.

I don't look back much on that night. My mom is still unaware that I am now one of every six women to be raped. I try to deny it but it is a reality I've learned to live with. Every time a boy looks at me, when I get drunk and feel that same veil of helplessness coming over my body. Every time I step into a cold dark shower. I think about how an arrogant 18 year old changed the trajectory of my life so drastically.

I have never had an intimate relationship. Instead of love and intimacy I feel fear and anxiety. I'm afraid to open up to people. Not just boys but everybody. Since that night I've had an invisible wall surrounding the real me. I choose to mask myself with humor and shallow flirtation rather than truth. By sharing my weakness and allowing myself to be vulnerable again I know that I will be hurt. I have taken control of my romantic life by turning it into a type of game—Playing with fire but extinguishing it before I can get burnt.

For this assignment, you may choose to write in either of two genres: literacy narrative or memoir. Please review the "Literacy Narrative" and "Memoir" chapters in The *Norton Field Guide,* and choose the genre you would prefer to try.

— Professor Keith DeRenzo

Anh Nguyen Quach

Little Things, Big Things

1.   2006.

I never knew how he did it, how he could answer all my rapid-fire questions while still maintaining control of his motorbike, cruising alongside fellow sour-faced motorists honking their horns as Saigon descended into rush-hour chaos. I never knew how he could observe the world so carefully, decelerate, and go nowhere as the *go somewhere* mood lingered in rapidly accelerating Saigon. All I knew was that I, cheerful and awestruck, was there with him, November sun in my eyes and the afternoon breeze in my hair, watching Saigon stir.

I was six years old, sitting at the front of Dad's motorcycle and going on an impromptu city tour after school.

As I sang, gawked, and asked questions, Dad told me all I wanted to know: how clouds formed, how engines worked, why colonial French buildings were painted yellow, why some birds flew but others didn't, and why all the birds seemed to have left the countryside for urban Saigon. Cruising on an old moped amidst the hysteria of a rapidly developing city, I was embarking on adventures. I felt I was in a documentary, with Dad as my own David Attenborough, plunging into the great unknown. I was curious, thrilled, excited. I was going places.

And then, in a narrow street full of narrow houses with gigantic windows, Dad braked. My songs stopped. Yet the rumbles of Vietnam's economic capital lingered.

"Why are we here, Dad?" I wondered.

"Look," said he. *Look.*

2.   2017.

From a window in my third-storey high school classroom, I saw everything. I saw 2016 Saigon – or the part of Saigon that could be seen from an open window above a street – stretch out below me, red brick roofs, shiny corrugated roofs, yellow French buildings, and tall skyscrapers sprawled under a cloudless, bleached-blue March sky. I saw green trees line grey streets under the serene morning air, their leaves bathed in the blazing sunlight. A lady wearing *nón lá* pushed a bicycle on the sidewalk as someone opened a window high up an old apartment block. You could hear the faint rings of her bike bell as she struggled to get past a student blocking her way. Yet, on that seemingly peaceful summer morning, I saw Industry 4.0 avalanche closer the moment the traffic lights turned green. Eight-thirty-a.m. Saigon trembled amidst revving engines, screeching brakes, and ear-shattering horns as cars, buses, and motorcycles sped past, kicking up rolling clouds of dust and plastic bags. Texters crashed into everything, forgot to talk, and filled the city with selfies and livestreams. Imagine the chaos.

Then, above me, something rustled.

It came as a surprise, rather nonchalantly, as if also on a daily commute, unaware that it was being watched. Clumsily yet surprisingly gracefully, it landed on an electric wire above the road, wings flapping, legs extending, an airborne feather ball from the very blueness of the sky. But for the ruffles of its feathers, heard loud and clear amidst the nonsensical rumbles of Industry 4.0, it made no sound. Casually, lifting one little leg at a time, the plump creature set off on the wire to a tangled green tamarind tree on the other side of the road, garbage in its beak, glossy feather gleaming in the heat.

It was *walking*, the thing. Or marching. Metronomically, almost Mozartian, in 4/4 time. The tempo was, perhaps, *allegro moderato*. One step. Two. Then three. Then four. One-two-three-four-one-two-three-four. A plump spotted dove baby-stepped on a rope to its nest in a tree on the opposite sidewalk. What a sight, indeed.

There was something special about that *Spilopelia chinensis*, perhaps. Or maybe it was just birds being birds. Yet, as a bus trundled through a narrow street and blasted its vuvuzela-like horn, as a blaspheming pedestrian dodged a taxi, as a motorcyclist jumped a red light, or while nearly everyone was too busy texting and commuting to watch, the dove carried on. Docile, unwavering, the little march continued in tempo: one-two-three-four-one-two-three-four. Two steps. Then one. One more to go.

Touchdown. Fluttering onto the nearest branch, the spotted dove disappeared into the tangles of leaves, tenderly depositing its cargo into a nest built out of garbage and the love of two birds. All *you need is love*, said John Lennon, *love is all you need*.

As leaves rustled, the dove took off and, armed with more garbage, re-commenced its pilgrimage for the millionth time.

All you need is love.

And some more garbage.

3.   2006 (revisited).

Look.

They were *here*. High above the now-golden sky, their white bellies and black bodies tinted gold and pink by the dusk, they'd emerge from mud nests in gigantic windows. They'd glide, gracefully, beautifully, above narrow streets and grey buildings. Ascending higher and higher to the pinkish-golden clouds, they'd spread their wings and sing their light, bright, silvery songs that meandered through noises.

Amidst the rumbles of Vietnam's economic capital, common house martins circled in the golden sunset.

How paradoxical these *Delichon urbicum* birds are, an adult me marvels. They'll soar high up in the sky, yet low enough for a dad and his daughter on a motorbike to stare at. Constantly at unreachable heights, they seem ephemeral but still tangible enough to color a child's imagination. And how ubiquitous they are, loud and all over the place, an integral part of Saigon, yet at the same time forgotten and awaiting rediscovery as the city accelerates.

Six-year-old avian-enthusiast me, however, wasn't philosophical. Climbing on my dad's moped while he held my legs to keep me from falling over, I'd wave and talk to the house martins, anxiously waiting for replies. Singing and clapping to their little silvery songs, I'd imagine them – my tiny tuxedo-clad opera singers and ballet dancers – on a golden-pink stage, warbling sweet melodies and twirling (to Tchaikovsky's *The Nutcracker*, perhaps) to a distracted audience of tired humans, dust-coated trees, and silent, trembling buildings.

The six-year-old avian enthusiast's rapid-fire questions reverberated through the dusk:

When do they come home?

What are they talking about?

And the house martins, still singing, glided through the pink clouds until darkness enveloped the Saigon chaos.

4.   Little things/big things.

Remember how you'd open your nearly-burst backpack one last time to check if you'd forgotten something, I tell myself as another day dawns, *and your stuff fell out? Remember how, days prior, you posted an Instagram story asking for advice on what to pack? Remember how you'd freak out, mid-security-check, about all the things you've left behind: your pathobiology book, your favorite pillow, your toilet roll? And remember how you'd spend your 23-hour flight to Philadelphia regretting that you couldn't fit everything in four suitcases and two backpacks that you were already barely able to carry?*

Such pressing matters these were. *Did I forget anything? How do I bring the un-bring-able? How do I pack the eighteen years of my life into bags without leaving anything behind, so I can move to another country in peace?*

Yet, watching the sun rise above Philadelphia once more, I find myself smiling. They're all here within me, these eighteen years, stored in those little fragments of Saigon's dichotomous nature: the rosy-brown speckled feather of that tightrope-walking spotted dove amidst the greyness of a typical urban landscape, the rumble of a city undergoing economic development under a pinkish-golden sky, Dad's Attenborough-esque voice rising above the chaos, and the little house martins' silvery songs filling the noisy air. These seemingly random and insignificant moments make up where I'm from and who I am. And on the bland canvas that is my wonderfully mundane college life, these little memories paint magnificent hues.

Look. Just *look.*

What is a question that you want to explore about deception and yourself?

Guidelines:
1. Include yourself. Remember that YOU are at the center of this research; make sure your audience knows this.
2. Address our class; your audience is the 21 people who have been talking together each week. You know us; write to us.
3. Include at least one primary source.
4. Include at least 3 secondary sources, one of which must be scholarly.
5. Cite works in your text and include a works cited page using either MLA or APA format (use Purdue owl guide).

—Dr. Karen Nulton

Alexis Washburn

Human Beings, Being Human

My dad is the strongest person I know. He is kind, he is wise, and he is resilient. He is the kind of person that, no matter how hard you kick him when he is down, he will always get back up again. If you saw my dad today, you would see a man with a stable job and a beautiful family, living in the suburbs. A regular guy who works a regular job, and occasionally smokes a cigar in his free time. The man who coached his daughter's soccer team, the guy who taught his son how to throw a fast pitch. The guy behind the grill at a neighborhood pool party. But things did not always used to be this way. At a point in time, my dad was homeless. His mother kicked him out of the house when he was 18 because of his frequent drug abuse. For years, my dad lived in abandoned houses, rehab centers, crackhouses, and Salvation Army's around the greater Philadelphia area.

My dad is the strongest person I know. He is kind, he is wise, and he is resilient. If you ask him how he is doing, he will look at you with a smile and tell you he can not complain. He does not let his past mistakes define him. My dad looks at the homeless in a way that you and I will never be able to. He does not call them dangerous, or dirty. He does not think of them as an annoyance or inconvenience when he walks down the street. He does not look straight ahead when he walks so as not to make eye contact with them. He gives them his change. He smiles at them. He acknowledges them, and for a moment, he makes them feel human, which our society has done a great job of doing the opposite of.

My father is no different from these men. He once sat in their place. He too, was once covered in dirt. He too, was once hungry. Now, my father can command a room with the mere tone of his voice. He can walk into a restaurant and not be denied service. When people pass him on the street, they are not afraid to meet his gaze. My father now has all of these social privileges, but he did not change. He did not do anything to deserve them. The only difference between my father and these men, is their situations. The hand of cards that they have been dealt in life. Our society is one that is inherently classist and elitist, and it can become so easy to forget that these people are not lesser than the average, but rather, people who are just really down on their luck. People who are in need of some *humanity*.

I have always known about my dad's history with homelessness, but never in full. Recently, I sat down with him at our kitchen table, in our little suburban house in South Jersey, and got the full truth about my dad's past.

My dad's story starts off in a small section of North Philadelphia called Germantown. He lived there from 1963 until 1980. When asked about his neighborhood, my dad described it as depressing. Most of the families in his neighborhood received some sort of government assistance or welfare, and the majority of the population was African-American, which surprisingly, he didn't really feel the effects of until after moving out. These racial and cultural lines were crossed almost daily, and my dad had a lot of black friends. In his neighborhood, gangs ruled the streets. He witnessed multiple shootings, drug deals, theft, and race wars. My dad got his start in drugs when he started seeing his friends and acquaintances participate in these activities. In his own words, he simply says "it's just the way of life there." He claims he was drawn to it because of the peer pressure. "Yanno how you have your group of friends. You have the cool group, the nerds, the jocks. My friends, they were the low-lifes, for lack of a better word. It's just the only way we knew. It was my environment. It was the only choice really."

In first grade, my dad was already getting in trouble for cutting class, skipping school, and fighting with classmates. He was kicked out of school multiple times, as were his sisters. He had to repeat the first grade a number of times. It is because of this, that he doesn't recall his actual age in sixth grade, when the drinking began. At the prime age of (around) twelve years old, my father was already an alcoholic. By the time eighth grade rolled around, he was regularly using marijuana, cocaine, and methamphetamine. Occasionally, he would use intravenous drugs, such as heroine. In light of his drug use, his mother kicked him out. She said that "she could not accept that lifestyle, or the heartache that comes with it." From about ninth grade, until he got sober at age twenty-four, he had no contact with his mother. The cops were called if he showed up to his house. He dropped out of school.

My father was forced to live wherever he could. Sometimes that meant a friend's house, sometimes that meant sleeping on a park bench. When asked about his experience with homelessness, he claims "it was the loneliest point in my life." He ate very little, but when he did eat, his diet consisted mainly of hot dogs from 7/11, cheesesteaks, or fast food. Eating usually only happened once a day - the rest of his day was reserved for getting high. All of the money he had was from "stealing, cheating, and lying." He achieved this by telling strangers that he could get them drugs, then taking their money and running, "borrowing, with no intentions of ever paying it back" from friends and family, selling his food stamps for drug money, borrowing money from people at bars, or on the street. However, he never panhandled. He "refused to go that low."

After a while, people got tired of his lying and cheating, and my dad was forced to live in crackhouses. He and his oldest sister Terry sold drugs out of her house for awhile, a practice he refers to as a "shooting gallery." Essentially, the house was a hub where local drug addicts would meet to shoot up heroine together. The people who came to her house "were not to be trusted. They were drug dealers, gang members, and addicts. They were all dirty and malnourished. Honestly, looking back, most of them are now in jail, or dead. More of them are dead."

On the streets, my dad lived a dangerous life. He was robbed multiple times for his money and for his drugs. One morning, after staying with my aunt Terry, he woke up to find his own sister had robbed him of his drugs and money. Often times after these encounters, he would be left with nothing. He had few belongings, and several times throughout the years he was robbed of literally everything he owned. Often times when he was intoxicated, my dad would pick bar fights. Broken noses, fingers, and limbs were among the injuries he sustained. He was even stabbed once, but being that he did not have a lot of money, he had to have a friend patch it up using a sewing kit and rubbing alcohol. I asked him if it hurt, but he claims to not remember the pain because he was too high at the time that it happened.

People in public treated him "like a scumbag." They would make fun of him and belittle him by making him do menial tasks for money. "Strangers got off on kicking me when I was already down on my luck. People would avoid me at all costs, they were afraid to associate with me. They wouldn't trust me. People would see me and go the opposite way."

My father finally decided it was time to get help. I asked him what made him change his ways, to which he said, "it was the loneliness that got me. I wasn't welcome at my own house. I got to a point where I had to seek help." At first, he was on welfare so he had free medical services. He went through detox at Valley Forge. He was in and out of various treatment centers for four years. "Detoxing is a scary, scary thing. Scary because I didn't think I would be able to do it, didn't know where I'd live or end up. But mostly I was scared of failing. Nobody can predict who will succeed. But through my efforts, and luck, I was successful at getting sober."

Interestingly enough, throughout all of this, he has never been arrested. He has had his phone wiretapped by police, and was under surveillance multiple times. His sister and partner in crime (who is now dead from an overdose) was arrested for selling meth to an undercover agent.

The process of getting back in his family's good graces was not an easy one. It started when he went to the Salvation Army, and demonstrated a sincere desire to get his life back on track. This meant changing his ways, getting a job, and staying clean. My grandmother was very cautious of my dad for a long time. It took two years of sobriety for her to believe in his efforts. My dad lost touch with a lot of friends, but made many more. Slowly but surely, people started letting my dad back in their lives and started believing in him again. Everything after that was positive. He was able to get sober, find employment, find his wife, and have a family. "Getting sober was the hardest thing I ever did in my life. It meant giving up everything I knew, and learning a whole new way of life. Looking back, I couldn't be any more blessed." Going back and telling me about his past brought up a lot of emotions, he said. Among these were shame, sorrow, and remorse.

My dad's experience is just one of a population of people argued to range from 250,000 to 3,000,000 (Dail, 1993). At an estimated increase of 24% each year, the homeless truly do not get the attention they deserve. The notion that street people choose the life that they live is one completely unsupported, and one that can be disproved with experiences like my dad's. Because of these stereotypes, it makes it easier for us to dehumanize this population. Often, we do not give thought to how these misconceptions can lead to political decisions, social norms, and public policies that negatively affect the homeless (Auerswald & Goldblatt, 2016). Its damaging stigmas can incite anger and hatred in the average person, for they are under the impression that these people are "lazy" or "hopeless." These people are no longer people with stories and families, they are daily inconveniences, and they make us very uncomfortable. So uncomfortable in fact, that we often can not spare them our change, or even muster eye contact.

Although we do not realize it, stigmas surrounding the homeless have caused many changes in our country. Last month, about a dozen volunteers were arrested in El Cajon, California for feeding the homeless. Just a few months prior, the city council had passed an ordinance prohibiting the distribution of food on city property ("The rules of the streets," 2018). This direct discrimination towards homeless people can be explained through society's attitude towards this population. "Criminalization that, creating stigmas, prejudices and stereotypes, in a sort of vicious circle, it feeds feelings of hatred that make it socially acceptable to perpetrate crimes against the weakest," ("Hate crimes against homeless," 2016). "Since 1999, more than a thousand attacks against homeless individuals have occurred. These attacks occurred in cities throughout our country in forty-seven states, the District of Columbia, and Puerto Rico. They know no boundaries and are not limited by coast, region, or state. These attacks have permeated every corner of our society, resulting in three hundred twelve deaths and eight hundred seventy-two non- lethal attacks including beating with golf clubs, rape, and setting victims on fire while they slept," ("Hate crimes against the homeless," 2012). Much like minority groups, the homeless suffer hate-filled attacks, stereotypes, and micro aggressions. However, unlike minorities, the homeless are not protected by law from this discrimination, being that they are not recognized as a protected class. "Thus, legislation that specifically targets the homeless can be enforced and upheld so long as it does not deny the homeless of other constitutional rights and the law is applied uniformly without bias toward one of the classes that are protected," ("Are there any special laws").

My dad said the worst part of being homeless was not the way his toes curled up uncomfortably in his shoes when it was cold and he slept in the park; it was not the detoxing, or the crackhouses, or the "sleeping with one eye open." It was the shame he felt. The shame that he still feels today looking back on his experience. Overall, my research showed me that this country suppresses its homeless population. Instead of trying to rehabilitate people, money goes towards other government programs. This is all because of the idea that people choose this lifestyle and, although this is true to a degree, people generally don't consider the many variables that factor into this. In my father's experience, the neighborhood he grew up in forced him into the only lifestyle that he knew. He fell into a system, one that so many others fall into each year.

In reality, it can happen to any of us. No one is safe from possible disaster, financial struggles, or drug addiction. According to the National Survey on Drug Use and Health, 21.5 million American adults (aged 12 and older) battled a substance use disorder in 2014 ("Statistics on drug addiction," 2018). Clearly, addiction does not discriminate. Why do we? Next time you walk down the street, and you see a man begging for change, pay him a smile, make eye

Drexel Publishing Group

Essays

Introduction

Researching, thinking, and writing are at the core of the College of Arts and Sciences. In every field, students must be able to find and evaluate the best evidence and information on a topic. Students must be able to form original ideas, and then write with a fresh approach.

The following essays were selected from student submissions to the Drexel Publishing Group Essay Contest. The contest was judged by faculty from a wide range of disciplines in the College of Arts and Sciences. The essays in this section of *The 33rd* explore diverse topics such as comics, artificial intelligence, education, philosophy, and medical research. These student writers demonstrate originality, skill, and passion, and do so in a variety of disciplines in the arts and sciences.

To honor the stylistic requirements of each field, we have reproduced the essays and articles in their original forms.

— *The Editors*

Amanda Christian

X-Men: A Commentary on Modern American Racism

Introduced in September 1963, the X-Men were a team of young mutants led by Professor Charles Xavier, their teacher and mentor. Throughout the comics, their goal is to fight super-criminals and other mutants, who are led by Magneto and strive to destroy humanity in an effort to protect mutant kind (Ciampaglia). However, rather than being a black-and-white battle between good and evil, the X-Men mutants were hated by the humans they defended. By exploring the stories of characters who were vilified by the majority for being different, Stan Lee "drove home messages of tolerance and acceptance while rejecting demonization and bullying" (Ciampaglia). Through releasing the X-Men comics in the early 1960s when the Civil Rights Movement was in full swing, Marvel took a strong stance on the intolerance of hatred and bigotry. Naturally, with a comic so controversial and racially charged, it contained elements which connected it to historical figures and event in American history. X-Men uses character dynamics and plot development to create a social commentary comparing the anti-mutant oppression to institutionalized racism in the United States.

The biggest general connection between African Americans during the 60s and mutants in the comics, is the perception of them as the oppressed "other." As X-Men readers and viewers, it is easy to see that other than their powers, they are no different from humans. They have the same emotions, face the same internal struggles, and interact with one another as any other person would. Long-time X-Men writer, Chris Claremont, stated that "the X-Men are hated, feared, and despised collectively by humanity for no other reason than that they are mutants. So what we have..., intended or not, is a book that is about racism, bigotry, and prejudice" (Lyubansky). As a result of the comic's release, the taboo discussions about race became more prominent in American culture. Those who empathized with the mutants and their yearning to be accepted for who they were, were forced to look in the mirror and analyze the way they treated people who did not look like them.

This concept of perceived otherness brings up the concepts of racial passing and covering, which are prominent issues facing African American community. Racial passing occurs when an individual classified in one racial group is accepted by a member of another racial group. In the African American community, this usually occurs when a person has a light skin tone. Racial covering occurs when a person alters their behaviors or physical appearance to fit into a racial group which is not their own, or disassociate from their own group. The act of racial passing and covering most likely evolved due to the Civil Rights Movement and the cessation of Jim Crow laws (King 5). "The fear or rationale that drives the need for covering or passing is relative to which aspect of their identity is deemed more of a threat" (King 5). In *X-Men Days of Future Past,* the two characters who struggle most with their physical identities are Mystique and Beast.

In her natural form, Mystique has blue textured skin and bright yellow eyes, which clearly sets her apart from the average human. With the power to shapeshift into anyone she wants, it makes it easy to pass as a 'normal' human; however, it makes it extremely difficult for her to accept her true identity. In a deleted scene with Professor Charles Xavier, he reprimands her for her behavior and says that she is giving humanity a reason to fear and hate mutants. She responds by transitioning to her true form and saying "Do you honestly think they'll ever be able to see me like this, and feel anything but fear? You can't even look at me!" Although Mystique is accepted in her human form, she believes she will never be excepted for who she truly is. Her struggle to accept her own identity due to outside forces is much too real for minorities in America, particularly African Americans. Even today with all the racial progress American has made since the 1960s, there is still an inherent fear and preconception of minorities.

Several of the characters found in the X-Men universe can be related to historical figures who were prominent during the Civil Rights movement. The two who most often fight due to their differing ideologies and methods of establishing justice are Professor Charles Xavier and Magneto, who are often compared to Martin Luther King Jr. and Malcolm X. Professor X is motivated based on his vision of harmonious human-mutant coexistence (Ciampaglia).

While his ideologies were perceived as unattainable and unrealistic, Xavier had an unstoppable drive which gained him an abundance of mutant and occasionally non-mutant followers. His ideologies and views on inclusivity draw a clear connection to Dr. Martin Luther King Jr. In his most famous speech, 'I Have a Dream,' he states that one day he hopes "little black boys and little black girls will be able to join hands with little white boys and white girls as sisters and brothers." In a world where black and white children could not even be in the same classroom, King dreamed of them loving each other. Today, this seems like a realistic goal; however, at the time, it was just as radical as mutants and non-mutants living in harmony.

In addition to Professor X sharing positive perceptions of MLK, he also shares the historically negative ones. Despite the incredible influence Dr.

King has had on America, part of the African-American population at the time felt that he was blaming them for their own oppression. In the same 'I Have a Dream' speech, King stated that the way to fight injustice was with love and peace, not hatred and bitterness. However, in a world which discriminates against people for no reason other than their differences, it is difficult not to feel negative emotions. Much like how African-Americans in the antebellum South were expected to accommodate racism "rather than demanding that the society itself become more accepting and less oppressive," being passive and peaceful is not always the answer (Lyubansky). Overall, Professor X is seen as the hero in the X-Men comics since the reader is rooting for equality between humans and mutants, but the hatred towards mutants spawns a more radical approach to mutant prosperity.

Magneto, the main villain in the X-Men comics, strives to fight for the liberation of mutants by any means necessary. As a character, he is predominately a sympathetic leader with understandable motivations but disagreeable methods (Parks). In the comics, Magneto lost his family in the Holocaust and survived extensive inhumane treatment in a concentration camp. Because of this, he understands the dangers of prejudice, racism, nationalism, and fear (Parks). Malcolm X suffered from a similar tragic childhood which shaped his motives as a leader. At a young age, his father was murdered by the Ku Klux Klan and his mother was placed in a psychiatric facility (Parks). After turning to a life of crime and "embrac[ing] the ideology and eschatology of the Nation of Islam," he began to follow Wali Fard who taught that "the original inhabitants of the earth were black and that white people were evil incarnate, the devil" (Parks). Clearly, both Magneto and Malcolm X came out of traumatic situations with extremist views on the world. Their distorted views and unrealistic understanding of contemporary race relations resulted in a hatred towards people unlike them and an inherently violent approach to establishing justice (Lyubansky).

Magneto and his army represent the aggressive approach to strengthening minority power, similarly to the black nationalist movements. As history shows, Malcolm X emphasized the urgency of the time and the consequences for restricting African-Americans racial and democratic equality. One of his most famous quotes regarding this is "If we don't do something real soon, I think you'll have to agree that we're going to be forced either to use the ballot or the bullet" (Parks). Magneto's approach to equality is just as aggressive, and even if he is defeated, he refuses to go down without a fight. In the film X-Men: First Class he states, "Peace was never an option... Whatever comes, I and mine will not go like lambs to the slaughter—but like tigers!" His strategy goes beyond simply fighting fire with fire, but creating a force far greater than the one it was meant to destroy. Although his motives of protecting his people are justified, his violent methods show the dangers and realities of oppression.

In addition to bringing in history through characters, Stan Lee and the other X-Men writers also used historical events to influence the X-Men storylines. In 1965, the X-Men series introduced The Sentinels, which were massive mutant-hunting robots. It is no coincidence that three months prior, readers had watched black Americans being beaten and abused by white police officers during the Watts Riots. The Watts Riots, also known as the Watts Rebellion occurred in Los Angeles in August of 1965 (History.com). The riots began after an altercation between a police officer and stepbrothers Marquette and Ronald Frye, which quickly escalated to include their mother Rena, and hundreds of other police officers and members of the predominantly black community. "The Watts Riots lasted for six days, resulting in 34 deaths, 1,032 injuries and 4,000 arrests, involving 34,000 people and ending in the destruction of 1,000 buildings, totaling $40 million in damages" (History. com). Even though the officers who were a part of the riots were significantly outnumbered by residents, they possessed clear advantages and used a tremendous amount of force against mainly unarmed rioters. This is similar to the power dynamic between the mutants and Sentenials, who were technologically advanced and possessed abilities such as flight, strength. In addition to their similarity in numbers, uniforms worn by the officers during the riots share many similar elements with the build of the Sentinels. Although the police were dressed in their typical uniform, their riot gear consisted of white helmets with dark brims (History.com). For the viewers at home, the dark brims shielded the officer's eyes, making them appear unhuman and disassociated with morality. This X-Men comparison is particularly powerful because it forces the public to acknowledge the corruption in their own political systems and law enforcement.

The X-Men mansion has been destroyed and rebuilt more than any other establishment in the Marvel comics. While many people associate this with the constantly changing racial climate, it can also be linked to the destruction of safe spaces in African American communities. Between 1900 and today, there have been 60 documented burning and bombing attacks on African American churches. In X-Men, their mansion is a place for them to feel safe and protected from the negative outside world. It is a place for mutants to learn, socialize, and strategize, surrounded by people who support them. Churches such as the Second Wilson Church of Chester in South Carolina served a similar purpose. In addition to holding services, churches, particularly in African-American communities during this period, were a safe and peaceful place. They were built around love and acceptance which greatly juxtaposed the hateful racial politics in America. The Second Wilson Church of Chester was gutted and completely leveled by fire, much like the X-Men mansion was in Uncanny *X-Men #154* (Lune). The destruction of a sacred place in order to silence the voices of the oppressed in not exclusive to the African American community, but is certainly prevalent in American history. This connection to the home of the X-Men shows that no matter how devastating the loss is, people can rebuild and grow back even stronger.

"The X-Men's struggles in a world defined by systemic persecution proved malleable enough to outlast the civil rights era" (Ciampaglia). Although their origin stems from the injustices faced by African Americans in the 1960s, the X-Men have been adopted by numerous minority groups, especially members of the LGBTQ community. In modern America where people should be accepted regardless of looks or preferences, the battles faced by these communities to be accepted for who they are far from over. "This was made explicit in the film *X-Men: The Last Stand* (2006) when the distraught parents of Bobby Drake, also known as Iceman, ask him, 'Have you tried not being a mutant?' It's a question that was painfully familiar to generations of LGBTQ youth"(Ciampaglia). Despite how easy it would be to fade into the background and mask individuality, the X-Men franchise carries on the value that it is not only okay to be different, it is what makes you a hero.

Works Cited

Ciampaglia, Dante A. "How Stan Lee's X-Men Were Inspired by Real-Life Civil Rights Heroes." *History.com*, A&E Television Networks, 13 Nov. 2018, www.history.com/news/stan-lee-x-men-civil-rights-inspiration.

History.com. "Watts Riots." *History.com*, A&E Television Networks, 28 Sept. 2017, www.history.com/topics/1960s/watts-riots.

King, Lauren Caryl. "Passing, Covering and the Role of Authenticity in Marvel's X-Men Universe." *Harvard Extension School*, Nov. 2016, dash.harvard.edu/bitstream/handle/1/33797395/KING-DOCUMENT-2016.pdf?sequence=1&isAllowed=y.

Lune, Matt. "X-Plosion! All the Times the X-Men Mansion Has Been Destroyed." *CBR.com*, CBR, 1 Dec. 2018, www.cbr.com/x-men-mansion-every-time-destroyed/.

Lyubansky, Mikhail. "The Racial Politics of X-Men." *Psychology Today*, Sussex Publishers, 5 June 2011, www.psychologytoday.com/us/blog/between-the-lines/201106/the-racial-politics-x-men.

Parks, Gregory S. "'A Choice of Weapons': The X-Men and the Metaphor for Approaches to Racial Equality." *Indiana Law Journal*, vol. 92, no. 5, 2017, pp. 1-27., www.repository.law.indiana.edu/cgi/viewcontent.cgi?article=11267&context=ilj.

Tori Popescu

Philosophical Reflections on American Students' Attitudes Towards Education

As an international student coming to the U.S., I was exposed to a lot of culture shock: different interactions, food, laws, work habits, fashion style, and the list can go on. However, the biggest culture shock I encountered happened in the classroom setting, and it goes beyond that to *the way American students view education.*

The story that made me want to write this paper happened at the beginning of my freshman year when, while in a class that was almost at its end, students vigorously started packing their things and left the room while the teacher was still speaking. First, I thought there was some sort of emergency that had made them rush out of the class. Soon, I realized it was just the American culture acting in such a disrespectful manner towards one of the aspects of life that matter the most to our development, *education.* Six months later, and I still was not able to understand why students felt so entitled to rush and to disrespect their teachers. Every ending of a class was another chance for me to be shocked by how students treated their education. Coming from a country where at the time the teacher comes in the class, you must get up and say loudly the proper salutation, I was shocked to see that students were not even saying "Hello" when entering the class.

Being truly disturbed by this situation, I started analyzing it from a more profound point of view. I chose to go to one of the professors and ask them if they thought this kind of behavior is normal. I was told that it is a part of the present American culture, and that ten years ago it was different. *What made it change? What is so different about today's generation that makes it so opposed to the idea of being in school and getting an education?* The students' attitude is more than leaving the class before the teacher is done talking. It makes it seem like they are going to college only because they are forced to do so. It shows that they are seeing college as a necessity, and not as something enjoyable. Personally, I believe their attitude towards education is not the right one and I see it as a first step into the way they are going to live their lives after graduation. I analyzed this issue from an ethical point of view, and I came up with three different philosophers that state theories which reinforce my claims. Education is important and I believe it should be treated with respect and dedication, *but what would Aristotle, Kant, and Mill say about this?*

First, Aristotle would be a huge advocate for the European educational system. In his book, Nicomachean Ethics, he talks about the power of habit (or "ethos"). He believes that the character of an individual is developed from childhood by reinforcing behaviors that demonstrate respectful attitudes which, in the end, lead to a "greater good". According to Aristotle, *"It makes no small difference, then, to be habituated in this way or in that straight from childhood, but an enormous difference, or rather all the difference."* Thus, the rigorous system of rules imposed in the European classroom is mandatory for creating well-behaved students that will show respect for their teachers. By promoting minor acts such as simply caring for your teachers, addressing them in a more formal way, and paying attention to the classes you are taking, the attitude towards education will experience a shift, becoming more positive. Aristotle believes that you *"become just by doing things that are just,"* thus you should act in a manner that you act knowingly, by choice, and not randomly. Aristotle's belief would be that your actions speak for yourself, therefore you must honor them, even if it might not be pleasant. By being forced to practice a behavior that takes you out of your comfort zone and challenges you to confront your natural laziness for the sake of recognition, knowledge, and growth, you will develop the power of advancing socially and intellectually, getting closer to achieving the good, an unattainable concept at which everything aims.

Second, I will begin Kant's analysis with the Categorical Imperative, which states that you should act only according to that maxim whereby you can at the same time will that it should become a universal law. Thus, students should ask themselves "Am I willing to be treated without respect by the people to whom I would share my knowledge? Am I willing to put so much time and effort receive nothing but a lack of interest?" If their answer is negative, then their maxim cannot become a universal law, and the Kantian process would make them realize the consequence of their actions, thus stopping them from behaving in that certain way. In addition, referring to the part of moral philosophy concerned with deontology, Kant would believe that showing respect to teachers and valuing education is part of our duty and our work towards the *"kingdom of ends,"* an ideal society where everyone is rational and acting ethically. In his view, the moment students treat education, thus professors, simply as means of achieving a career, they lose the joy of purely enjoying the process. This is well described through the *humanity formula:* *"Act in such a way that you treat humanity, whether in your own person or in the person of another, always at the same time as an end and never simply as means."*

Last but not least, the need to educate society is present in Mill's work, which promotes the achievement of higher faculties and the avoidance of a lower level of existence. In his utilitarian view, it's essential to have the people educated, and the perfect world would be one in which there is free universalization of education. Therefore, in order to get to the ultimate end of *"an existence exempt as far as possible from pain, and as rich as possible in enjoyments, both in point of quantity and quality,"* you have to make people conscious about the more elevated faculties available to them and make them strive for mental cultivation. Mill would believe that the students' attitude is not following the Greatest Happiness Principle, which states that the right actions are the ones which promote happiness, and by happiness he refers to the higher pleasures which can only be accessed once you cultivate your mind. Possessing such a mind will make students find infinite sources of interest all around themselves, whether it is in art, nature, poetry, or other noble pursuits, thus achieving greater happiness.

All things considered, American students' attitude towards education doesn't promote superior achievements nor getting closer to the highest good, and it's not a maxim that they would be willing to universalize. This goes beyond their studies to their way of living, in a culture that makes the majority of them not satisfied with their work, while feeling pressured to follow certain steps, without thinking about enjoying the process. By showing a sense of superiority derived from the idea that everything is a business – in the given case paying for college means they can act however they want – they deprive themselves of the cultivation of nobleness of character, therefore from achieving the desired state of happiness. Personally, I believe that all the philosophical concepts mentioned in this paper should be applied to the way American students are educated: *enforcing a respectful attitude since childhood, being taught to think about the universalization of their maxim, and being more exposed to the benefits of mental cultivation.* By doing this, students would not see college just as a necessity anymore. They would actually find pleasure in being educated, eventually being able to enjoy listening to their professors until the class is done.

Tracy Marcelis

What's the Point of Same-Sex Education?

When I was in eighth grade and deciding where to go to high school, I was told that sex-same schools are one of the best choices for teenagers, especially girls. There are no distractions from boys, one can feel confident in the classroom being in a room of all women, and the girls do not have to worry about dressing up to impress boys. All these statements were selling points for same-sex education, but where was the proof that this education was ultimately better for me than co-educational? This topic has been debated by educators, students, and even politicians for decades, with no true conclusion as to whether single-sex education is more beneficial to students compared to co-educational schooling. Having attended a co-ed grade school and an all-girls high school, I have had experiences with both types of educational settings. From my experiences, I believe that single-sex education helped me in areas like self-esteem and confidence, however, from an academic standpoint, I do not know whether I would have done just as well in a co-educational setting. The common questions over the effects of single-sex education focus on how female students are impacted by single sex-education in the areas of math and science, how confidence and self-esteem differs between students in single-sex schools versus co-ed schools, and whether or not single-sex education in itself is a sexist system and limits students' success.

This issue goes far beyond my own education, with some educators and policy makers arguing for same-sex education in public institutions, not just private. The basis for some of the supporters of same-sex educators is that single-sex classrooms would help alleviate the gender gap in areas like science and mathematics. In an experiment conducted in Switzerland where half the students in a school were placed in a same-sex classroom and half were placed in co-ed classrooms, girls in the same-sex setting on average had a greater improvement in math scores (Eisenkopf). As proponents of single-sex education believe, this could be due in part to stereotype threat, which is an anxiety brought on by stereotypes about certain groups and the fear that comes from trying to not conform to that stereotype, in this case that females do worse in mathematics than males (Eisenkopf). By only having females in the room, the threat is eliminated and female students can do better than those in the co-educational classrooms. This conclusion, however does not hold true for all studies that have been conducted. According to Bigler and Signorella, in another study testing the effect of stereotype threat on girls, girls in the coeducational high school did better than boys on a given math test, while in the single-sex schools, the boys did better than the girls on the same math test. In this case, stereotype threat had the opposite effect on the scores of girls. This is possibly a result of girls being more motivated to beat the stereotype, rather than feel threatened by it. For me, in high school I did not face stereotype threat, being in classrooms of all girls, but in grade school and college classes, I was and am in classrooms with men, and to some extent I do feel motivated in subjects like math to do well in part based on the stereotype that men are better than women in mathematics.

Along with mathematics, the sciences are an area where males dominate and many believe that same-sex education could help give girls the boost to take higher level science courses, and ultimately pursue more STEM careers. In a study that looked at the courses taken by Israeli Jewish high school students in co-educational schools and all-girls schools, it was found that attending an all-girls institution made no difference in the amount of higher level science and math courses taken, except in physics and computer science (Feniger). This study found that in comparison to girls at co-ed schools, those in all-girl schools took advanced-level computer science and physics courses at higher rates, but those at co-ed schools took advanced level biology courses a higher rate (Feniger). The level at which the girls at same-sex school take higher level computer science courses is equal to the frequency of male students, however as Feniger points out, this does not seem to be a result of the all-girl environment but rather the requirements all-girls schools have for taking such courses. Again, this shows that all-girls education has very little impact on the advancement of women in STEM fields. The STEM gap, according to Gross-Loh, seems to be closing in areas of biology on its own, without the help of all-girls schools. Being a biology major myself, I look around me in my lectures and labs, and see mostly women around me, from both co-educational schools and same-sex schools, so I can see first–hand that women are beginning to dominate fields like these, and attempt to advance into previously male-dominated careers of research and medicine.

While there has been little conclusive evidence as to the beneficial effects of same-sex classrooms on academics themselves, supporters of single-sex education believe that this type of schooling makes a significant difference in confidence and self-esteem of both girls and boys. Having attended an all-girls high school, I believe that the experience helped boost my self-confidence because I was not comparing myself based on looks as much, considering we all had to wear the same ugly uniforms. Depending on what the environment of the school is, I believe that same-sex schools give girls the chance to focus less on looks and appearances, and more on developing character. As a woman named Pippa Biddle states in an article written by Christine Gross-Loh, "I could wake up five minutes before class, pull on clothes, and feel just as beautiful as I would have with full hair and makeup. The value was put on who we are, not what we look like." Many studies have shown that girls thrive in same-sex schools because they feel safer and more confident in their environments (Anfara and Mertens). This research, however, is based more so on personal accounts from those who have attended such schools rather than empirical data. From these accounts, there has been a significant number of students, mostly women but also men, who attribute single-sex education as a benefit to their self-esteem and confidence in the classroom because it is easier to take risks and participate without the fear of embarrassment (Anfara and Mertens). While this viewpoint is consistent with my own, that is not the case for all students and is not supported by all data.

While some studies show that single-sex education is beneficial, other show that there is little to no difference in the confidence levels between co-educational and single-sex schools (Anfara and Mertens). In the majority of research, attitude and self-confidence are either impacted positively or not influenced at all by single-sex education, however, in the area of body image, single-sex environments could be harmful. In one study, while the prevalence of problems with body image and eating disorders were similar for single-sex and co-educational schools, girls who attended all girl schools "endorsed a thinner ideal body type than girls who attended coeducational school" (Bigler and Signorella).This ties into how the type of schooling females attend may influence their expectations of femininity and gender stereotypes. Would being at an all-girls school lead to more comparisons of body and appearance more so than at co-educational school? For some girls, an all-girl environment may be more toxic to body image considering they are constantly surrounded by other girls to compare themselves to, but for other girls, this type of environment may be less intimidating because there is less social pressure to look a certain way which is typically more present in co-educational settings, which was the case for me.

Opponents of single-sex education disagree with the supposed "benefits" because of the lack of conclusive evidence. It is almost impossible to have a concrete methodology in conducting an experiment because there are so many factors involved, such as having students randomly assigned to attend single-sex or coeducational schooling. This is not possible with the education system today, where one must attend a school voluntarily, and attending same-sex schools is most likely influenced by economic background and family income because single-sex schools are not public institutions (Gross-Loh). As it can be seen from all the studies mentioned previously, there are so many conflicting results, especially in regards to academic performance. So, if there are no definitive positive results, why continue to separate boys and girls?

Many believe single-sex education is a sexist system, where gender stereotyping continues to be reinforced because all-boys schools cater to the "typical" ways boys learn, while all-girls schools cater to the "typical" ways girls learn, and many educators take these stereotypes as the absolute (Gross-Loh). While boys and girls typically do learn slightly differently, it is harmful to strictly teach to one or the other stereotype of learning because the majority of students do not learn one specific way. Other opponents of single-sex education relate it to racial segregation in schools, saying that by being separate, the schools cannot be equal (Anfara and Mertens). There are many arguments against this view however, due to the fact that single-sex education is a choice. Many also believe it does level the playing field for girls when they attend single-sex schools. As Burch Ford, an educator, administrator, and counselor at multiple schools, discusses in Gross-Loh's article, because these girls attend same-sex institutions, there is no possibility for certain gender roles to infiltrate the classroom. Gender stereotypes that exist between males and females that may influence things like who speaks in class, who performs certain tasks for assignments, or whether boys or girls are better at a certain subject, do not play into the dynamic of an all-girl or all-boys school because students are required to do all things regardless of the gender stereotypes associated with certain tasks (Gross-Loh). At my school, I was required to speak in class, I was encouraged to do dissections in lab, I was required to do my best in gym class, and I was expected to voice my opinions. I was not given the opportunity to feel stereotype threat when performing these tasks because I was not in an environment where that could directly impact me, considering I was not in the room with male students.

While I believe that my all-girls education was an experience that benefitted me in my personal growth and development, it is difficult to say whether or not academically I was influenced significantly. While I believe that self-confidence and the feeling of safety do play into academic success, many studies lack conclusive evidence that same-sex schools definitively improve academic success alone. Through analyzing how the gender gap in STEM fields is related to same-sex education, how confidence and self-esteem is impacted, and how the system can be seen as a pathway to gender stereotyping, there can be no true conclusion drawn as to whether is it more advantageous to send a child to same-sex schools, which is why the debate still continues to this day, and why public institutions have yet to segregate schools in this manner.

Works Cited

Anfara, Vincent A., and Steven B. Mertens. "Do Single-Sex Classes and Schools make a Difference?" *Middle School Journal*, vol. 40, no. 2, 2008, pp. 52-59. ProQuest, http:// ezproxy2.library.drexel.edu/login?url=https://search-proquest-com.ezproxy2.library. drexel.edu/docview/217434298?accountid=10559. Accessed 22 Oct. 2018.

Bigler, Rebecca S., and Margaret L. Signorella. "Single-Sex Education: New Perspectives and Evidence on a Continuing Controversy." *Sex Roles*, vol. 65, no. 9-10, 2011, pp. 659-669. ProQuest, http://ezproxy2.library.drexel.edu/login?url=https://search-proquest-com.ezproxy2.library.drexel.edu/docview/898231300?accountid=10559,do i:http://dx.doi.org.ezproxy2.library.drexel.edu/10.1007/s11199-011-0046-x. Accessed 22 Oct. 2018.

Eisenkopf, Gerald, et al. "Academic performance and single-sex schooling: Evidence from a natural experiment in Switzerland." *Harvard Kennedy School: Journal of Economic Behavior & Organization*, 2015, pp. 123-43. http://gap.hks.harvard.edu/ academic-performance-and-single-sex-schooling-evidence-natural-experiment-switzerland Accessed 26 Oct. 2018.

Feniger, Yariv. "The Gender Gap in Advanced Math and Science Course Taking: Does Same-Sex Education make A Difference?" *Sex Roles*, vol. 65, no. 9-10, 2011, pp. 670-679. ProQuest,http://ezproxy2.library.drexel.edu/login?url=https://searchproquest. com.ezprox y2.library.drexel.edu/docview/898227313?accountid=10559,doi:http:// dx.doi.org.ezproxy2.library.drexel.edu/10.1007/s11199-010-9851-x. Accessed 22 Oct. 2018.

Gross-Loh, Christine. "The Never-Ending Controversy Over All-Girls Education." *The Atlantic*. 20 Mar. 2014. https://www.theatlantic.com/education/archive/2014/03/ the-never-ending-controversy-over-all-girls-education/284508/. Accessed 26 Oct. 2018.

Kyle Prekeris

Time: Reality or an Illusion?

What is time? Is time part of our reality? Or is time a fabric of our imagination? Time is a challenging concept for us to completely understand – it really can be anything that we make of it. Depending on how it is perceived, its meaning can change for us – is it constantly flowing or does it have turbulent aspects? Three theories of time try to help us understand the question of, what is time?

A-theorists believe that time is dynamic. Time flows and there is a moving now that is a real, objective, moving entity. Reality changes because of the passage of time. There are two different A-theories – Presentism and the Growing Universe View. Presentism states that only the present is real – the past and future do not exist – and the present itself is unique. However, it can quickly be rejected due to the fact that present events are caused by past ones – "If A caused B, A and B both exist. Hence if past event X caused present event Y, X exists; ergo past events exist" (Garrett 78). The Growing Universe View states that the present and the past are real, but the future is unreal. The present moment is not unique because past moments are real as well. As time progresses, the present becomes the past and the past becomes more of the past – layer upon layer is added to the growing past. An objection to this theory is that it allows for the possibility that we are living in the past. We could think that we are living in the present, but it could actually be the year 4000 and thus we are actually living in the past (Garrett 79).

B-theorists, on the other hand, believe that time is not dynamic. Time does not flow and there is no moving now. Rather, "an utterance of 'now' merely refers to its time of utterance, just as an utterance of 'here' refers to its place of utterance" (Garrett 71). For them, the past, present, and future are equally real. Because all times exist, the present moment has no privileged status. For B-theorists, we travel along a timeline – this is why the past and future are real. Because they believe time runs along a timeline, they tend to be determinists because the future for them is already laid out and we're just going through it. One objection for this theory is that events never change their B-series location – it will always be true that World War II ended on September 2, 1945; this event cannot change.

Henri Bergson presented another view of time. He said that through the perception of change, one can understand the reality of time. In "The Perception of Change," Bergson had four main theses. First, change is indivisible – it cannot be divided, only space can be divided. Second, change is absolute and radical, without support – it is fundamental. Third, the present varies according to attention to life. Time is malleable; by making the world more present to us, it makes it present. Lastly, the past is preserved in itself, automatically. The whole past itself is real. Our brains are a filter to the past – they focus on the things that are important to us and filter out the rest. This is useful for us because we could not survive if we attended to our whole past. And so, we do not have to store or know the past for it to be real because the past is always retained. For Bergson, everything is moving in time – the appearance of it being immobile is how we perceive it. Reality itself is change – we only perceive change when it reaches a certain threshold. For instance, let's say a ceiling fan is going to fall. It could be falling slowly, but we don't perceive it; we know and perceive the change when it falls all at once. Bergson also said how our inner life is like a melody – a continuous stream of change. All of our moods and our thoughts are constantly changing and when we introspect we can perceive this change. Bergson said that change is constantly adding to itself. Time isn't succession – it is fluid. When time is spatialized, then we see specific states and we go from one to the next in succession. Time builds on itself like a spiral – as more of time becomes the past, it grows and grows. Bergson's theory is probably the most sound, as it allows for the past, present, and future to be real and also for the future to be opened rather than predetermined.

I like to believe that time flows like a river and at certain points on that river it can be turbulent – so depending on where I am in time, it could be smooth and calm for me, but fast and chaotic for you. I do not agree with Presentism or the Growing Universe View – I believe that there is definitely a past and there is a future. However, I like the principle of adding layers to the past, as stated by the Growing Universe View, because it is true – the past is continuously growing more and more as time progresses. Although B-theory seems like it is the most widely used theory, as it says that past, present, and future are real and that time runs along a timeline, I do not agree that the future is already laid out. I believe that we have a say in what our futures can become and depending on what path we choose, we travel down a different realm of possibility.

All of the theories, with the exception of Presentism, states that there is a past, which I agree with – the past exists and has existed; it exists in our memories and in time. We can see evidence of the past by looking at the Earth and its many layers, at fossils and how species have evolved, and at the rise and fall of empires with the Babylonians, Romans, Mayans, Incans, etc. And so, there should be no debate on whether or not the past is real.

I do not think that the future is determined as B-theorists would believe – I think that there are possibilities that can be taken and depending on which possibility is chosen it can lead to a different set of possibilities. Although we cannot perceive the future like we can the past, I believe that time does not just stop in the present – it continues on into an unknowable future.

Finally, I think that there is no present – only past and future. The future comes towards us and once it reaches us, it becomes the past. I do not think there is a way for us to perceive the present, as any time we view something through our eyes, or feel something at our fingertips, it takes time, albeit a very short amount of time, for our brains to process what we see and what we feel. With that being said, it would be true to say that we always live in the past. However, the present may just be the instantaneous change between past and future, which is something that we cannot perceive, but we can understand. And so, this would mean that there is a present. If there is a present, then I would have to agree with Bergson's view of it – the idea that the present varies depending on how much attention is placed on it and that the brain is a filter for the past and it only keeps information that is important to us. Thus, it can be inferred that Bergson's "present" is any event that your brain focuses on and allows you to perceive or remember. For instance, let's say someone that you care for has passed away. Your brain keeps this event in your mind, and so the attention that you and your brain are giving it is making it your present, even though the event itself is in the past. So now, their death is your present for as long as you keep it in your mind – once their death is accepted and is no longer focused on, it is no longer your present but is now completely part of the past. From that understanding, it seems as though my definition of "present" is different from Bergson's because for Bergson, an event in the past can become your present while also staying in the past, while for me, the present would be considered to be the here-and-now or the instantaneous change from future to past.

Time is a fickle thing – it is ever-changing. Depending on how we perceive it, time can be constant or it can be turbulent. The different theories present for us ways to interpret and understand time; however, we may never truly know what "time" is. Even then, many of us can agree that time is real and that it changes depending on how it is perceived.

Reference

Garrett, Brian. *What Is This Thing Called Metaphysics?* 3rd ed., Routledge, 2017.

Heather Heim

A Process of Approval: The Development and Acceptance of the First Birth Control Pill in the United States, 1950-1970

Before the development of the birth control pill in 1959, many couples, and women in particular, had to worry about having too many children and supporting big families. Those who tried to prevent conception had to rely on other methods that could be dangerous or unreliable, and unwanted pregnancies often resulted in illegal abortions or shotgun weddings. In the 1950s, persuaded by feminist Margaret Sanger, and funded by feminist Katherine McCormick, Gregory Pincus researched and developed the first birth control pill. Though the FDA eventually approved the pill, it was met with much criticism from the Catholic Church as well as from government officials, all who felt the pill was immoral. Regardless of these concerns of morality, many couples began to use the pill and despite its initial controversy—a controversy that has yet to die out—the first birth control pill had a massive impact on society. Not only did it allow for family planning, but it also gave women a new freedom and position in society, which led to a broadening of women's rights.

Following the end of World War II, America and several other nations experienced a massive baby boom; couples were marrying young and having children right away. However, the combination of new opportunities being made available to women outside of family life and the growing trend of sex before marriage, made women desire more control over their sexual activity and over their bodies (May, 3). In her book, *America and the Pill : A History of Promise, Peril, and Liberation,* author Elaine Tyler May notes that before the development of the birth control pill, men controlled the most common methods of contraception: condoms and withdrawal (May 4). In addition to abortion and surgical sterilization as more extreme ways to prevent pregnancy, May notes, "Potions and remedies of various sorts appeared on the market in the nineteenth and early twentieth centuries. Sold as a means to 'regulate' the menstrual cycle, they often came with bold warnings that their use might prevent pregnancy or cause miscarriage" (May 4). These ineffective and/or dangerous methods of birth control made a reliable and effective method of contraception necessary.

Such a method was developed by Gregory Pincus in 1959, in the form of Enovid, the first birth control pill. However, it was almost a decade earlier, in 1950, that the idea was first planted and the research first began. In his article "Gregory Pincus and Steroidal Contraception Revisited," author E. Diczfalusy provides a timeline for "the birth of the birth control pill," starting with Margaret Sanger's persuading Pincus to test contraceptive steroids in animals and Katherine McCormack's funds (Diczfalusy 10). May goes into greater detail about these women, noting that far from researching birth control methods, "Many of the developers of the pill were trying to find a cure for infertility" (May 14). She credits Sanger and McCormick (both lifelong feminists and both in their 70s at the time) ironically as the "two mothers" of the birth control pill. Sanger had been advocating for women-controlled contraceptives since as early as 1912, and in 1916, she "went to prison for opening the first birth control clinic in the United States," after which she developed a new strategy of working with doctors, to lend her movement legitimacy (May 18-19). McCormick was also an activist, and being born into money, was able to study biology at MIT; this was an opportunity that was uncommon for women at the time (May 21). Sanger first approached Pincus, who did experimental biology, to research contraception. She then approached McCormick, who promised Pincus $10,000 per year and oversaw the progress of the project (May 24). May notes, "McCormick ended up contributing more than $2 million to the pill project over the years— the equivalent of about $12 million in year 2000 dollars" (May 24).

With Sanger and McCormick's influence and money, "Pincus recruited two partners—M. C. Chang, a longtime colleague, and John Rock, the chief of gynecology and obstetrics at Harvard Medical School" (Thomas 149).Working from the findings of chemists Carl Djerassi and Russell Marker, who synthesized progesterone from yams, Pincus and his partners tested the synthetic hormone, called progestin, for its ability to inhibit ovulation (May 24). In 1951, they would carry out their first rabbit experiment, publishing their results two years later (Diczfalusy 11). As their research progressed, Pincus began clinical trials in Puerto Rico with Dr. Rice-Wray (Diczfalusy 11). In his book *A New World to be Won: John Kennedy, Richard Nixon, and the Tumultuous Year of 1960*, G. S.Thomas explains, "Pincus recruited 221 volunteers in Puerto Rico. Not one became pregnant during the first eight months. Equally important was the fact that 85 percent of the women who stopped using the pill became pregnant within four months, proof that Enovid did not induce infertility" (Thomas 149). In 1957, the pharmaceutical company G.D. Searle, would get Enovid approved by the US Food and Drug Administration (FDA)—but only for "menstrual regulation," not for contraceptive use (Diczfalusy 11).

The director of clinical research at G.D. Searle, Irwin Winter, stated "Even that much came about, in part, because the medical director of the

FDA was a friend of mine" (Thomas 149). Initially, fearing the opposition the of the Catholic church, "Searle didn't dare ask the FDA to clear Enovid for contraceptive use" (Thomas 149). Moreover, the government's widespread lack of support for birth control prevented Enovid from initially being approved for its true purpose. In 1959, President Eisenhower stated, "I cannot imagine anything more emphatically a subject that is not a proper political or government activity or function or responsibility...The government will not, so long as I am here, have a positive political doctrine in its program that has to do with the problem of birth control. That's not our business" (May 22). Despite Enovid's being approved solely for menstrual regulation, its contraceptive potential was not lost on consumers. The FDA required Searle to label each container with a warning that Enovid prevented ovulation (Thomas 149). Winter described the warning as being "like a free ad" (Thomas, 149). May notes, "half a million American women suddenly sought medication for 'menstrual irregularity,' a condition rarely treated prior to the availability of the ovulation-suppressing remedy" (May 5).

In 1959, Searle tried to get Enovid approved as a contraceptive. Searle's policy counselor, James Irwin stated, "We were going into absolutely unexplored ground in terms of public opinion...My fear was that this would provoke an avalanche of letters" (Thomas 149). Thomas notes that Irwin "planted stories about Enovid's birth control powers in Reader's Digest and *Saturday Evening Post* and braced himself for a violent backlash," but ultimately, "Nothing happened" (Thomas 149). A formal hearing took place in Washington in December of 1959. The FDA reviewer assigned to the case was Dr. Pasquale DeFelice, who May describes as "a young obstetric gynecologist who was still completing his residency" (May 33). DeFelice noted, "There I was...a thirty-five-year-old, qualified but not yet board-certified OB-GYN man. Standing before me was John Rock, the light of the obstetrical world" (Thomas 150). Thomas notes, "The two men would recall the hearing differently— Rock remembering it as a tense debate of moral issues, DeFelice as a straightforward discussion of scientific minutiae" (Thomas 150). DeFelice later stated, "I knew what was going to happen once we licensed it...I knew that birth control pills would be flying out the windows. Everybody and her sister would be taking it" (Thomas 150). After the hearing, DeFelice even considered buying stock in Searle, but decided this would be unethical (Thomas 150).

The FDA took its time in making a decision. DeFelice said, "Even though the pill had been through more elaborate testing than any drug in the FDA's history, there was a lot of opposition...we were in no hurry to put the FDA stamp of approval on it" (Thomas 150) Five months after the hearing, in May of 1960, Enovid was finally approved for contraceptive use. Still, the FDA tried to separate itself from the drug's function. *The New York Times* article officially announcing the FDA's approval, shared the carefully worded message of the

FDA's Associate Commissioner, John L. Harvey: "Approval was based on the question of safety...We had no choice as to the morality that might be involved. When the data convinced our experts that the drug meets the requirements of our new drugs provisions our own ideas of morality had nothing to do with the case" ("U.S. Approves Pill for Birth Control").

Once Enovid was on the market as a birth control pill, its biggest opponent was, perhaps, the aforementioned Catholic Church. Before the FDA even announced its approval of Enovid, *The Washington Post* printed an article that stated, "The chancery of the Catholic Church here yesterday said 'no' to the possibility Catholics might be able to use a birth control pill which prevents conception by 'natural means'" (Catholics reject birth-curb pill). May notes, "many Catholics took the pill anyway" (118). Throughout the 1960s, the issue would be debated at the Vatican, but in the end, papal approval wouldn't be granted (May 125). However, May notes "By the end of the decade, many American and western European priests were openly giving their married parishioners permission to use contraceptives, in defiance of the Pope's decree" (125). Notable Catholic supporters of the pill were John Rock—who, despite being a developer of Enovid was also a devout Catholic who had "separated biology from theology quite early in [his] life...and never confused them again" (Thomas 149)—and John F. Kennedy, America's first Catholic president, who had been elected shortly after the FDA's approval of Enovid (May 125). It's unclear how much government and religious approval of Enovid affected how many women used it, however, Thomas notes "400,000 women sought contraceptive prescriptions within" its first year on the market and the "number shot up to 2.3 million by 1963" (Thomas 151).

Though it took a long time for Enovid to get FDA approval and widespread acceptance in the U.S., the process was an extremely important one for American women. Famous playwright, journalist, and politician, Clare Boothe Luce believed that "The pill would release women from the all-encompassing demands of ever-expanding families, allowing them to pursue their creative and intellectual interests," and stated "Modern woman is at last free...as a man is free, to dispose of her own body, to earn her living, to pursue the improvement of her mind, to try a successful career" (Thomas 150-151). May shares this sentiment about the pill, stating, "women used it as a powerful tool not only to control their fertility, but to change their lives" (May 171). Though there is much progress to be made in terms of women's rights to privacy and control regarding their bodies, the approval and acceptance of the first birth control pill, nearly 60 years ago, started a much-needed conversation.

Works Cited

"Catholics reject birth-curb pill." *The Washington Post,* 1960.

Diczfalusy, Egon. "Gregory Pincus and Steroidal Contraception Revisited." *Acta Obstetricia Et Gynecologica Scandinavica,* vol. 61, no. S105, 1982, pp. 7-15.

May, Elaine T. *America and the Pill: A History of Promise, Peril, and Liberation.* Basic Books, New York, 2010.

Thomas, G. S. *A New World to be Won: John Kennedy, Richard Nixon, and the Tumultuous Year of 1960.* Praeger, Santa Barbara, Calif, 2011.

"U.S. Approves Pill For Birth Control." The New York Times, 1960, pp. 75.

Viktor Kim / Bibhav Pradhan

Work Culture in Japan: How Overworking is Burning Out the Young Generation

Japan has made miles of economic progress in the last decade and has risen to a global force with major influence in trade and power. This rise to power can be attributed to several different factors, one of which is Japan's tirelessly working young populace and the work culture they have. The beliefs, thought processes, and attitudes of the Japanese youth have brought about positive changes in Japanese society and made the country an economic powerhouse. But under the veil of prosperity, the work life of the Japanese youth shows the darkness hidden under the success. Overworking has taken away the pleasures of life among the young population and made it comparable to a grayscale image. The country has undoubtedly benefited from this hard work, but there are numerous drawbacks to the Japanese work-culture that need to be brought into the spotlight. Taking a quick look at the employees' lives shows that the quality of life among the Japanese youth has gone downhill, thanks to the intensive work expected from them. Working beyond their limits has disturbed the balance between the physical and mental aspects of life in the Japanese youth ranging from age 20 to 30 and unpaid work hours have exacerbated the issue. No matter what, action must be taken now so that the present young generation can get the chance to work under the right conditions and receive right compensation for overtime work.

Young people in Japan are increasingly suffering from severe cardiovascular diseases (Takashi, Toru, and Hiroyuki p.1). Their workaholic attitude leads them to push themselves beyond their limits which causes severe problems to their body. High levels of stress can lead to increased blood pressure and cholesterol, which increases the risk of heart failure. In Japan, corporate workers and salarymen have a tradition of lifelong job security, but this advantage comes at a cost. They are expected to work long unpaid hours, which induces sleep loss and gets in the way of healthy eating habits. An increasing number of Japanese youths are sleeping on the job as a result of working long hours, which shows how sleep-deprived they are. Polar Electro, a Finnish fitness technology company, analyzed sleep habits of polar users from 28 countries which showed that Japanese users logged 6 hours and 33 minutes of sleep per day, the least of all the countries analyzed. Not having enough sleep results in decreased cognitive functions and heart problems, which has been plaguing the young Japanese generation for a long time. The combined effects of sleep deprivation and heart problems have also resulted in the death of several people, even young adults.

Translated literally as overwork death, Karōshi is the unexpected loss of life associated with a person's occupation. Different from occupational fatality, the main cause of Karōshi deaths include heart attack and stroke that results from extreme stress and a starvation diet. Recent deaths include Miwa Sado, a 31-year-old journalist for the news network NHK, who died from heart failure after she logged 159 hours of overtime per month. Karōshi deaths also include suicide, as of 24-year-old Matsuri Takahashi, who jumped off her employer's roof as a result of overworking. This is also known as Karou-Jisatsu. Working long hours, which is often unpaid, and devoting everything to the company you work for is driving people to death, especially the young population who carry the burden of expectations of their family and friends. Karōshi and Karou-Jisatsu are common problems in Japanese society and the work-life balance isn't getting better. Karōshi deaths are estimated to be in the thousands, and there are new cases every year (Adelstein 2017).

Furthermore, the Japanese youth has also been haunted by mental issues associated with overworking. In addition to acute effects such as memory issues, impaired attention, and mood changes, overworking can lead to depression and mood disorders, which are pretty common issues for the Japanese populace. According to IMS health, between 1998 and 2003, the use of antidepressants rose by 56%. Suicide rates have also risen in Japan, alongside the use of Selective Serotonin Reuptake Inhibitors (SSRIs), which are drugs to treat major depression and anxiety. A 2018 paper published in Industrial Health mentions that over a half of the individuals receiving compensation for mental disorders were in their 30s or younger and about 47% of mental disorder cases were compensated due to work-related factors. To add fuel to the fire, mental illness is very stigmatized in Japanese society, which makes it very difficult for people suffering from depression to get help in time (2003).

Nearly a quarter of Japanese companies have employees hitting the 80 hours overtime per month mark and a significant chunk of these employees also cross 100 hours overtime per month, which most probably is the root cause of mental illness among the Japanese young population. A survey on 10,000 companies published in Japan's first white paper on Karōshi found that more than 20 percent of the companies exceeded 80 hours per month mark (Tomoko 2016). The Industrial Accident Compensation Insurance (IACI) claims for mental disorders went up to 1586 in 2016 from 155 in 1999, which is a clear indicator of depleting mental health. The impact of long unpaid working hours has also had detrimental effects on the employees' social lives. Young people, who should be enjoying life, are having their social circles cut down due to their work. Parents don't get to see their children, and old friends can fall out of contact, building up emotional stress. As leaving before one's colleagues or boss is frowned upon, this demanding work culture has caused several mental illnesses like anxiety and depression in the people of working age. In many cases, this pent-up stress has led to various mental issues and in severe cases, people taking their own lives.

Due to this issue, a new culture of 'Freeters' has come into existence. It refers to the people who lack full-time employment who choose not to be a salaried worker even though jobs were available. Freeters deliberately choose not to join the traditional Japanese work environment and desire to live life to the fullest. In addition, they might have aspirations that might not align with the Japanese standard of working. While adopting the freeter lifestyle offers a lot of personal freedom and professional independence, most freeters live on a disposable income and don't get any union or employment benefits (Japanese 17). The freeter lifestyle gives a privilege of personal choice, but the tradeoff is that sustainable life and career development for a freeter is hard to achieve. While this movement might be a step towards change, the excessive influx of people into this way of life may be detrimental to the crucial corporate structure of Japan.

While it is true that the Japanese government and companies have applied some work reforms and creative strategies to combat overworking, there hasn't been any significant change. Prime Minister Shinzo Abe declared in 2017 to launch work-life balance reforms that is aimed towards cutting overtime hours and better pay. In 2018, the Abe government passed the "Work Style Reform Law" which has regulations regarding the restriction of overtime hours (100 hours per month) and a stated purpose of increasing productivity at the same time. Many companies, including Japan Post Insurance, have issued company policies to turn off the lights after a certain time to encourage workers to go home. Japanese drone company Blue Innovation has developed T-Friend, a special drone which plays loud music and takes pictures of any staff working late and reports them to management. Steps have been taken for the welfare of young workers' physical and mental health, but analyzing the outcomes is difficult, considering the fact that these efforts are quite recent.

Meanwhile, to ensure a solid outcome from the recent reforms and bring about positive changes to their physical and mental health of young Japanese employees, the new government work regulations and labor laws must be enforced efficiently by concerned authorities. Companies should be instructed by the government to monitor their employees' working hours actively and should document them effectively to prevent the employees from burning themselves out. Workplace workshops and awareness info sessions regarding overworking and health issues must be made mandatory, especially for young people. Additionally, the power of social media must be harnessed to the fullest in order to spread awareness on this issue. Counseling services must be made available to the employees who are feeling overwhelmed with work and having serious workplace issues. Also, compulsory paid leave must be taken seriously by companies and employees alike. The technological solutions like drones and cameras must be given priority as they can be effective tools to identify the overworking employees.

To put it briefly, the Japanese youth working overtime beyond their mental and physical limits, which is usually unpaid, bring about serious health complications. The cardiovascular diseases and mental disorders induced by such work on them have counterproductive effects, and in dire cases, lead to untimely death. This work culture must be changed by personal and governmental efforts for the benefit of all young striving Japanese employees to maintain a proper work-life balance.

Works Cited:

Adelstein, Jake. "Japan is Literally Working Itself to Death: How Can It Stop?" 30 October 2017.Web. 8 March 2019. https://www.forbes.com/sites/adelsteinjake/2017/10/30/japan-is-literally-working-itself-to-death-how-can-it-stop/#59add2c22f14

Asian Boss. "Why Japanese Die from Overwork (Karoshi)." 13 February 2017. Web. 8 March 2019. https://www.youtube.com/watch?v=UxMlGRThKws

Desapriya, EBR, Iwase Nobutada. "Stigma of Mental Illness in Japan." The Lancet. 2002. Web.   8 March 2019. https://www.thelancet.com/pdfs/journals/lancet/PIIS0140673602087019.pdf

Fleming, Sean. "To combat Japan's sleep debt, some firms allow tired workers to nap on the job." Web. 21 February 2019. https://www.weforum.org/agenda/2018/11/this-japanese- company-pays-its-employees-to-get-a-good-night-s-sleep/

"Japanese social security measures to support the retiring aged." International Research Convention on Social Security, Helsinki. 25-27 September 2000. Web. 8 March 2019. https://www.issa.int/html/pdf/helsinki2000/topic2/2katsumata.pdf

Lane, Edwin. BBC World Service, Japan. "The young Japanese working themselves to death". 2nd June 2017. Web. 21 February 2019. https://www.bbc.com/news/business-39981997

"Polar Analyzes 6 Million Nights of Sleep to Reveal the Sleep Habits of 28 countries." 16 March 2018.Web. 21 February 2019. https://www.polar.com/en/about_polar/press_room/polar_analyzes_6_million_nights_of_sleep_to_reveal_the_sleep_habits_of_28_countries

Otake, Japanese. "1 in 4 firms in Japan say workers log over 80 overtime hours a month." The Japan Times. 7 October 2016. Web. 8 March 2019. https://www.japantimes.co.jp/news/2016/10/07/national/social-issues/1-in-4-firms-say-some-workers-log-80-hours-overtime-a-month-white-paper-on-karoshi/#.XILo_xNKhdg

Weller, Chris. "Japan is facing a 'death by overwork' problem — here's what it's all about." 18 October 2017.Web 21 February 2019. https://www.businessinsider.com/what-is-karoshi- japanese-word-for-death-by-overwork-2017-10

Yamauchi, Sasaki, Yoshikawa, Matsumoto, and Takahashi. "Incidence of overwork-related mental disorders and suicide in Japan". 11 August.2018. Web. 23 February 2019. https://www.ncbi.nlm.nih.gov/pubmed/29897506

Yamauchi, Takashi, Toru Yoshikawa, and Hiroyuki Yanagisawa. "Cerebrovascular/cardiovascular diseases and mental disorders due to overwork and work-related stress among the local public employees in Japan". 2018. Web. 21 February 2019. https://www.semanticscholar.org/paper/Cerebrovascular%2Fcardiovascular-diseases-and-mental-Yamauchi-Yoshikawa/227bd7969d9126985235e89a4ef3bb7cd2871d05

Jie Zhi
Evolution of Race and Ethnicity in Superhero Comics

Comics, to the casual eye, may seem like just a form of entertainment and simply offers an escape from reality into fantasy. But in fact, Superhero comics, and other Superhero mediums, can often be a reflection and rhetoric on society, culture, and socio-economic issues. Over the years, comics have served as a creative outlet for the narrative on issues such as crime, war, and female and minority empowerment. The industry has portrayed and represented races differently throughout the years, following the shift in attitudes about race and stereotypes in America. The first Superhero comic was created in the early 1930s, since then the Great Depression, World War II, Civil Rights Movement, Vietnam War, September 11, and election of the first black President occurred. Race relations and society's views on them have changed and shifted since the 1930s. However, this does not necessarily mean that minorities feel equal and not discriminated against, or that all Superhero comics accurately portray minorities without the use of stereotypes themselves today.

It is not a secret that the majority of comic book writers, artists, and Superheroes are white. Black Panther is widely considered as the first black Superhero, due to the success and popularity of the recent marvel film Black Panther (2018). However, even before Black Panther, the first black Superhero appearing in newspaper comic strips was Lothar. Although his appearance was modest, he first appeared as the partner of Mandrake the Magician in 1934 [1]. Lothar was introduced as a savage man with immense strength, resistance to heat and cold, and poor English. The creator's aim to project him as an uncivilized African man reflected in the initial pictures of Lothar, in which he wore short pants and leopard skin. As for his origin, Lothar was of royal African descent, and in various regions of Africa, the leopard skin or fur is associated with masculinity and power, much like a royal crown [2]. However, the setting of the comic was in America, although he had this history and reputation in Africa, he was sometimes referred to as "giant black slave" of Mandrake [3]. Much of America in the 1930s had a shallow and superficial view on blacks, judging them based on their skin color, regardless of their background. Naturally this raises questions about the creator Lee Falk and artist Phil Davis' treatment of racism and ethnicity.

With the Civil Rights movement of the 1960s and the death of Phil Davis in 1964, Fred Fredericks replaced Davis and worked as the artist alongside

Falk. Fredericks understood that the portrayal of Lothar with the leopard skin and other stereotypical characteristics would not stand in the new Civil rights era [1]. In the comics, Lothar began to speak proper English and grammar, for example, no longer using the words "Me this, Him that, She where." Fashionably, he went from the leopard skin and shorts to a leopard shirt and long pants. The most drastic change was that Lothar was no longer treated like Mandrake's servant, but rather his equal and friend. Lothar was one of the first racial characters to develop into a progressive hero, offering a hint of hope to the industry for minorities at the time.

A few years after the Civil Rights Movement ended, the first comic book series to have a black character as the protagonist and comic book title was created [5]. Luke Cage Hero for Hire (1972) was created by Stan Lee, who has constantly challenged social issues with the makes of other comics too, such as X-Men and Black Panther. It is known that most Superheroes have origin stories to their powers, Superman was an orphan and from Krypton, Spiderman and the death of Uncle Ben, Batman and death of his parents, etc. In the Luke Cage comic series, the young Carl Lucas was involved with street thugs, gangs and even had the goal of becoming a Harlem boss himself [6]. Lucas was eventually prisoned by being framed for possession of heroin. At the prison, he becomes the target of two men working on a top-secret cellular regeneration experiment due to judgement on his build and aggression. Of course, after Lucas gains superpowers from the experiment, he breaks out of jail (making him an escape convict), goes back home, and changes his name to Luke Cage, in hopes to start a new life. He begins to charge people money for his superpower services, thus the name "Hero for Hire."

Although Stan Lee created Luke Cage to reflect on the struggle of blacks in society in at the time, Cage is also a character who is created based off stereotypes of blacks in society. In the comics, Luke Cage is displayed as an angry black man with an afro, metal cuffs, thick chain belt, and an unbuttoned tight shirt. This description clearly creates the allusion of slaves, to be more exact, slaves escaping their owners and seeking revenge through anger [8]. Cage's origin story involving gangs and crimes and escape convict label can be closely tied with stereotypes as well. In the industry, many of the white Superheroes save lives and protect the country because of what they believe is the right thing to do, and of course for free, but not Luke Cage. His choice of mercenary and using his power for monetary gain plays heavily on the stereotype that black masculinity is partly defined by the acquisition of wealth or jobs [9]. Although much of his comic representation is based on stereotypes, Stan Lee is able to reflect on the social fears of blacks in the series. For example, the wrongful conviction of Carl Lucas is representative of the fears of African Americans during the Civil Rights Movement and racial disparity.

Luke Cage is the first black Superhero to have his own comic, but Black Panther was the first to appear in mainstream comics. Created by Stan Lee and Jack Kirby, T'Challa first appears in Fantastic Four #52 in 1966. He then later appears as part of the Avengers and earns his own comic series in 1977, 5 years after Luke Cage Hero for Hire [10]. In Fantastic Four #52, the members of the Fantastic Four were invited to Wakanda by a "mighty, masked Jungle mystery man" [11]. Black Panther and the Fantastic Four first meet in conflict. The purpose of the invite was so that the Black Panther could gauge his strength and powers against them. This can be representative of the notion that Africans are often competing with the dominant white race, whether in academia, professional settings, or just looks. The results of the battle were inconclusive, hinting that both parties were equal.

Unlike prior black Superheroes who were set in America and African Americans, the Black Panther and his people were "just" Africans in an African country, Wakanda. A direct quote from a research paper by Martin Lund states that "Wakanda reproduces notions about Africans as peoples without history, whose opportunity for progress and a future – their way out of their 'savage' past – comes from engaging in international trade, ignoring the fact of centuries of intra-continental trade and of European complicity in keeping Africa underdeveloped" [11]. The lack of racism, commercialism, and capitalism can be attributed to the success and prosperity of this underdeveloped country and the happiness of the people.

Black Panther was a revolutionary representation of minorities in the Superhero world. The character did not have a stereotypical appearance or origin story. The movie adaptation was released in 2018 and grossed a total over 700 million, becoming #1 in Marvel Cinematic Universe series franchise and #3 all time in the U.S [12]. The film features an all black cast and (mostly) all black crew. It gave society something different with a predominately black cast and non-stereotypical representations of Africans and African countries. Wakanda was underdeveloped, but they were technologically advanced and well off. Black Panther maintained a similar origin story to other white Superheroes, unlike Luke Cage. He was of a wealthy and noble background and the death of his father sparked his heroism.

There is some criticism on whether Marvel created this movie as a diversity move or money move. Sean Combs described *Black Panther* as a "cruel experiment," [13] as Marvel was able to capitalize the rising popularity of diverse films and turning African culture into revenue. The *Black Panther* comic book series suffered poor sales when issued. But, Marvel was able to use their reputation and the fact that *Crazy Rich Asians* was successful to "experiment" with *Black Panther* due to low risks. Regardless of their intentions, *Black Panther* paved the way for more minorities, whether it be race or gender, to be represented in the big and small screens and other mediums.

Throughout the years, there have been attempts by the Superhero industry giving well-known and established Superhero titles racial diversity. For example, Isaiah Bradley as Captain America and John Stewart as Green Lantern. In 2010, Barack Obama had been elected as President and was holding office, and Donald Glover was dressed in Spiderman gear in NBC comedy "Community." The result of Glover's skit caused fans over social media campaigning for Glover to become the new, and first black, Spiderman in *The Amazing Spiderman*. Although the campaigning failed, in 2011, Michael Bendis created a new Spiderman alias, Miles Morales, inspired by Obama and Glover [14], and first appeared in Ultimate Fallout #4. Everyone knows the origin story for Peter Parker Spiderman, an orphan, bite of a spider, and death of Uncle Ben. Besides also getting a spider bite, Miles Morales does not follow the origin story of Peter Parker. Jefferson Davis, Miles' dad, is of African descent and used to live a life of crime prior "turning it around" and becoming a Brooklyn cop. On the contrary, Aaron Davis, Miles' uncle, resumed the crime life. Rio Morales, Miles' mother, is of Hispanic/Latino descent, thus, making Miles Afro-Latino, the first ever bi-racial Spiderman.

In Spiderman #2, there is a line where Miles says, "I don't want to be the black Spider-Man. I just want to be Spider-Man." Then, six issues later in Spiderman #8 when Miles meets Luke Cage, Luke says, "Hey kid! Spider-Man is a kid of color now. That is cool. It's important. Don't screw it up" [15]. Although these quotes show the diversity and cultural significance of the series, there are a few things wrong. Miles clearly exclaims that he does not want to be acknowledged due to his color but rather his actions. At the surface, this is a great point to make, but if you look deeper, this quote undermines his representation of minorities, which is not the purpose of Miles Morales as Spiderman. Imagine former President Barack Obama saying, "I don't want to be the First Black President, I just want to be The President" [16]. The fact that Barack Obama was the First Black President changed the world, in a positive way. This type of minority representation matters and serves as a catalyst for minorities around the world. Luke Cage's quote basically says, "You're not white Spiderman, you're different, you have to act differently and not mess up because you are of different race and a minority." Analyzing this quote, as a minority challenging the status quo of a predominately white role, it is important that the person is aware of this fact and that all eyes are on them. Any mistakes can instantly spark criticism and ruin it for other minorities. Miles does not and will not get the same treatment as Peter Parker due to his racial background, which is still reflective on society today. Even though there have been cultural and social shifts, there are instances where minority groups will be stereotyped and erratically judged.

Miles Morales is not black, he is Afro-Latino, yet throughout courses of the comic series Miles is referenced as black, due to his exterior appearance. Even his own quote in Spiderman #2 says "... black Spider-Man." Miles' grades declined after his role of Spiderman took off and his grandmother, Gloria, presumed that Miles was dealing drugs. During an argument between Jefferson and Gloria due to this, Gloria asserted that "this is your half of him we're dealing with" [18]. The idea and stereotype of criminality and Africans/blacks is presented in this statement. And although Miles' is Afro-Latino, he is being racially stereotyped and profiled as black.

Race and ethnicity in Superhero comics do not only refer to skin color, but also has an impact on wealth, origin stories, and how they are treated within the comics. Although Superhero creators try to use diversity as a way to represent minorities, their origin stories are often created using stereotypes. The root of this problem could perhaps be the creators' inability to relate to these characters, since most creators are of white origin. This shallow understanding and prejudice had led to racial inaccuracies in many comics. Perhaps one reason why the Black Panther film was so successful was due to the racial cast and crew, allowing them to have a personal connection to the film.

Much of this paper discusses those of black racial groups, however, another race severely underrepresented in both the big and small screens and in comics are Asians. Marvel recently announced the first Asian Superhero film for Shang-Chi (created in the 70s). Shang-Chi is considered to be the Master of Kung Fu, the greatest non-powered and enhanced fighter in the Marvel universe. Shang-Chi wasn't a popular Superhero in the comics and was obscured until now. Of course, Marvel is first a business more than anything else. They are trying to capitalize off the movement for Asians due to the success of *Crazy Rich Asians,* and *Black Panther,* knowing that this is not a big risk to try to pull into theaters. Marvel plans on making the cast and makers of Asian descent, similar to *Black Panther.* Some people may feel that there is a hint of racism and stereotyping with Marvel picking an Asian Superhero that's also a martial artist. Generally, the biggest Asian names have all been associated with action/Kung-Fu movies (see Jackie Chan/Donnie Yen).

Minorities were portrayed as insignificant Superheroes or side-kicks in the earlier years of Superhero comics and film. Today, we see more and more minority protagonists, however, they are still often portrayed with stereotypes. It is important to note that the Superhero industry is at first, a business and a market. Whether it is the industry strongly pushing for diversity in the world, seeing that diversity is bringing in the money, or both, is debatable. Regardless, this movement is opening doors for what was, but still is, a pre-dominantly white area for minorities. It is important to appropriately portray characters of different races and genders in Superhero comics as they can shape and affect the idea of children about humanity and morality. Although we see a cultural shift in how racial Superheroes are represented in comics and films, just like in society, there is still room for improvement.

References

[1] M. Carlson-Ghost, "Before Black Panther, there was Lothar! - Mark Carlson," *Mark Carlson-Ghost*, 03-Sep-2018. [Online]. Available: https://www.markcarlson-ghost. com/index.php/2018/02/10/before-the-black-panther-lothar/. [Accessed: 14-Mar-2019].

[2] K. Ryder, "The Meaning of Leopard Print," *The New Yorker*, 21-Jun-2017. [Online]. Available: https://www.newyorker.com/culture/photo-booth/the-meaning-of-leopard-print. [Accessed: 14-Mar-2019].

[3] "Black Heroes/Sidekicks," *History Revealed*. [Online]. Available: http://www. historyrevealed.eu/africa-new/african-diaspora/black-heroessidekicks.html. [Accessed: 14-Mar-2019].

[4] "Lothar (Character)," *Comic Vine*. [Online]. Available: https://comicvine.gamespot. com/lothar/4005-61659/. [Accessed: 14-Mar-2019].

[5] K. R. A. DeCandido, "A Brief History of Luke Cage in the Comics," *Tor.com*, 30-Sep-2016. [Online]. Available: https://www.tor.com/2016/09/29/a-brief-history-of-luke-cage-in-the-comics/. [Accessed: 14-Mar-2019].

[6] M. N. Kleinhenz, "Luke Cage's Origin Story: Comics vs. TV Show," *ScreenRant*, 05-Oct-2016. [Online]. Available: https://screenrant.com/luke-cage-netflix-origin-story-comics-changes/. [Accessed: 14-Mar-2019].

[7] G. Baker-Whitelaw, "A Reader's Guide To Luke Cage Comics," *The Daily Dot*, 24-Feb-2017. [Online]. Available: https://www.dailydot.com/parsec/luke-cage-comics-reading-guide/. [Accessed: 14-Mar-2019].

[8] D. Bogle, *Toms, Coons, Mulattoes, Mammies, and Bucks: An Interpretive History of Blacks in American Films*. (Fourth ed.) New York: Continuum, 2001.

[9] R. Lendrum, "The Super Black Macho, One Baaad Mutha: Black Superhero Masculinity in 1970s Mainstream Comic Books," *Extrapolation*, vol. 46, (3), pp. 360-372, 2005.

[10] "Black Panther (1977) #1," Comics | Marvel.com. [Online]. Available: https://www.marvel.com/comics/issue/17855/black_panther_1977_1. [Accessed: 16-Mar-2019].

[11] M. Lund, "'Introducing the Sensational Black Panther!' Fantastic Four #52-53, the Cold War, and Marvel's Imagined Africa," *The Comics Grid: Journal of Comics Scholarship,* vol. 6, (1), 2016.

[12] "Black Panther (2018)," *Box Office Mojo.* [Online]. Available: https://www.boxofficemojo.com/movies/?id=marvel2017b.htm. [Accessed: 16-Mar-2019].

[13] C. Carras, "Diddy Calls 'Black Panther' a 'Cruel Experiment'," *Variety,* 11-Jul-2018. [Online]. Available: https://variety.com/2018/film/news/diddy-black-panther-cruel-experiment-1202870736/. [Accessed: 16-Mar-2019].

[14] I. Lagman, "6 Fun Facts about Miles Morales, the New Spider-Man," When In Manila, 17-Dec-2018. [Online]. Available: https://www.wheninmanila.com/6-fun-facts-about-miles-morales-new-spider-man/. [Accessed: 14-Mar-2019].

[15] B. Jacob, "Spider-Man #8 – REVIEW," *Amazing SpiderTalk A SpiderMan Website RSS,* 16-Sep-2016. [Online]. Available: https://superiorspidertalk.com/spider-man-8-review/. [Accessed: 14-Mar-2019].

[16] "Miles Morales vs. Spider-Man: When You and Your Blackness Disagree," *Black Nerd Problems,* 21-Dec-2018. [Online]. Available: http://blacknerdproblems.com/miles-morales-vs-spider-man-when-you-and-your-blackness-disagree/. [Accessed: 14-Mar-2019].

[17] JK(Zi-O), "Spider-Man #8 | Comics Amino," *Comics | aminoapps.com,* 14-Sep-2016. [Online]. Available: https://aminoapps.com/c/comics/page/blog/spider-man-8/DViP_uMezvqlKj5kolpoz5Qnvwb4Ek. [Accessed: 14-Mar-2019].

[18] G. A. Cruz, "Superheroes & Stereotypes: A Critical Analysis of Race, Gender, and Social Issues within Comic Book Material." , ProQuest Dissertations Publishing, 2018.

Kevin Karnani

Automation: How Will it Affect the Workforce?

This notion that the rise of sentient machines will overtake humanity one day is one that has dominated many aspects of human culture. The science fiction books about artificial intelligence, movies such as the Terminator trilogy and The Matrix using AI as a crucial underlying theme, and the plethora of articles and editorials that point out AI as a threat are a few examples of the many ways this sentiment is rather dominant in modern-day society. However, both the antepenultimate and penultimate take on fictitious and extreme case scenarios, whereas only the ultimate of the three elements mention one of the more realistic issues that the use of AI will bring about: the rise in unemployment rates. In the past, automation meant computers would run the same algorithms to perform repetitive work in factories, but today, computers can land aircrafts and even trade stocks. This raises a critical question: How long will it take for computers to become better than humans in every single line of work?

Some say we are entering an era of automation unlike anything we have seen before in the past, while others say that automation has been around for decades and that nothing has changed (Bostrom and Yudkowsky, MIRI). In the past, humans used many innovations to produce more resources and ease the workload off themselves. While this rise in productivity eliminated many of the older jobs, it also created many new jobs for the growing human population. This started as a gradual process; however, the rise in the rate of innovations over time led to the Industrial Revolution, which then led to a huge change in the workforce from agriculture to factories. As automation became more popular, machines took over industrial and production jobs while humans moved into service jobs and "more complex roles" (Bossmann, World Economic Forum).

It was only a few decades after the Industrial Revolution that humanity entered the Information Age. However, even in this small amount of time that humans have spent in this era, everything has changed considering how machines and computers are now taking over jobs at a rate that is much faster than anything humans have encountered in the past. In fact, according to a 2013 study (Frey and Osborne, 44), approximately forty-seven percent of jobs in the United States could potentially be automated in the next twenty years. To make a comparison, in 1979, General Motors employed about 800,000 people to make around 11 billion dollars, while Google employed 58,000 in 2012 to make 14 billion dollars (Sinha, Medium). This is a prime example of how modern innovations do not compare to older innovations as the modern is not only creating new jobs but is also eliminating old jobs at the same time.

Another example of a modern industry relative to this topic is the Internet. While many argue that this innovation is on par with that of electricity, the Internet does not create enough job opportunities to make up for the industries that it has killed off. For example, in 2004, Blockbuster made 6 billion dollars with 84,000 employees, while in 2016, Netflix made 9 billion dollars with only 4,500 employees (Sinha, Medium). While these statistics are astounding on their own, the mere fact that a new wave of automation with a new generation of machines that is slowly approaching us should instill terror into our minds. If nothing is done about this, we will find ourselves outcompeted by our very own creations to the point where humans will not find any work, and as such, will not be able to sustain themselves.

To understand how computers will overtake the workforce, one must understand how computers could autonomously complete complex tasks without human supervision. However, this is simple to see as computers operate in the same manner that humans have done for eons: through the division of labor. Through the passage of time, humans have had many breakthroughs, which led to further specialization of jobs. No human can create one product on his own as it takes many specialized people with the proper training to construct said product, a concept that applies to computers as well (Sinha, Medium). While computers cannot take on complex tasks immediately, they are much better than the specialized human at completing narrowly defined tasks. Machines are decent at breaking down complex tasks into narrow ones, but once AI reaches the point where they do it effortlessly, will we have any more areas in which humans can specialize themselves?

This leads to a discussion of the way in which machines have been able to better their skills, which is through a process called Machine Learning. This process includes the constant analysis of data in order to acquire new skills and information, something which is easily accomplished since humans have started to gather data on everything and anything (Sinha, Medium). Considering how even shopping patterns are recorded, a machine could gradually learn what other items to recommend to a user in hopes that it will catch their eye, which is precisely how online marketing has functioned. However, in addition to behavioral patterns, humans also record weather patterns, medical data, personal information, and communication data, all of which could contribute to an "archive" or "library" that any computer could access in order to learn how humans operate as well as learn how to operate more efficiently.

Having said all this, there are a plethora of varying viewpoints on the matter. While evidence shows that the possibility of a rise in unemployment rates is quite high, some believe that this will not be a problem whatsoever. For example, Erik Brynjolfsson, an MIT economist that authored the book that details the aforementioned history of technological changes, has said, "If you look back to the first machine age the vast majority of Americans worked in agriculture. Now it's less than two percent. Those people didn't simply become unemployed, they reskilled" (Heath, TechRepublic). Alan Manning, a professor from the London School of Economics, noted "If I take a historical perspective then technical change has always destroyed some jobs and created others, and this would in some sense be no different from that." Similarly, some viewpoints call to attention that a solution may already be in our system. For example, "unemployment in the US is at its lowest level in 16 years... while automation today is associated with job losses in manufacturing, it is associated with overall job growth in other sectors" (BU School of Law). Additionally, this article implies that automation will not change anything as it has been going on for years, so it must be other factors that hold up the economy. However, sentient AI will create an entirely different context than non-sentient computers as we will be dealing with computers that have their own thoughts and ideas, which makes the two contrasting perspectives irrelevant to the context of the situation.

Finally, the ideal viewpoint, one supported by the comparisons made earlier, is one that calls for multiple things: human oversight (Lufkin, BBC), staying transparent, as well as the creation of "initiatives already working on understanding AI technology and its foreseeable impact" (Beall, WIRED). If we make sure to spend as much time as possible in analyzing the ways in which AI works as well as stay transparent about implemented automation algorithms (Beall, WIRED), we should be able to harvest the many benefits that AI brings about. However, while AI will bring about many benefits, it would be catastrophic to create an AI without any of the following guidelines: understanding how it works, supervising it, or communicating the way in which the code was implemented. An example of a lack of any of the three aforementioned guidelines occurred when certain developers "deploy[ed] an autonomous vehicle... at the chip maker Nvidia went on the roads in 2016 without anybody knowing how it made its decisions" (Beall, WIRED). This is dangerous as it shows lack of understanding by the developers who implemented such code as well as a transparency between developers on how the code works. If we are to let AI take over our jobs with no supervision and no understanding of what the AI has done to create the product, what is to say that there will not be any mistakes?

The aforementioned examples have shown a wide range of applications and implications that will come about due to the rapid development of AI.

Current trends demonstrate a loss of company workers and a gain in company profits. If companies allow this trend to continue, once AI are proficient at functioning within any line of work, mass layoffs could occur, which would contribute to a widening of the already existing socioeconomic gap. To prevent such layoffs and other consequences, we should implement a system in which humans are required to adhere to the previously mentioned guidelines of understanding through initiatives, supervising, and communicating the manner of code implementation. At the end of the day, it is important to realize that technology is going to upgrade over time no matter what, which is why we must understand the effects of what we create with such initiatives as well as supervise the actions of said AI.

Annotated Bibliography

Bossmann, Julia. "Top 9 Ethical Issues in Artificial Intelligence." *World Economic Forum,* 21 Oct. 2016.

This article from the World Economic Forum annotates the top nine ethical issues that the topic of artificial intelligence will bring. The article points out that many technologically advanced companies as well as a few individuals believe that now is the time to discuss the landscape of this topic as this is a new frontier in the technological realm. In addition to this, the article then lists the top nine issues as well as describes how or why they are an issue. However, to conclude, the article makes it obvious that it isn't entirely against the prospect of the development of AI. I will use this article to show contrasting points of views.

Beall, Abigail. "It's Time to Address Artificial Intelligence's Ethical Problems." *WIRED,* WIRED UK, 24 Aug. 2018.

This article from WIRED begins by highlighting all the good that AI has brought as well as how well AI would be able to serve us in the future. However, the article then begins to mention all the possible dangers it could produce by referencing other articles and giving examples of current uses of AI where issues have been raised. Furthermore, the article goes on to mention a few organizations who participate initiatives in which they partner up and dedicate themselves to researching AI. To conclude, the article stresses that since we barely understand it right now, mistakes are bound to be made, which is why humans have the responsibility to use AI correctly and for the good. I will use this article for my solution.

Bostrom, Nick, and Eliezer Yudkowsky. *The Ethics of Artificial Intelligence.* Machime Intelligence Research Institute.

This paper, published by the Future of Humanity Institute (Oxford University) and a non-profit organization called the Machine Intelligence Research Institute (MIRI), has an abstract and 6 sections, all describing the ethical issues and manners in which humans can ascertain nothing catastrophic occurs. In the first section, the authors merely highlight the different issues that AI will bring about. In the second section, the authors outline the different challenges that arise in ensuring that AI operates safely. In the third section, the paper goes over the circumstances in which (or whether AI should) have a "moral status". In the fourth section, the paper goes over how our ethical assessments might cause differences between humans and AI. The paper then concludes with the possibility of creating an AI that is more intelligent than a human and goes over how to ascertain that this AI is used for good. I will use this scholarly piece to define my issue.

Lufkin, Bryan. "Future - Why the Biggest Challenge Facing AI Is an Ethical One." *BBC News*, BBC, 7 Mar. 2017.

This article from BBC introduces us by mentioning that AI is a current issue due to the impact it has on our lives even today. With this, the editorial then transitions into a discussion on how AI will affect human autonomy as every system will become much more complex. The article mentions that there aren't any common practices as of right now in how to oversee the development of AI, which will remain troublesome until one is implemented. Moreover, the article explains that AI might have a negative impact on humans, finishing off by stating that technology should help humans, not replace them. I will use this editorial to give a part of my solution.

Heath, Nick. "Why AI Could Destroy More Jobs than It Creates, and How to Save Them." *TechRepublic*.

This article from TechRepublic mainly goes over the varying viewpoints from multiple professionals on the matter of the effects on jobs due to automation and AI. In addition to mentioning a few viewpoints, it also describes the context behind them with the use of graphs, pictures, and many explanations of both the former and latter. It also talks about the types of jobs at risk, the roles that machines would do better than humans, if those who lose jobs will find other jobs, and the current effects of technology in the workforce. I will be using this article to talk about the various viewpoints of my paper.

"Why Isn't Automation Creating Unemployment?" Boston University School of Law. 05 Mar. 2019.

This article, posted by an unknown author, is a research summary conducted under the Boston University School of Law that goes over topics such as: the boost of employment rates due to automation, the change in demand over time that creates new jobs in each respective "Industrial Revolution", and the current effects of automation based on new informational technologies through the use of graphs and explanations. The article goes on to counter the fear that AI will take over our jobs mainly since the unemployment rate in the US is at its lowest level in 16 years. I will be using this paper to show the counterarguments to my solution and demonstrate the fact that there are various viewpoints on the matter.

Frey, Carl B, and Michael A. Obsorne. *The Future of Employment.* Oxford University, 2013.

This paper, published by Oxford University, is similar to the aforementioned paper co-published by the Future of Humanity and Machine Intelligence Research Institute in terms of the purpose of the paper. This paper consists of an introduction, the history of technological revolutions, the technological revolutions of the 21st century, the measure of the impact of automation, and employment in the 21st century. The paper attempts to categorize occupations in terms of their susceptibility to automation, then uses this to predict the probability of automation of said occupations in order to analyze the effects this could have on the US labor market. I will use this paper to provide statistics and examples.

Sinha, Siddhant. "My Thoughts on the Fourth Industrial Revolution." *Medium.com,* Medium, 16 Sept. 2018.

This blog, published under Medium, uses a variety of credible sources to show his thoughts on automation and the effects that have been noticed in the last few decades. He includes the perspectives of many professional economists on the matter. Sinha also uses a video, one that was based on many books by professionals mentioned in my essay and the Frey/Osborne study mentioned above, to describe the history of the changes in technology as well as the workforce. The blog mainly seems to mention the negative aspects of the upcoming "Fourth Industrial Revolution", however, Sinha highlights that there still is a possibility of positive changes that it could bring about. I will use this blog to go over the history of technological changes.

Karim Khaled Mohamed

Stained White Coat

For generations, society has held medical professionals in the highest regard. From a slight cough, to terminal illnesses, we regularly depend on doctors and related medical professionals to provide us with a high standard of care. This standard of care, which is upheld by the AMA and its strenuous requirements for medical practice throughout the states is essential to the public's faith in the American medical system. Although it isn't a currently a major debate topic, academic and financial greed plague the medical research industry just as any other. Over the past few years, a series of incorrectly conducted studies regarding END (e-cig) use prompted my research into the field of medical research. Little did I know, that the financial powers at play in the END research industry weren't isolated to that area of medical research. Despite the general public confidence in the white coats and their explorative research, a plethora of nefarious practices plague the pharmaceutical and medical research industries, specifically with company-sponsored research. From financially greedy research participants, to desperate researchers and statisticians, it's better now than ever to revisit the topic of primum non nocere.

The pharmaceutical and medical industries as a whole rely primarily on exploratory and comparative research to establish efficacy of experimental drugs in humans. Typically these studies are conducted using a double-blind placebo controlled approach, the most reliable type of study designed to test efficacy. In these studies, an independent source randomly selects whether each study participant receives a placebo or the drug in question; the statisticians and researchers are kept completely in the dark regarding which subject receives which treatment until the study is completed. Ioannidis comments on the ideas of power and bias, which determine the strength of a studies results and are highly dependent on sample size and study design (Ioannidis 124). Ioannidis comments on the largest problem of all, the lack of confirmation for studies simply because the statistical tests within that study point towards statistical significance of results. Just as research articles are peer-reviewed, the lack of confirmation of results by other studies greatly reduces the reliability of the majority of medical research being published today. Similarly, human bias (leading to the statistical form) tends to present itself in the form of research findings (data points) that are reported despite knowingly being unreliable. Typically, statisticians use a confidence level of 95% to determine whether a study's findings are statistically significant, yet when human bias in study design comes into play, studies with significantly lower true significance (<95%) are often passed off as >95%. This problem is ultimately the result of studies deliberately designed in a fashion that promotes statistically significant results despite the lack of an actual basis for these findings. Based on these observations, it's reasonable to conclude that there are specific factors that influence the reliability of a study. These include human bias, financial incentives, replication, the popularity of an area of study, and the effect of the study. The popularity of an area of study and whether that study is replicated are highly dependent on each other. Seemingly, these "hot" areas of study are highly dependent on independent research findings and almost counter-intuitively result in a lack of replication due to competition. Financial incentives lead to human bias in study design, and often result in vague terms defining study outcomes and classification of results (Ioannidis e125). Research regarding tobacco in the 20th and 21st century provides a classical example of these factors at play.

Tobacco research is a hot area of study that comes along with tons of controversy due to the large effect of these studies and the financial interests at play. In 2018, an organization named "Foundation for a Smoke-Free World" was established by PMI, manufacturer of Marlboro cigarettes in order to conduct public health research and "reduce the public health burden of smoking related diseases" (qtd. in Rubin 123). Expectedly, the organization was met with backlash from organizations such as the Truth Initiative, which specializes in maintaining research integrity in the tobacco industry. The nature of tobacco research in the 20th century leads the ethical research industry to believe that PMI's latest attempt at providing research funding is a mirror image of its last. In the late 1960s and 1970s PMI and other big tobacco organizations provided large grants to amenable researchers to misdirect research regarding lung cancer and tobacco smoke. The Tobacco Industry Research committee continued these practices from 1954-1999 when they were ultimately banned from providing research funding. The ban, combined with the large effect of these studies prompted the backlash surrounding PMI's 2nd attempt at research funding. 17 of the largest research schools have already signed statements saying they won't accept funding from FSFW, and the World Conference on Tobacco and Health has barred FSFW from attending (Rubin 125). However, PMI's recent interest in the non-combustible market indicates some interest in harm reduction. Nevertheless, the unreliability of the tobacco industry's research funding in the relatively new field of ENDs and "heatables" shouldn't mix, simply due to the large implications and malleability of public opinion regarding ENDs. In spite of the backlash with this organization, smaller drug development trials studies with lesser "effect" often slip through the cracks.

Recent research regarding Bisphosphonates, a class of drugs designed to treat osteoporosis (brittle bones) has come into question due to the unreliable study design in blatant disregard for practical context. These studies, all RCTs (double blind, placebo controlled) and the subsequent phase II and phase III trials that resulted in the FDA approval of all of these drugs were later discovered to inadequately identify long-term effects. Unsurprisingly these studies were designed by the companies who provided the funding for the clinical trials of these drugs. Knowing the long term adverse effects of these drugs, these companies deliberately designed the studies to be short-term (Marx 38). Study designs can bias a study towards positive results by incorporating vague language or deliberately leaving out important suspected effects in the studies. For example, the zoledronate and pamidronate studies excluded observation of exposed bone in the mouth and thus resulted in misleading safety profiles. Similarly, randomization criteria were designed by the sponsor in bisphosphonate research resulted in plausible deniability when the long term safety was brought under question. The adverse effects such as osteonecrosis later were blamed on previous cancers which deteriorated bone health (and these subjects were conveniently removed from the study) as well as poor oral hygiene (Marx 39). Conducting studies that effectively remove any long-term effects of the drugs often is a result of financial interest and the relative "need" for the drug. For example, the onset of dementia for Detrol and Elavil took long enough to only show up in FDA reports in the late marketing phase, significantly later than their approval (e40). Although the development of these drugs was necessary for treatment of postmenopausal osteoporosis, a carefully conducted long-term study should have been conducted in spite of need of the drug at the time. However, deception in studies isn't isolated to the researchers, financial interests, and statisticians. Study participants often fake symptoms or conditions for financial gain when participating in studies.

Twenty-five percent of research participants who participated in four or more studies in the past 3 years admitted to exaggerating symptoms, while 14% pretended to have a health problem to be eligible for a study (Resnik and McCann 1192). Although federal law prohibits falsifying data or research, there are no guidelines regarding research participants misinforming researchers. A database of repeat offenders, or participants who take part in studies as a source of income simply doesn't exist. However, financial gain isn't the only incentive to lie. Embarrassment regarding previous mental health, medical conditions, and drug abuse often prevents research participants from disclosing this vital information (1193). The inclusion of participants who never had a health condition often is indicative of poor study design and subject vetting from a lack of quantitative tests for indicators of the condition in question. Although this isn't the fault of the researchers, there are certain measures such as blood testing and other diagnostic tests that would prevent these participants from throwing off results. However, lack of funding and time tend to discourage researchers from doing this. As a result this amplifies the distrust of medical research at no fault of the researchers.

These practices bring the conversation back to the concept of primum non nocere, the direct translation of which being "first, to do no harm." This part of the Hippocratic oath that all medical practitioners take refers to the possible harm their actions might cause (DeAngelis and Fontanarosa 1196). According to the bioethics definition of primum non nocere, it is better not to take action to rectify an existing problem if the possible risk is greater than the benefit. Although it is a seemingly simple idea, physicians and the like are in a constant battle between harm and benefit. Would it be better to prematurely release drugs in hopes of solving an imminent problem, or to wait and let many die in the process? Knowingly releasing drugs that cause long-term harm is a different story, and often is only known to the sponsors of the study who often conduct internal studies prior to providing grants. By reducing sponsor involvement in design of studies, increasing replicability, and appointing independent committees to analyze studies and practices such as the Truth Initiative, confidence from doctors and the public on medical research can be restored (1198). These steps, among others, would ultimately work to remove the "stain on the white coat" that is unreliable research, and restore the high regard that the medical profession is held.

Works Cited

DeAngelis, Catherine D., and Phil B. Fontanarosa. "Ensuring Integrity in Industry-Sponsored Research: Primum Non Nocere, Revisited." *JAMA*, vol. 303, no. 12, 2010, pp. 1196-1198

Ioannidis, John P A. "Why most published research findings are false" *PLoS* medicine vol. 2,8 (2005): e124.

Marx, Robert E. "The Deception and Fallacies of Sponsored Randomized Prospective Double-Blinded Clinical Trials: The Bisphosphonate Research Example." *The International Journal of Oral & Maxillofacial Implants*, vol. 29, no. 1, 2014, pp. E37.

Resnik, David B., and David J. McCann. "Deception by Research Participants." *The New England Journal of Medicine*, vol. 373, no. 13, 2015, pp. 1192-1193.

Rubin, R. "New Foundation Revives Debate about Health Research Funded by Big Tobacco."*JAMA-Journal of the American Medical Association*, vol. 320, no. 2, 2018, pp. 123-125.

Drexel Publishing Group
Creative Writing

Introduction

Creative writers take their experiences and observations and transform them into written journeys for their readers. The following works were selected by faculty judges from student submissions (of creative nonfiction, fiction, humor, op-ed, and poetry) to the Drexel Publishing Group Creative Writing Contest.

These pieces engage with issues of gender, culture, mental illness, current controversies, and personal struggles. They are as varied and diverse as the students who wrote them. You may marvel at the insight, compassion, humor, and humanity these writers possess. The writers whose works appear in this section are brave and generous in their desire to share their work. Please enjoy the writing they shared.

—*The Editors*

Isabella Pappano

Dissolution of Self

1. I crave scarcity. Or, perhaps, I detest living in a world of excess. As a baby, I would fall asleep in bustling rooms, as if protecting myself from the *rushing*. My mother tells me this story often, marveling at how my body knew what it needed, questioning when it forgot how to care for itself.

2. I lived for a long time attempting to escape consumption. If I could design my perfect existence, I would require nothing from this world.

3. Yet, life requires energy. At least, biologists claim this in their list of the characteristics of life. (Gather twenty people, put them in a room, and tell them to scrawl down the definition of life. What would they write?)

4. What is biology? I think it is philosophy disguised as science.

5. In my one of my labs, I work with infections. These fragments of disease possess the ability to lyse open cells; they infect and they reproduce and they evolve and they are nonliving. Almost like a reflection of life in a mirror, they subside on the essence of living organisms while in themselves, holding no life of their own.

6. If I was in a room of nineteen strangers and had to define life, I would first mention contribution. Life cannot simply take and destroy like a virus.

7. My obsession with emptiness was bound to overcome me. I like bare walls and white sheets far too much. I enjoy the hollow echo of shoes on tile. I confuse the word hungry with holy.

8. Life demands that those who possess it remain aware of it. I feel my blood pound in my wrists, an ever-present thrum. Life consists of a constant rhythm of reminders that I am here.

9. Biologists claim that movement marks life and I agree. Why else would our pulses sound like rivers except to remind us that we are journeying somewhere?

10. To cease moving is to die; it halts the streams running through the body. The faucet turns off and the rivers sit. These waters with no direction,

they breed. Disease and death multiply within the stillness. Yet, stagnancy sometimes feels safer than the rushing flow of life.

11. I think I wanted to be a girl forever. Youth possesses a lightness of being, hovering and shaking like a dragonfly over the floods of existence. I desired to remain frozen in a moment of waiting.

12. (Shouldn't everyone be a little terrified of progressing forward and leaving the known behind?)

13. I learned that if you sacrifice dinner to the garbage disposal gods, they reveal the secret of controlling time. Hear the rumble when you flip the switch? They want to escape so they can crawl into your ears and lay eggs in your brain. Soon, those eggs hatch and the hive is born.

14. Brain scientists take pictures of the blob of neurons in the skull and gene scientists translate the nucleotide language of DNA to reveal a secret message. They can explain how the visual cortex and the self-control centers of the brain work overtime in order to produce a girl who wakes up dizzy every morning but with an irrational sense of accomplishment. What they cannot explain is the hive and the ever-present buzzing I hear in my mind.

15. When confronted with the bizarre, humans flee to intellecualization or romanticisation. Scientists like to explain it away; writers enjoy the dwelling. I am both, stuck between two streams, split down the middle.

16. At twelve years old, the buzzing began reverberating against my skull, and a hive planted itself underneath my bed. Lightning would burst through my vision if I stood up too quickly from my desk. At night, I slept under countless blankets, the space heater in my room set to burning. Breakfast consisted of a cup of black coffee; lunch a diet soda. I survived on the inescapable swarm in my head and the steaming hot baths I took at night, my naked body steeping like a tea bag. The steam would condense and drip down the tile, but I could still not seem to get warm.

17. Science demands that life must beget life. The study of life intrinsically relies on reproduction, because observation of the dead becomes boring after a while.

18. Since I couldn't reproduce, was I not alive? (Maybe that was the point of it all.)

19. I vacillate between minimization and comprehension, between denial and acceptance, between dwelling and departing. Do I miss floating amidst that dirty water, the muck tangled in my hair? I do not know. I do know that stagnancy yields the comforting slowness I covet.

20. Reworded, did I want tragedy to define my life? Would I allow death to coil around my waist, pulling me under to drown like Ophelia? (Must women drown in order to be relevant to a story?)

21. Starving people cannot register thirst. Soon after the manifestation of this malfunction, the body's imbalance of fluids and electrolytes causes the electrical currents which produce heartbeats to fail.

22. Almost like a different type of drowning, a drowning devoid of water.

23. The Ophelia complex, a concept proposed by Gaston Bachelard, associates the feminine with liquids, and explains Ophelia's fate as a dissolution of self. Almost as if she placed herself in a tub of acid and allowed herself to disintegrate.

24. Scientifically, solvation involves the breaking down of molecules within a liquid. Bonds form, bonds break, molecules reorganize. Ions dissociate.

25. (Why do girls feel they must tear themselves apart in order to find their fate?)

26. Women are expected to birth, to sacrifice, to consistently dilute themselves into tiny pieces. To occupy less space, to be a comma in the story of a man. Perhaps I was scared of that watery shape of womanhood I observed. Maybe I almost allowed myself to drown in it.

27. Womanhood possesses some type of shape, of that I am certain. Not the shape of a fragile girl, her collarbones straining against her skin. Not the shape of a puddle, or a shadow. No, if I were to give the feminine a shape, it would resemble a flame.

28. I learned to burn the sickness from my life. Boiling the waters I thought would kill me. Evaporating the disease into the air. Setting the hive aflame, scattering the bees across the wind. Allowing a fire to burn and build in my stomach. This is my growing up, this is me coming into my own.

29. What is fate except for choice?

Tracy Ng

Is it the American Dream, or the American Nightmare?

When you think of the word nightmare, what is the first thought that pops up in your mind? A dream? A surreal experience? For some, a nightmare may be ghosts, zombies, or vampires. For others, a nightmare may be falling down a rabbit hole of financial debt, staying employed in a job they passionately hate, or losing the love of their life. For my mother, however, her everyday life transformed into her own personal nightmare.

My mother's life has always been filled with difficult decisions: To stay silent about a manager who is beginning to show her true colors and slack off, or offer a hard-working restaurant co-worker the chance to rise up in the ranks? To stay in the homeland of China that she has known for 29 years of her life since she was a baby, or immigrate to America for her husband and his fallible promise that she will never again have to work a day in her life? To bring her beloved mother to America, or choose the delinquent son of her brother in hopes of repairing severed familial relationships?

"Of course I chose the latter options," my mother, now aged 54, recalled upon her younger self's naivety. "In fact, I should have never come to the United States."

"Why?" I inquired, immediately floored by her bluntness. "Didn't you want to have a chance at the American Dream, too?"

"Your father did," she replied. Her eyes smiled softly at me and portrayed the same, intense sadness whenever she reminisced about China. "I did not."

Perhaps her life drastically changed even before the moment she stepped foot on American soil. After all, she had made the decision to step away from her close family and friends to pursue the unknown with her husband. In 1989, her husband flew by himself to America and stayed at his distant relative's house while working towards obtaining some financial stability and, most importantly, a green card. For three consecutive years, my mother patiently waited for him and waited Cantonese teahouse tables to sustain herself. My mother chuckled to herself and said she would have been lying to herself if the thought of him never coming back had not crossed her mind—because it did, more times than she could count on her fingers. Back then, the one and only form of communication they had was through a telephone using an international phone card. Although her doubts constantly plagued her mind, he returned to China with a new green card and brought her overseas in 1992. Uncoincidentally, 1992 was the year the force of gravity felt the heaviest on my mother.

Here, on the second floor of house number 235 on 11th and Vine Street, the weight of my mother's reality gradually transformed into a living, crushing nightmare. From Monday to Friday, she would travel to SCS School on Market Street in order to learn English with other foreigners, including Russians, Hispanics, Vietnamese, and Chinese. Straight afterwards, she would head to a Chinatown factory and take up sewing work. What she could not bear most, however, was not the fact that she had schooling or that she was given the false hope of never working again. These did not phase her because she had worked her hardest, every damned day of her life. No, what she could not handle were the feelings of loneliness and guilt that slowly enveloped her. This cycle repeated until one day, everything piled up and she broke down.

Drip. Plook. Drip. Except for the leaking bathtub faucet, her surroundings— from the scrapes of car tires on pavement to the chatter of passersbys on the street—sounded like white noise to my mother. With her knees bent on the stone cold bathroom floor and her hands in the bucket of clothes, she remained still as a statue as her fingertips pruned in soapy water. Memories of her family, friends, and hometown flickered through her mind like a roll of film on repeat. All at once, every emotion flooded her senses. In that hollow apartment, she was truly alone and nothing could hold back her tears—not even the baby in her growing stomach. Her eyes overflowed like the thunderous cascades of Niagara Falls until my mother felt emotionally—and physically—numb.

Eventually, similar to how the dark clouds clear up after the rain has ended, her nightmare subsided. Once three months passed, they finally moved out of the cramped one-bedroom, one-kitchen apartment and into another temporary living arrangement in Cherry Hill, New Jersey. The thunder from the stormy days were starting to simmer down as my mother discovered solace in my newborn sister and newfound friends, who had experienced the same feelings as she had when they first arrived in America, from her English-learning class. In the same spectrum, she started a new job at Pincus Bros.-Maxwell, a clothing store where she learned to enjoy her work for eight continuous years. Throughout those eight years, the company graciously covered my mother's medical fees for all three of her children, including me. Ironically, shortly after having me and quitting her job to care for all of us, their clothing factory closed down—which signaled the end of an era for both itself and my mother.

"Despite everything," my mother momentarily paused and looked into my already glistening eyes. "I am incredibly grateful to have raised three beautiful and intelligent children." As I studied my mother's slowly aging features, I still could not believe how much conflict she had to overcome. All I could see was a woman with a past that always caused my heart to squeeze in pain. All I could see was a woman who radiantly smiled and wholeheartedly laughed, just like the rest of us. All I could see was my mother—a person who I look up to—and no matter how many hardships she has faced, she has always cared for others. Hence her everlasting motto, which has been ingrained in my daily life: "Be kind and do what you love".

The purpose of my mother's story is not to invoke pity or sympathy, but simply to address the fact that your past and your challenges will always be there. You could view your life as a piece of art and your adversities as blemishes or stains on the canvas. Alternatively, those adversities could be viewed as brush strokes that add depth to your work and enhance your colored canvas in hindsight. In other words, you are the person who chooses whether to see the glass half empty or half full. For my mother, she gradually overcame her demons and definitely emerged as a stronger woman. Do not let the past define you or become an obstacle in your present life. You may have been shaped by those events, but ultimately you decide how you react. Embrace your bad times, but do not forget that you are much greater and full of life than those moments.

Although our nightmares can become recurring, the amazing aspect about nightmares are that they always have to end—whether that be in the next second, or over the course of decades. No matter how long, it will get better.

Upoma Chakraborty

Yes, No, Very Good

"Yes. No. Very good. If you know these words, you'll be set in America, *bhai*, or should I say, in English, brother," Shuvo reassuringly told Roni in Bangla. Tonight, Shuvo was leaving Roni to tend to the store all to himself for the first time ever.

Shuvo owned a large convenience store in Jackson Heights and he was the one giving Roni, his younger brother, his first job in America. Having just come to America four months ago, he was living with Shuvo who had come decades before him. While long ago, Shuvo still recalled those days and wished he had someone that would have helped him. Yet here he was now, with his whole family in America, all living and working under the same roof, and for that he was thankful.

Shuvo had a stable income as the owner of his family operated convenience store and was excited to have another family member help with the store. Unlike many who squeezed their families into small one bedroom apartments, he owned a home in New York. His spacious home was then filled with family members who Shuvo trained to learn English, work in the store, and be productive members of American society. He made sure his family ate well, slept in large comfortable beds and always made sure they had winter coats for New York's harsh weather. He never let them be without. So when it came that Roni, his youngest brother and the last of his family to arrive in America, Shuvo made sure he and his pregnant wife had ample space.

Shuvo was proud of the empire he built. He had systems and schedules set up so that everyone in the house knew their own respective roles. Children, of course, were expected to go to school and earn high marks, and if they had time to spare they would work at the store after school. Women, while they were trained in managing the convenience store, instead cooked and cleaned at home. The exception was Shuvo's wife, Shelpi, who handled the finances in the store and spent much of her time crunching numbers in the store's office. She was a sharp looking woman who knew how every dollar entered and exited the store; perhaps that's why Shuvo loved his wife, she was meticulous and measured. Lastly, were the men who took different shifts working at the store starting from 6 in the morning to midnight, 7 days a week.

The two brothers wasted no time trying to make sure Roni was up to speed with what happened in America's past couple years.

"A tragedy called 9/11 where many Americans died and then war was wagered on people who look like us, but are not us," Shuvo told Roni. "There are Americans are angry towards people who speak broken English and have dark skin."

Roni could understand this anger and hostility, he had seen it within his own country. It was always easier to blame a group of people as opposed to one person. And so with that, Roni had kept quiet. He had never had a real conversation with an American except for the time he had trouble filling his MetroCard. An old white woman who had a mellow voice helped him and told him to "have a good day, sir." She had said it so sweetly and with such a lovely smile, it had to be a nice thing. *But then again,* Roni thought, *Americans did smile too much.*

Roni abided by what his brother told him and when he could understand the basics of an English conversation, it was his turn to work in the store. The week before Roni was supposed to start, Shuvo taught his younger brother everything, and like the good student Roni was, he paid attention with all of his might.

"This is where the eggs are," Shuvo said while pulling on the freezer door, letting all of the cold air spill out to the floor. "If you see a carton past the expiration date, pull it from the shelf immediately, but don't throw it away. Tell me or Shelpi first, then throw it away."

Roni had no idea that eggs even expire. In Bangladesh, people ate whatever they could get. But Roni quickly understood that in America there were regulations and standards. He liked these rules very much. They made him feel safe.

After the week of training, it was now Roni's turn to work. His brother gave him the easiest shift to work, the closing shift. Shuvo, wary that his brother may mess up, also made sure his son, 16 year old Nikhil, would be with his uncle. Nikhil was a strange unsocial kid who did not have many friends in school and unknowingly to the family, had poor grades. Nikhil would being home fake report cards so his parents wouldn't make a fuss. He would also take three showers a day just so the smell of cigarettes wouldn't linger on him; no one in his family knew he smoked. He wasn't a bad kid, just a lost one.

The shift began promptly at 8:00 PM, with Roni and Nikhil standing in front of the register. Shuvo left after his shift and left the reminded Roni that the words yes, no and very good, would get him through the evening. Roni was so proud when the first customer walked in, purchased a bag of chips and a large soda and then left. He felt as though he accomplished something. He didn't need Nikhil's help at all. Roni counted out the man's money, 3 dollars in ones, and gave him back his change, 2 quarters. *Counting money is the best part,* Roni thought. There was something about counting money that made him feel important. It made him feel as though he was contributing to the household.

The hours between 8 PM to 11 PM went by uneventfully. People came and went, buying no more than the typical chips, candy, cigarettes and soda. They didn't say much either.

Hi.

How are you.

Okay, thank you.

Bye.

Roni knew these words. This job, which was so menacing and seemed to have so many tasks wasn't so bad. Roni was proud of himself when he realized he didn't need his nephew's help.

Eventually, 11:55 PM rolled around; five minutes until Roni was supposed to lock up the store. Closing took at least thirty minutes since Roni was given a plethora of tasks: sweep the floor, make sure the aisles have been straightened out, count the money in the register then put it in the safe, the list went on.

Just as Roni was about to walk up to the front door to lock it, a gaunt, loud man came through the door, "Lemme in! I gotta buy a pack of cigarettes! Marlboro, please! It'll take two minutes!" Cigarettes. Marlboro. Roni understood that the man wanted cigarettes, specifically Marlboro. Truthfully, Roni wanted the man to leave because at this point the store should be empty, it was time to lock up. But when he looked at the time and saw it wasn't midnight just yet, Roni let the man in. And so he walked over, grabbed the pack, scanned it and announced the total, 7 dollars and 89 cents.

"Ya got change for a hundred?" the man asked while pulling out a fresh hundred dollar bill.

Roni did not understand. The man spoke too quickly and was waving around a hundred dollar bill, which the store would not accept. Surely he would know that since the sign of what bills were accepted was to the man's left, right where his cigarette packet laid. Roni remembered his brother's words "Don't ever accept hundred dollar bills, especially if their total is under 10 dollars, they might try to scam you and give them more change back than what they deserve." The man repeated what sounded like the same question and Roni said no quietly.

The man blew air out of his nose loudly and put his hands on his hips, "No?! Well why the hell not? It's a freaking hundred dollar bill, it's valid American currency!"

There was not a single word that Roni understood. He pointed his finger to the sign that said no hundreds were accepted.

The man grew red. "Well I see that! I'm asking why goddammit. Why!"

Roni understood the man's simple question, but he didn't have the words to explain why.

"Because it no good..." Roni started. "It will be...."

It will be a problem is what he wanted to say. But how did you say problem in English? In Bangla the word was *shomosha*. It was the kind of word that naturally rolls out of your mouth when something goes wrong. But in English? Roni tried to think and think, but it seemed the more pressure he was under, the less English he remembered.

The man felt his ears growing warm. "You goddamn immigrants don't speak a word of English do ya? And yet they still hire ya! You're completely useless. Where are the jobs for the people who belong here?"

Roni towered over the man physically, but he was the one who felt small. Where was Nikhil? Roni squeaked out to the man "One minute, you wait," then turned his back to call for his sleeping nephew, *"Nikhil, oi Nikhil, koi tui? Ai na tui, ekhane ektu ai!"* Roni called repeatedly for Nikhil. He wanted his nephew here. He wanted to hear his nephew speak English to this man to resolve the matter. But to no avail, Nikhil did not show despite the fact that Nikhil was known to be a light sleeper. Roni turned to the man and was embarrassed, "I'm sorry, my English no good... " Roni wanted to say more but there were no words to fill the embarrassment.

At this point the man was screaming, "Dirty ass immigrants! You're good fr *nothing*. You bring nothing but crime here! You don't even pay taxes. You take all of the jobs but can't speak English! You're probably an illegal alien aren't ya? That's why ya can't speak English!" The man's eyes were a dark shade of blue but the red veins surrounding his iris made the blue look sinister. Roni had always liked blue eyes until now.

The man leaned over the counter and looked directly into Roni's brown sad eyes, "I hate terrorists like you. Go back to your own f***ing country and stay the f*** out of mine." The man turned around as if nothing happened and left; slamming the door on his way out. The pack of Marlboro cigarettes remained on the counter, next to the sign of what bills were accepted. The number 7.89 was still on the register screen.

Nikhil had heard everything. He woke up when the man yelled for what cigarettes he wanted. Nikhil wished he was brave. He wished he could tell the man to get the f*** out of his store and give him the middle finger. But he froze. Nikhil had never heard words like that; at least in person. He didn't know people could hate like that. Sure, some kids at school would call him Osama's son after 9/11, but never did they say they hated him. *Because the guys at school were joking, right? They didn't actually mean those things, did they?* Nikhil didn't know anymore.

The shaken 16 year old stepped outside from the back office into the store. It was there he found his uncle silently crying while sweeping the floor. Roni did not look up from his task. "Why didn't you come when I called you?"

Nikhil had no response. He couldn't think of a single valid thing to say. Not one.

Roni leaned the broom against the wall, out of place where it should have been. He knew this was not where the broom elongated. While only 28 years old, Roni suddenly felt decades older, but in the worst sense. He felt as though he had seen it all and was tired of this life; it was time to move onto the next.

Roni calmly stated what he intended to do, *"Ami ei kaj ta chere dechi."*

Nikhil had never heard of such a thing; a family member quitting? The store? The store that provided for their family? Impossible. Nikhil responded in English, his preferred language, "You're quitting? Why?"

"Is that the word in English?" Roni started in Bangla, then continued in English. "Quitting? I quit. Okay? I am quit. Quit. Quit. Quit."

The word felt strange in English. It was too short and Roni didn't like the way it sat in his mouth after saying the word so many times. *English was not a pretty language,* Roni thought.

Nikhil tried to plea with his uncle as Roni grabbed his things. Nikhil pleaded in English. In Bangla. With tears. Without them. It was of no use, Roni had decided to quit working at the store. Nikhil didn't understand why his uncle was going, but Roni fully understood his place in this cold cruel country.

As Roni was walking out of the store, he realized something— he had learned a new word.

Kate Stone

Stuck

Twenty-three is a weird age. Some of my friends are getting engaged and others are blacking out four times a week at the bar. Me, I'd say I'm somewhere in between. Not quite an alcoholic, not quite a true adult. I'd fall in the middle of the spectrum: average.

I work six days a week as a waitress at Chester's, a mediocre diner that's regulars consist of no one below the age of 65. I don't mind it though. I kind of like listening to them repeat stories of all the crazy things they did when they were my age. Sometimes I think about what stories I'll tell when I get old and it makes me anxious. I have a fear of falling into a routine where my days blend together in a mundane fashion until one day I wake up and I'm alone with a cat still working the lunch shift at Chester's.

When I was a little girl I used to dream of being a famous ballerina. I wore pink tutus to the grocery store, school, and even church on the rare occasion that my mother broke down and let me. She was a beautiful dancer. We would turn on classical music in the kitchen and pretend to be on stage in New York City at the American Ballet Theatre. We would leap and twirl and laugh until we were too tired to go on. Sometimes I get rocketed back into that kitchen when I hear the sound of a violin on the subway platform, only to be brought back to reality by the swift gust of wind hitting my skin as the train arrives.

Every Monday at approximately two-thirty in the afternoon, I meet my friend at a coffee shop on the corner of 9th and Union St. Her name is Claire. She recently graduated from NYU with a degree in screenwriting. Unfortunately, despite four years of throwing everything she had into her education, she is collecting unemployment and living in a studio apartment with six other artistic So-Ho twenty-somethings. The thing about Claire is that she still believes she's on brink of fame. Today as we sip on our vanilla chai lattes, she's going on about some new sitcom idea she has, but I can't stop thinking about the song playing in the background. It was the song "Vienna" from Billy Joel's album *The Stranger*. I can still remember my mom pouring a glass of pinot noir from the boxed wine in the fridge and turning on the record player in our living room. She always loved Billy Joel; she told me once that listening to him was like escaping from reality for a little while. Right now the speaker blared his voice "And you know when the truth is told that you can get what you want or just get old." I was never one to believe in magical signs from up above, but sometimes it's hard to not feel like she's trying to tell me something.

"Annie, Annie, are you even listening to me?"

"Hey, sorry I'm back. I zoned out for a minute."

"Well, I was just asking you how things with George have been going?" Claire said after rolling her eyes.

"Good, well fine, I guess, I don't know."

I honestly didn't know, lately I've just gotten bored. Not just with George, but with the direction my life's been going in. I always figured I'd be engaged by 26 married by 28 and pregnant by 30, but now I don't even know what I want. Apparently "I don't know" wasn't a good enough answer for Claire though.

"You don't know how things are going with him? What the f*** kind of answer is that Annie? You can't keep just staying in one place because you're afraid. If you're over it then you're over it, but if you actually love him you should start acting like it."

Claire was right as much as I didn't want to hear it, but I was thankful that she dropped the subject and went back to focusing on her own life. Twenty minutes, and two life altering realizations later, Claire's rant came to an end. I looked down at my watch and realized I had promised George I'd meet him at his apartment by four and it was already three-thirty. Claire made me promise I'd stop being complacent and sent me on my way.

When I got off the subway and walked down to the rundown apartment in Brooklyn that George was renting it was already twenty minutes passed four. I prepared myself for our reoccurring argument about the value of punctuality and rang for him. He buzzed me in and I took a breath and knocked on his door, he opened it with a huge smile.

"Annie, finally, I was starting to think you forgot about me," he said still smiling.

"I'm sorry, I know I'm late, but I was with Claire and just lost track of time."

He leaned in for a kiss and I was caught off balance. I wasn't sure why he was in such a good mood, but I figured I should just be happy that I avoided a fight.

Pulling back from me he whispered, "I have a surprise for you. Close your eyes"

He reached in his back pocket, pulled something out and placed it in my hands. It was light with sharp edges, clearly made of paper.

"Open your eyes."

I opened them and looked down at the two tickets I was now holding. They had the words American Ballet plastered across a photo of dancer. I didn't say anything.

"Annie? Aren't you excited, you used to love going to the ballet? I thought you'd be happy."

I heard what he was saying, but my mind was already somewhere else. The last time I danced was two years ago at the final performance of my third year at Julliard. I thought I would be able to do it. I thought I could muster up the courage to complete my routine, but when the lights hit me and I looked at the faces of the people in the crowd, I broke down. Tears rolling down my face I ran off the stage. It was the first time, that I knew she wouldn't be in the audience, couldn't be. They told me that she was watching me from up above, always rooting me on, but I thought that was a load of bullshit. I wanted her to really be there, in the front row, smiling at me.

"Annie?" George mustered, concerned.

"I -uh, I am excited, it's just, it's been awhile since I thought about dance."

"I know, that's kind of why I bought them. I thought maybe watching them would reignite that spark that died in you. That's what she'd want Annie. It's what I know you want."

I agreed to go, to keep from having to discuss it any longer, but as he cooked dinner I mulled over what he had said. How the hell did he know that's what she'd want? That's one of those things people always say after you lose someone. She obviously didn't give a f*** if I made it as a dancer or not, if she did she would have stuck around to watch me get there.

It was an average Tuesday afternoon when I got the call. I remember the beginning of my day vividly, I had just gotten out my music theory course and was headed back to my apartment when my aunt's name popped up on my phone.

"Hello, Aunt Jen." I answered.

Her voice was shaky when she said, "Hi Annie," and she fell silent for a minute.

"What's wrong?"

"It's your mom Annie."

Growing concerned I mustered "What about my mom Jen?'

"She's dead Annie," Jen replied sobbing.

I don't remember much about that specific moment other than the fact that I dropped my phone and stood completely stoic for a few minutes before my body caught up with my brain and realized that I should be crying. I'm not sure when I stopped crying, but I know it wasn't because I had adequately relived all my sadness, but rather because I had exhausted my supply of tears. That was two months before I took the stage for the last time.

At seven-thirty that night we arrived at the theater. We took our seats and George squeezed my hand. He had filled the vacant space with conversation for the past few hours, as I sat unable to pretend to be present. I didn't know how it would feel to sit in the audience and watch people perform in a show I was destined to be a part of. Some of them were my classmates. When I walked off that Julliard stage I never came back. I was three years into my degree, but it felt meaningless when I found out my mother had overdosed. They ruled it a suicide through the use of prescription pain killers. Everyone told me that she was sick, that there was nothing I could have done, but I resented the fact that I was hundreds of miles of way when she needed me the most. I resented that I wasn't enough to keep her alive.

The show started and I closed my eyes for a moment taking in the sound of the classical music. Visions of my mother in the kitchen filled my head and I opened my eyes letting a tear drop down as I watched mesmerized by the beauty. I leaned on George, resenting the fact that earlier I didn't realize how much I loved him. I think I had tried to distance myself from feeling any emotions at all.

After the show I made George wait outside with me, so I could say hello to an instructor I had at Julliard who was a part of the performance.

"Hi, Georgia!" I said as she walked outside.

Smiling, she hugged me and said "It's been too long Annie."

"You were magnificent tonight," I replied.

"You should have been up there with me."

"I know, I didn't realize how much I missed it until tonight. I needed a break, but two years was a bit much," I laughed.

We left the theater and hailed a cab. George gave the driver our address and we sat back as he turned the radio up.

"Tell me why are you still so afraid?" it sung. I looked up and smiled.

Christopher Bream

Golden Delicious

At the bottom of the hill sat a green pickup truck. It had an extended bed and was half full of wooden, square apple crates, each initialed with "RP" in fading paint. On the opposite end of the truck, facing the trees and appearing to talk to them, stood Mr. Pearson. He was tall, just about 6'4", quite thin for his age and the amount of beer he drank. He wore a white button down. It was fleece-like, buttoned only half way. His thick chest hairs were freely protruding.

Owen made his descent towards the truck, lengthening his strides now as his father's voice rang out in his head, "Move with a sense of urgency!"

"Hi, Mr. Pearson!" Owen's voice burst out.

"Good Morning, Owen. Nice of you to finally join us," Mr. Pearson replied. Owen hadn't noticed until he reached the bottom of the hill that Mr. Pearson wasn't talking to the trees but, rather, a group of men scattered within them. They stood with undivided attention, like a group of farm cats when the door of their feeder springs open. The men were short in stature, some able to stand beneath the lowest hanging branches. Their faces were worn, for which the sun was responsible. Owen looked at them with eyes of embarrassment and insecurity. He did not know them, and that was enough for any 15-year-old boy to be made uncomfortable.

"I am truly sorry, Mr. Pearson. I assumed you'd be up at the house," Owen said. Mr. Pearson then let out a grunt of dismissal and continued loading full crates atop his truck bed.

"I'll need you here by six every morning. Can you do that?" Owen opened his mouth in protest, but Mr. Pearson's face suggested no opportunity for debate.

"Yes," Owen said, closing his mouth. He considered the deep pain of rising this morning and wondered how much more deeply it would hurt to awake even 30 minutes earlier.

"Good. Now it's very simple. You grab an empty crate." Mr. Pearson held the crate out for Owen to take as he did. "You walk over to a tree. Place the crate beneath your feet like such," Mr. Pearson demonstrated, "then you begin picking. You have a ladder already, along with an over-the-shoulder bag, if that's more appealing." Owen looked past the men to where Mr. Pearson was pointing. A tree stood, just the same as the others, supporting a ladder cut from what looked like the same wood as the crates. The ladder was old and chipped, but visibly sturdy.

"Any questions?" Mr. Pearson asked.

"No, sir," Owen replied.

"Good to hear." And with that, Owen began.

. . . . .

Apples have a funny way of looking perfect. Good pickers reach their hands out, plucking the stem straight from the nutrients and warmth of the mother tree. The red delicious may spin with the slow-motion beauty of a Disney cartoon princess or a carousel lighting up the cotton candy-covered face of a four-year-old. The skin of the fruit may seem taut, tight, and tenacious. But raise the food of knowledge of good and evil to your lips and take a bite—if you'd truly like to be dissatisfied. For deep within this apple grew a tiny worm. A worm whose bite had spoiled a spot and bruised the whole lot through.

. . . . .

Owen spit the apple out with urgent velocity. His coworkers turned their heads in mild confusion, and Owen's face began to sweat. He was a nervous boy and had many years to learn the lifelong lesson of caring little for what others think. He looked down at the apple, examining it. How could he have missed such a large mushy spot. Ever since he was a boy he had hated the mushy spot. His father often mocked his deep-seated disgust of bruised fruit in a hideous, teasing screech, "BUT DADDY IT'S BROWN!" Owen shed a half smile remembering how swiftly his father would snap a bite of decaying banana or pear, triggering the sensitive gag reflex of his thin six-year-old throat. Mr. Pearson had his head turned, and just as swiftly as his father's bite, Owen threw the apple deep into the heart of the dark and shaded orchard. He nearly fell off his ladder.

Mr. Pearson showed Owen to his tree a few hours ago, and Owen had about two bushels to show for it. He moved timidly, holding on to the ladder, only removing his supportive hand when his knees ceased their wobbling. He'd pick until he'd find each apple just beyond the comfort of his reach in a Da Vinci-esque semicircle. Owen would then climb down, slide his ladder to the next sturdy spot and arise back to a position of elevation and control. He cared little for how much slower he was picking but couldn't help but notice his neighbor had descended with at least eight bushels since Owen's observations began. He became distracted with the speed and precision of which his picking companion picked. He reached with confidence in his fingers and balance deep within his toes. Although he seemed to sway and shift on the ladder, it appeared his bellybutton remained firmly pressed against the center of the top rung. He wore army green cargo pants with a torn pocket near the knee of his left leg. His shirt was a dirtied grey, and his hat was a faded red, nearly pink. Owen stared at his hat for a moment too long, for the worker had caught his glimpse. They shared a second of observation, as a squirrel might look at a chicken, with no predatory interest, but interest just the same. Owen noticed that the face of the worker was taut like the skin of the mushy apple he had bitten into. His eyes held no baggage, and his cheeks remained elevated in the position they were born in. "That's no man," Owen's eyes exclaimed, "he's like me!" The fellow teenager felt this realization in the rapid fluctuation of confused facial crevices and arching eyebrows that Owen made no effort to suppress. He looked away quickly in embarrassment, hiding behind the extension of his fading red—pink—hat.

Owen's first instinct was to talk, as he opened his mouth. And words would have escaped had the flustered reaction of his newly discovered peer not stopped him in silence. "Why did he turn away like that?" Owen thought. "Perhaps he doesn't speak English good," Owen's prejudiced little mind suggested. Owen opened his mouth once more to speak but closed it slowly just the same. The embarrassment of the boy had spread into the blood vessels of Owen's forehead. Oh, what it was to be a pubescent teenage boy—one would never be quite as alive as in those years.

The apple picking continued until lunch break was signified by a mumbled "Let's eat y'all," from Mr. Pearson. Everyone descended from their ladders, placed their partially full crates at the trunk of their tree and headed in the direction of Mr. Pearson's truck. Owen found himself first off the ladder, causing Mr. Pearson to shake his head in temporary disapproval, which Owen missed entirely due to his ravished focus on the apple and PB and J sandwiches his mother had packed the past evening. He chowed with a newfound lack of energy. The boy had worked for only four hours yet already burned the calories of an entire day's worth of video games. He tore and gnashed at both PB and Js, feeling discontent when he reached into the bag to discover he had already eaten his second sandwich. He settled on the apple, which had lasted five bites at best.

He looked over his right shoulder into the shade of the overgrown orchard. Underneath a tree sat the boy with his hat removed, releasing neatly hidden handfuls of flowing black hair. The boy sat next to a man, much smaller than he, who had wrinkled cheeks and slouching shoulders. Owen assumed this must be his father as the boy appeared a spitting, stretched-out image of the withered man sitting beside him.

As Owen observed the two, a radiant yellow jacket landed smoothly on the apple core Owen held. The pesky insect was unbothered by Owen and was consumed by the succulent sugar of the apple the boy had failed to bite into. Owen raised the core to his lips, stretching his teeth out within centimeters of the fruit before his eyes caught the shining yellow and black of the dangerous intruder. "Dammit!" Owen yelled, tossing the core quickly away and digging his heels into the dirt in an effort to jump backwards.

Mr. Pearson turned his head along with the others. "Hey, Owen! Cut it out! These are God's fields, and I won't have you out here using that language. Not around my apples, and my workers, even if they don't speak a lick of English! Got it?"

Owen's wished he could simply shrivel up and disappear. "Yeh...yehh.... Yes, sir Mr. Pearson. I'm so sorry I didn't mean to, it's just..."

"Just don't let it happen again," Mr. Pearson said, and with that, all went back to normal. Owen felt sweat slowly drip from his armpits down the ripples of his emerging rib cage and into his waistband. He surveyed his surroundings, catching the eyes of many of the workers. Something told him they all spoke a "lick" of English.

Eventually Owen's heartbeat settled and he dared to turn his gaze back upon the Mexican Boy. The boy's cargo pants were ripped at the knees, and his shirt hung with age and dampness. Owen had heard about migrants on the news and was surprised to be with some, especially one his age. He wondered if they were "illegals," as his Uncle Tom often referred to them. Uncle Tom told dinner table stories about the violence and drugs that were being brought across the southern border into Texas and New Mexico.

"They don't look 'illegal'," he thought. He pictured the running silhouettes plastered on Channel 8 News with captioning in bold lettering at the bottom of the screen "MILLIONS OF ILLEGALS ENTER SOUTHERN BORDER." He pictured the brown-skinned men being detained by Border Patrol and wondered if his coworkers had ever faced such circumstances. He couldn't believe Mr. Pearson would be housing fugitives. "There's no way they're illegals." Owen finally concluded. But afterwards, he found himself at a loss for words for what exactly he would call them. He could hear them speaking to one another in the smooth-flowing, quick-syllabled Spanish dialogue. Owen wondered what they were talking about, especially when the Mexican Boy had shot him a quick glance while mumbling to his father.

Lunch soon ended, and each worker simultaneously ascended the rungs of his ladder and began picking. Owen felt an after-lunch grogginess despite consuming far less than he had wished to. He peered over his shoulder at the others in distrust, not knowing the content of their conversations.

The men and boys picked underneath the comforting clouds of a cool September day. It was quiet picking. The only sounds to be heard were the rustling of the wind through the leaves and the snapping of the apple stems from the nutrition of their branches. SNAP! SNAP! Occasionally, the pickers would pick in accidental unison creating a sound similar to that of a cracking back. The American boy picked slowly and poorly, bruising half of the apples he threw into his crate. But this mattered little as the Mexican boy picked at four times this speed, bruising hardly any. The two boys contrasted deeply. They held the weight of different skin and the color of different language. Culture fueled their identity, but upbringing lit their perspective.

The end of the day came, and the pickers started walking toward the gravel road that ran alongside the orchard. Owen was tired and hungry. He decided to pluck the low-hanging fruit of a tree at the brink of the orchard. He raised the apple to his mouth but stopped at the feeling of a hand on his shoulder. He turned to the reassuring face of the Mexican boy. "That one's brown," he said in perfect English. He then handed Owen a fresh apple, firm as his heart, and threw the rot deep into the orchard.

Timothy Hanlon

A 2,000-Year Pandemic

There is a pandemic spreading around this Earth so silently that it has gone undetected by the media, scientists, and maybe even the government for over two thousand years. The earliest documentation of this disease points back to the Roman Empire and it likely arose many years prior to that. By now the disease is so wide spread that I guarantee each and every one of you reading this has been affected by it in some way. *Pater Iocus* – or Dad Jokeitous – is no laughing matter and the only killer thing about the disease is the jokes.

Pater Iocus is clinically defined as "an infectious rewiring of the brain causing compulsive behavior, impulsivity, hyperactivity, and/or a lack of restraint leading the infected individual to present *seemingly* harmless jokes, puns, and other plays on words." Typical symptoms include, but are not limited to:

• A substantially increased understanding of language

• An inability to withhold contributions of terrible jokes, puns, and other word plays

• A collection of New Balance 624 Cross Trainers or alike tennis shoes

On top of these listed symptoms, individuals with the disease are often characterized as "witty" or "Rain Man with words". It is also important to note that this disease does not discriminate. While it is most commonly seen within male individuals who have children, it can be seen in males and females of any age with no regard to whether or not you are a father.

During the course of a conversation, those with the disease generally do not have a lot of time to come up with jokes or puns. Instead, they are given maybe a few tenths of a second to formulate and begin to deliver the joke. A common classic is the "Hi Hungry, I am Dad" response to someone saying they are hungry. In this instance, the infected has been able to successfully realize that in the absence of the adjective feeling, the person who is supposedly "feeling hungry" has actually identified their being as hungry. Therefore, the individual has triggered a response within the infected exposing a previously undiscovered understanding of language.

The inability to withhold terrible jokes is best exemplified through an experience I have gone through in real life. During my senior year of high school, I was diagnosed with Sacral Chordoma – which is essentially butt cancer. If you know anyone with Dad Jokeitous, you know exactly the types of jokes that can arise from a situation like this and let me tell you they came from the person I least expected them from. During my very first appointment with Dr. Brozovich, in his lead up to reveal my diagnosis, he looked me dead in the eyes and said, "Well, this is a pain in the butt, isn't it?" Dr. Brozovich, Marc if I may, a man who received his MD from Temple University, fundamentally summed up the quintessential Dad Joke, and second symptom of *Pater Iocus*, in ten words. During every appointment thereafter Marc made this same joke, without fail, at some point throughout my visit.

Before going into surgery, Marc said to me, "Now, we are about to have a knife fight, except you will be asleep and I will be the only one with a knife." As we can see in both of these instances involving Dr. Brozovich, *Pater Iocus* can cause the infected individual to experience sudden outbursts of jokes or puns, thus creating a sense of awkwardness triggering bystanders to feel second-hand embarrassment for them. After the surgery, when the doctors tried to wake me up, I suffered a seizure. While many medical professionals have chalked this up to an allergic reaction to the anesthesia, the only true explanation is that a hyperactive strain of the disease was transmitted from Marc to me at some point throughout the surgery. Just prior to leaving the hospital that day, Marc had asked me what I thought of his new New Balance sneakers. At the time I thought this to be a simple question with no underlying message; however, after many hours of research into the disease, I have come to realize this was a flagrant cry for help.

If you, or anyone you know, has created a desire to purchase and/or wear a pair of New balance 624 Cross-trainer tennis shoes, or any alike shoe, I urge you to report to the ER immediately. By putting these shoes on you are guaranteeing yourself the infection, and once they are on, they are the only shoes you will wear for the rest of your life. This is especially detrimental if you accompany this outfit by wearing a pair of jean shorts and yell at people in your household if they even *think* about touching the thermostat.

This disease not only affects the beholder but also those near and dear to them. If you take to YouTube and search "Dad Joke survivors" (https://youtu.be/FAQjbMK-5I8), you will hear the stories of four children who all have fathers with the disease. These kids, no older than twelve years old, have all experienced a traumatic event that will take thousands of dollars and years of therapy to recover from. Isaac now despises the film industry. Could you imagine not being able to watch a movie for the rest of your life simply because you and your family are unaware of the dire consequences of *Pater*

Iocus? Abbey has developed a phobia from what, in the mind of the disease, seemed like a harmless joke. And let us not forget poor Holly. Is she a girl, or is she a sandwich? At this point, she still does not know.

While there are currently no vaccines to prevent the contraction of this disease, there are some steps that can be taken to significantly decrease your chances of being exposed and ultimately infected. The first step is to avoid constant exposure. If you know anyone who is showing signs of the disease on any level, it is best for your health to avoid them at all costs; say so long to your friends and family and hello to solidarity—you cannot be taking any chances with this. The second way to avoid this disease is to tell well thought out and developed jokes that are actually funny. Honestly, just be like Jerry Seinfeld, Ellen DeGeneres, or John Mulaney. Entertaining millions of people and constantly being in the limelight really cannot be that difficult after all. The final step, and probably most tangible step, is to avoid fatherhood. The moment a child is conceived, the father's infection begins. While it is not apparent at first, partially because this strain of the disease takes nine months to develop, it is the most sever. To avoid getting this strain, it is advised that you head down to your local urologist's office to schedule a vasectomy as soon as possible—why they don't hand out vasectomies like circumcisions at birth to avoid this disease is beyond me.

Although *Pater Iocus* is arguably the most entertaining disease out there—as I find many of the jokes and puns quite comical—proper attention to those with the disease is required and can only be obtained through further research. Primitive research will probably look at those living in a monastery since everyone there lives a similar lifestyle and the rate of fatherhood is significantly higher than anywhere else. With your help of donations sent to my Venmo (@timhanlon1), we will be able to stop this wicked disease from spreading to the next generation.

Medina Talebi

Why I'm Superstitious About Lying About Superstitions

The expectation for exoticism can definitely get a little old at times. Between awkwardly accepting abrupt and cloyingly sweet compliments about my hijab and explaining how halal food isn't limited to just chicken-over-rice, I think most people from some kind of relatively diverse background can empathize with the experience of explaining yourself. And by empathize, I mean share that feeling of wanting to slam your hand in a car door every time someone asks if the "secret spice" in whatever homemade dish is cumin.

Every culture has its weird idiosyncrasies, and I think one of the most fascinating ones to talk about is superstitions. Not to me though. No, I wasn't brought up terribly superstitious; I just had a grandma who tried to convert me into a believer of her old wives' tales. Despite the efficacy of her home remedies—I don't know why Big Pharma isn't trying to recruit more grandparents—I bet they could use some homeopathic health care consultants—I would dismiss her other pieces of advice the same way I would the myths that they used to explain the seasons or tides or whatever. She has an explanation for everything and rejects a lot of what modern science has to say. I'm sure someone, probably the cumin junkies, would find that poetic and sweet, how she holds on to traditional stories and all that jazz. Me? I just find it conspiratorial.

I wonder if my grandma's a flat-earther.

Even if I don't heed her advice, my white friends do and boy do I tell you that they eat that stuff up. It all began sprinting up the steps one sweltering day in the spring of sophomore year and I accidentally had stepped on the back of my friend's shoes.

"Jesse, give me your hand," I request, with all the nonchalance of someone who had just robbed a bank for the first time.

"I know you want to hold my hand, but now is not the time," and before she could finish her sentence I was about to lose it. I grasp her hand and shake it, not too unlike the one I would have perfected by the end of all my co-op interviews, which was unbeknownst to me at the time obviously. Before she could demand a restraining order, I had already started explaining myself.

"Listen, we have this thing in my culture where if you step on the back of someone's shoe and don't shake their hand, it means that their gonna be enemies forever, and that's no bueno."

She nodded slowly, digesting what I thought was a bizarre justification for this random assault on her person, but it turns out that people are way more accepting than I previously thought.

And so I *gradually* filled my friends in on all the superstitions I had grown up with. And when I say gradually, I mean gradually. Unpacking them all at once would be almost as oppressive as making them live with them like I do. We started with the softballs I'll admit; priming them with some more innocuous ones like not to jangle your keys in the house (otherwise there would be an argument in that room), or the not to vacuum/dust at night (otherwise you'd start getting more gray hairs). Then somewhere around "whoever sits down first at a wedding reception, bride or groom, will make the decisions in the marriage," I started to transition into the major leagues. At this point, they'd pay rapt attention when I would casually mention how visiting a sick person on Wednesdays wasn't in your best interests since you're more likely to contract their same disease, or how you should *never*, under any circumstances, wear socks to sleep.

Because if you did, you'd go blind eventually.

Once my friends started mentioning to me how they were so sure their eyesight was improving since ditching socks before bed, I decided to test the waters a bit. Perhaps I exaggerated a superstition here or there, or even fabricated one or two. Still, they garnered attention. It was only when I mentioned how eating different foods of the same color on Fridays was sure to lead to losing money did I feel bad as they picked at their lunches halfheartedly. The next day I corrected myself, telling them that it would actually lead to a good fortune or a pay raise.

"You sure you've got it right this time? I was avoiding salad yesterday because I wasn't about to risk it," asks Jesse dubiously.

"Now would my grandma lie to you?"

"No, but you sure as hell would," and it was then that I knew they wouldn't be joining the flat-earthers any time soon.

Nicole Robinson

This Generation's Captain of Industry or Robber Baron: Amazon's Monopoly Effect on Small Businesses

Jeff Bezos, founder and CEO, of Amazon has been compared to several of the pioneers of industry. Some may say his accolades draw similarities to that of J.P. Morgan and the success of U.S. Steel. Others conclude his methods possess likeness to the collusion of John D. Rockefeller's Standard Oil. Despite the differences of industries, Jeff Bezos can be considered a captain of industry or robber baron depending on who is telling the story.

Over the last several decades, Amazon's business has expanded globally to provide merchandise to the average consumer. This online retailer's profitability has increased due to the influx of demand for quick and easily accessible products. The gradual progression of this company has transformed into one of the biggest monopolies in this generation. As Amazon rises, small businesses fall short in competition with the e-commerce giant's lower prices and online presence. Keep a lookout! The doors of the local store in your community just might be closing and Amazon just might be the reason why.

Amazon has profited off the rise of electronic commerce. The business has received it's recognition for selling books, music, movies, housewares, electronics, toys, and many other goods. The creation of the Kindle took the business to even bigger height (Hall). Flash forward to present day, Bezos is buying out other companies to expand his empire. The ideology of "purposeful Darwinism' reign"(ValueWalk) in the infrastructure of the company. The instinct to survive and prosper in today's economy led to purchase of Whole Foods' shares. Whole Foods is recognized for their "squishy, very un-Amazonian ideals—such as employee happiness and workplace satisfaction" (ValueWalk). This making the buyout even more controversial than if Bezos decided to control the shares of an internet-based company.

In the last decade, Amazon has inserted its dominance in the market of consumer goods. More than half of online shopping searches originate from the site. "The United States is much less a nation of entrepreneurs than it was a generation ago. Small, independent businesses have declined sharply in both numbers and market share across many sectors of the economy" (Mitchell).

This monopoly has forced thousands of small or midsize businesses to go out of business or to depend on Amazon to market their products. Small businesses are expected to adapt to this new wave of change. If a business is to prosper in the age of e-commerce promoted by online retailers such as Amazon, they must create an online presence. Amazon can help small businesses succeed, but not without taking away the satisfaction of growing their company or brand in a city near you.

Amazon is the third biggest digital ad seller and have made changes to applying for these ads in hopes of making it easier to understand. Although, digital ads assist in keeping sinking businesses afloat, it still takes away from more traditional advertising options. Also, there are just some products that cannot be sold online. Digital ads would replace the common hospitality and experience of going into a store and choosing a product.

Local businesses thrive of societal support and fellowship and online shopping takes away this element. "Between 1997 and 2012, the number of small manufacturers fell by more 70,000, local retailers saw their ranks diminish by about 108,000, and the number of community banks and credit unions dropped by half, from about 26,000 to 13,000 (Mitchell)." The shift in the U.S. economy challenges the anti-monopoly policy and its function. Small businesses produce job opportunities, distribution of income and supports the middle class. The more powerful the monopoly becomes; the poorer middle class becomes.

Whether Jeff Bezos is a captain of industry or robber baron is entirely up to who is benefitting from it. His success is costing small business across the country to face the reality of going out business. Just keep that in mind the next time you make a purchase on Amazon Prime for free shipping, rather than visiting your local convenience store.

Works Cited

D'Angelo, Matt. Staff Writer. "Countering Amazon's Impact on Small Business." *Business News Daily: Small Business Solutions & Inspiration*. 21 Nov 2018. Web. 30 Nov 2018. <http://www.businessnewsdaily.com/11161-amazon-changing-small-business.html>.

Hall, Mark. "Amazon.com." *Encyclopedia Britannica*, Encyclopedia Britannica, Inc., 1 Nov. 2018, www.britannica.com/topic/Amazoncom.

Mandelbaum, Robb. "Is Amazon Good Or Bad For Small Business?" *Forbes*, Forbes Magazine, 1 Apr. 2018, www.forbes.com/sites/robbmandelbaum/2018/03/31/is-amazon-good-or-bad-for-small-business-yes/#1b7cb4c14467.

Meraay, Hibba, and Nick Stumo-Langer. "Statement on Amazon's Small Business Impact Report." *Institute for Local Self-Reliance*, 16 May 2018, ilsr.org/amazons-small-business-report-may-2018/.

Mitchell, Stacy. "Monopoly Power and the Decline of Small Business." *Institute for Local Self-Reliance*, 10 Aug. 2016, ilsr.org/monopoly-power-and-the-decline-of-small-business/.

ValueWalk: Amazon: E-Commerce at any Cost. Newstex, Chatham, 2017.

Hasala Ariyaratne

Free Speech Matters

The question that those who call for censorship fail to answer is this: who is going to decide which ideas are worth serious consideration? Their various ill-conceived answers given with good intention, pave a path towards complete silence. The censors argue that in the interest of the "community", free expression must be suspended. Especially if speech is coming from the class of "oppressors", however vaguely defined. But what if it is a community of racists and the dissenters are in a numerical minority? Does communal opinion supersede individual liberty?

In the United States of America, the First Amendment to the Constitution protects free expression. This ensures that the government cannot act as a censor, unless under exceptional circumstances. Therefore, when someone is calling for censorship, they are essentially calling for the state to act as a censor. It will not always be those you agree with who will hold political power. You cannot censor without risking censorship for yourself. Silencing differing opinion would also lead to a situation where only one side of the argument is heard. As Mill pointed out "he who knows only his own side of the case knows little of that."

From our scientific explorations of the mind, a strong case could be made that the primary purpose of language is thinking, not communication. It is an internal process of creativity that is not seen in other animals. Speech is fundamentally human. This is what Orwell, albeit not scientifically, recognized in 1984, that freedom of speech is freedom of thought.

To see people, attack the very principles that allow dialogue, is disappointing. Ironically, I will defend their free speech rights to say that free speech is not worth defending. One of the supposedly strong arguments against my position is from the philosopher Karl Popper, whose paradox of tolerance is popular among those who advocate for censorship. The paradox states that intolerant people make a tolerant society impossible and the intolerable should be taken away, presumably by the state. I go back to my original question—who decides what is intolerant? There seems to be no agreement among any two people about what is and what is not acceptable speech. Even among the most reactionary, there are major disputes on ideas. Given such a reality, it is not wise to give up on free speech.

We do not have to choose between a society that defends free expression and a society that values justice. The ends of a just society do not and cannot require the means of surrendering free speech as silencing opinion is unjust. Free speech does mean that there will be material that most people find appalling. This is, however, an inadequate excuse for censorship. You can use your own speech to counter such speech or ignore it completely.

We must defend the right to free expression for everyone. Many tyrants have been in favor of free speech when they agreed with the content. If we do not defend free expression, especially for those whose views we consider most hateful, we are not defending free expression at all. Thomas Paine, famously wrote in The Crisis, "though the flame of liberty may sometimes cease to shine, the coal can never expire." The goal is free speech, the foundation of all liberty.

Chris Faunce
Growing Close

When your last name is Brickman,
    people expect you to be built strong,
even when your foundation is constructed on
    the steps of seventeen orphanages,
where large cracks are faithfully avoided
    and children are forgotten.

Enduring a childhood accompanied by sad faces,
    which you left before you met,
and never received visitors, never felt kept,
    you must have begged for any emotion.

When a wife and two daughters did not suffice,
    you reverted to alcohol,
and when beating your wife no longer felt right,
    you hung yourself in a prison cell,
perhaps seeing a more magnificent place to dwell.

Sophie Geagan

Rise

Tell me to sing of happy things,
of birth and bouquets of roses.
I could paint you worlds soaked in sunshine,
yellow dripping through the edges,
Or pastels
Pastels are my specialty.
I could color in all the spaces
people were careless enough to leave blank,
Stuff the cracks with tissue paper
And wrap it all in winding ribbon,
If you'd like a little extra decor.
All the weights that pull me into the earth
I could leave them behind,
I could put my heavy words in a bottle
And toss it far away into the foaming sea
To spin a life of dreams
With you.
So don't think for a second that I expect
you to take me as I am.
I would bend the sky for you
And I would cut these strings of gravity and rise.

Literature
Essay

Introduction

The essay in this section is the winner of the Literature Essay Contest. Essays must be submitted by (or nominated by) faculty teaching literature courses. Literature faculty are asked to select no more than two essays per class that demonstrate excellence in writing. These essays explore a variety of literary topics. The editors are pleased to include the winning literature essay in *The 33rd*.

—*The Editors*

Heather N. Heim

Colorism and Women in the Harlem Renaissance

The Harlem Renaissance represents an era in which African Americans were able to thrive for the first time. Opportunities were plentiful and from a troubled history, a black middle class arose. However, with this vibrant new community came a new set of issues. While people of color were finally being celebrated, light-skinned African Americans enjoyed more privilege than dark-skinned African Americans. To be light-skinned became a beauty ideal. This discrimination was especially salient for dark-skinned black women, who had a harder time finding work and marrying. As much as the prominent leaders of the Harlem Renaissance discouraged discussions of colorism — which they feared would make the black community look bad — authors like Zora Neale Hurston and Wallace Thurman used their writing to show that this discrimination did exist and to demonstrate how public attitudes caused dark-skinned African American women to feel ashamed of their skin color.

In the era of the New Negro and the Talented Tenth, writers like W. E. B. DuBois believed in using their writing as propaganda that would further the African American race. To them, there was no room for writing that would embarrass the black community. So even though color-based discrimination occurred between African Americans, to publicize this issue was frowned upon. In her article "Re-Evaluating 'Color Struck': Zora Neale Hurston and the Issue of Colorism," H. L. Classon notes, "in a time when White racism was being collectively attacked, and Black pride was fiercely asserted, Black audiences neither expected nor welcomed criticism from within the community" (13-14). However, Hurston breaches the issue in her play Color Struck, which she was able to disguise as "a play celebrating the folk spirit" (Classon 13-14). The fact that Hurston had to "disguise" her work to get it published shows how little the issue was acknowledged.

At the beginning of the play, the dark-skinned protagonist, Emma, and her light-skinned counterpart, Effie, are portrayed similarly. They are vibrant, outgoing, and good at dancing. Classon writes, "The characterization of Emma works against the usual depictions of dark-skinned women. Instead of being a desexualized 'mammie,' Emma is flirtatious, sexy, and, to John at least, physically attractive" (17). John says to her, "You certainly is a ever loving mamma-when you aint mad" (Hurston 709). Even the women's names, Emma and Effie, are similar. Yet, their difference in skin color is the one thing that sets them apart. Effie is viewed as being more desirable. All the men on the train comment on her beauty. Classon notes, "In the opening scene of Color Struck, without the presence of a single white person, the stigma of racism is poignantly felt in the Jim Crow railroad car" (16).

Marriage was a goal for many women in the early twentieth century, which worsens Emma's fear that John is more attracted to lighter-skinned women and may not want to be with her long term. This feeling of inferiority that Emma has internalized because of her darker skin affects her ability to be in a healthy relationship. Classon believes that Color Struck was a way to validate and acknowledge these types of feelings of inferiority. She writes, "To see Emma in a sympathetic light, to understand her obsession, one needs to acknowledge the existence of colorism. Hurston assumed her audience would know this form of prejudice, and at the same time, challenged her audience to face its ramifications" (11).

Moreover, the cakewalk contest demonstrates an opportunity to further comment on color politics. The cakewalk dance is a dance that's meant to mimic and mock white slave owners (even though white people didn't realize this at the time). Emma's refusal to participate in a dance that mocks white people almost symbolizes an internal respect for them, or perhaps a desire to be them. This sets up readers for the end of the play, when they meet Emma's light-skinned daughter. Classon notes, "Emma's near white daughter also suggests a white or half-white male presence. Because she is not married, Emma may have been raped by a white or near-white man, or she may have deliberately sought out a white heritage for her offspring in order to save her child from the 'curse' of dark skin" (Classon 16).

The fact that Color Struck is a play is important, because during the Harlem Renaissance, the roles of black dancers and actors were usually performed by light-skinned African Americans. Classon notes "In addition to the theatrical reinscription of the color caste system, the film industry developed its own color "casting" system for Black actresses...The popularity enjoyed by movies only highlighted the appearances of light-skinned Black actresses as the romantic interest, and, the darker skinned actresses, in contrast, as maids or other minor roles" (12). Though Color Struck was not performed in Hurston's lifetime, it would have forced the female lead role to be performed by a darker-skinned African American woman, breaking away from the norm. Moreover, the stage directions use lightness and darkness to give a visual representation of colorism. Scenes with Effie are described as bright and vibrant while scenes with Emma are sad and dark. In the final scene, when John finds Emma years after the cakewalk contest, the stage is so dark that he can barely see her. He must ask her several times to "make a light" (Hurston 715). Classon notes, "the influence colorism exerts upon Emma is the unifying force of the whole play...

only when the stage is stripped bare of color and excitement in the last scene is the pathos felt most forcefully. Emma's desolation is materialized on stage through the darkness" (11).

Wallace Thurman's *The Blacker the Berry* makes no attempt to disguise the social commentary in its discussion of colorism. As Daniel M. Scott suggests in his article "Harlem Shadows: Re-evaluating Wallace Thurman's *The Blacker the Berry*," "more directly than other fictional works from the Harlem Renaissance, suggests in a self-conscious mode...that such articulations of race and sexuality have often been denied critical recognition and open discussion" (336). In one scene, Thurman explains the prejudice through his characters, who have a heated discussion about color-based discrimination within the black community. One character, Truman, notes "you can't blame light Negroes for being prejudiced against dark ones. All of you know that white is the symbol of everything pure and good...the God we, or rather most Negroes worship is a patriarchal white man, seated on a white throne, in a spotless white Heaven..." (Thurman 642-643).

Later, Truman notes "since black is the favorite color of vaudeville comedians and jokesters, and, conversely, as intimately associated with tragedy, it's no wonder that even the blackest individual will seek out some one more black than himself to laugh at" (644). Emma Lou, Thurman's dark-skinned protagonist takes offense at this casual discussion of what she considers a painful subject: "She couldn't see how these people could sit down and so dispassionately discuss something that seemed particularly tragic to her...She wasn't sure that they weren't all poking fun at her" (645). Just like Hurston's protagonist, Emma Lou is constantly paranoid that people are judging her dark skin. Scott notes, "Caught up in the hierarchy of color and performance...Emma Lou sees her own skin as a mask that prevents her from being who she really is" (332).

Unlike Hurston's Emma, who seems to be imagining much of the discrimination she endures, readers actually see the color-based discrimination that Thurman's Emma Lou faces. She grows up in a family of light-skinned black women, with her mother and grandmother both being light-skinned. The narrator discusses that Emma Lou wasn't the only one who, "regretted her darkness" (Thurman 636) and that "It was an acquired family characteristic, this moaning and grieving over the color of her skin" (Thurman 636). Thurman also comments on how dark-skinned African American women faced harsher discrimination than dark-skinned African American men: "She should have been a boy, then color of skin wouldn't have mattered so much, for wasn't her mother always saying that a black boy could get along, but that a black girl would never know anything but sorrow and disappointment" (636). Scott notes, "always on the lookout for hypocrisy, Thurman found it in the uneven way that color prejudice is applied to dark-skinned women" (327-328).

The discrimination she feels in her family is not alleviated when she leaves home. When she starts dating a man, Alva, he does not introduce her to his friends, nor does he take her to any social affairs. The narrator notes that he couldn't risk "taking her out among his friends, for he knew too well that he would be derided for his unseemly preference for 'dark meat'" (Thurman 638). Alva saves his friends and social occasions for "Geraldine with her olive colored skin and straight black hair" (639), and only dares to take Emma Lou to uncomfortable rent parties. Through Alva's attitude, Thurman shows a social pressure that men felt to date and marry lighter skinned women. So not only were dark-skinned women discriminated against, but the men who went out with them were as well. Just like Hurston's protagonist, Emma Lou makes drastic decisions in the face of discrimination (whether that discrimination be real or imagined), such as using all sorts of products in an attempt to lighten her skin. Her routine for getting ready is described as "applying various creams and cosmetics to her face in order to make her despised darkness less obvious" (639-640).

Similarly to the way Hurston uses stage directions to demonstrate colorism, Thurman conjures up images of whiteness and the "goodness" it symbolizes. Truman says, "Ivory Soap is advertised as being ninety-nine and some fraction percent pure, and Ivory Soap is white. Moreover, virtue and virginity are always represented as being clothed in white garments" (Thurman 643). Furthermore, when Emma Lou graduates from a school where she is the only black student, she sits in a sea of white-robed white students, bringing to mind Classon's discussion about the lack of dark-skinned performers: "the black chorus line was...distinguished by the fact that its members were almost *cafe-au-lair* cuties...In photographs of the old chorus lines, occasionally a brown face appears, but there is never a dark one" (12-13).

Though discussions of colorism within the black community were discouraged during the Harlem Renaissance, Wallace Thurman and Zora Neale Hurston were not afraid to acknowledge and reproach the phenomenon in their writing, thereby, validating the feelings of insecurity and unbelonging that many dark-skinned African American women surely experienced. Looking back on these texts, written many decades ago, allows readers to see the strides that have been made in society since their publication, but also illustrates the progress that can still be made as dark-skinned black women are still massively underrepresented in popular culture.

Works Cited

Classon, H. L. "Re-Evaluating 'Color Struck': Zora Neale Hurston and the Issue of Colorism." *Theatre Studies*, vol. 42, 1997, pp. 5-18. ProQuest Literature Online.

Hurston, Zora Neale. *Color Struck. The Portable Harlem Renaissance Reader*. New York, NY: Penguin Books, 2008, pp. 703-719.

Scott, Daniel M., III. "Harlem Shadows: Re-evaluating Wallace Thurman's *The Blacker the Berry*. MELUS (Univ. of Southern California, Los Angeles). Vol. 29, no. 3/4, 2004, pp. 323-339. Proquest Literature Online.

Thurman, Wallace. *The Blacker the Berry. The Portable Harlem Renaissance Reader*. New York, NY: Penguin Books, 2008, pp. 636-649.

Writers
Room

Introduction

Writers Room launched in 2014 and from the beginning offered a monthly writing workshop, open to all, held at the Dornsife Center for Neighborhood Partnerships. Since then, Writers Room has expanded to offer many workshops and events and has become a true hub for learning, storytelling, and conversation. Recent initiatives have involved local high school students, who are given opportunities to interact with Drexel students as well as neighborhood residents and to thus forge intergenerational friendships. The campus studio space (first floor MacAlister) opened in the fall of 2017.

These offerings for *The 33rd* represent storytelling in different genres: poetry (Hymms, Kimball), fiction (Roman), and nonfiction (Hajo, McCullough) and showcase the talents of community writers, current and former Drexel students, and faculty. Hajo's "Layers in Three Parts" (III) describes her experience at Writers Room and, we hope, conveys the open and collaborative spirit of this place.

Valerie Fox, Ph.D.
Faculty Writing Fellow

Natasha Hajo

Layers in Three Parts

I

Sometimes hiding but, more often than not, trying to make watching look discreet. Watching. Looking out, taking in. Taking of. Mental notes, that is. Mental notes of others and pictures of me. Watching myself. Selfie. In the passenger seat of Sam's car, swimming in an XXL jacket. Red scarf wrapped, paprika. Red eye-shadow smudged, brick. Smiling behind bouquet of flowers from Sam. Gift paired with mace spray, just in case. Happy Valentine's Day.

II

Things left under wraps—layers made of turtlenecks, wide-leg jeans, draped scarves. Preserving my parts in oversized clothing. Keeping secret behind fringe bangs, a shag maintained for "style" but mostly for easy creeping. My second skin is much looser, flowing around and swaying behind. It's far less fleshy but just as knotted in its threading. Heavy boots help to avoid floating too far. Gold adornments from an auntie in Syria remind me of home. There are changes with the seasons and with which parts look best. Last spring highlighted collarbones. The fall found my waist or the space before cherished love handles. It'll still be loose in the summer, my sweaty second skin, but salt helps preserve meat so I'll be cured in the sun.

III

The one place I feel most free to be me is gray. Its lighting is dim but adjustable. The space is filled with wooden desks and swiveling chairs. Metal shelves are lined with books in its library, which is tucked behind a velvet curtain in the back. Writers Room. Open to all. There's no shortage of things for me to do there: I listen, write, read, get work done for classes. Avoid work for classes. Sometimes I go in just to focus on breathing. I drink coffee with Lauren and joke with Jen. I learn a little bit more about Kirsten. Dejah tells me about her day while Keyssha shares her philosophies. I get schooled by and hug Rachel, because I'm past being "past that." If I'm lucky, I hear Norman's stories. I think Writers Room—the space, the work, the people—is what makes me feel whole. Not "whole" in the sense that it completes me, it doesn't always have to be so deep. What I mean is that it never reduces me to a part—it sees my layers and recognizes me as a body of moving pieces. Pieces I've learned to be proud of. Writers Room is where I feel most free because it's allowed me to be all of me.

Elizabeth Kimball

I Exited the Speedline

and looked around
at the 8th and Market station. This was my stop:

the El stop to where I had my first job out of college at 7th and Chestnut.
Now, 20 years later,

I couldn't remember what to do next. I'd come from the other direction, east,
(then I lived in West Philly),
across the Ben Franklin Bridge and out of the suburbs. 8th and Market is where,
if you're from New Jersey, you can transfer to the rest of Philly on SEPTA.

I couldn't remember what to do. Was this a stop with different sides to pick the
right one, or did you go down and then get on the right train. Was there a token
machine. What had I read about those cards. The SEPTA sales office, buy those
packs of tokens, little plastic bags.

I'd leave work with my work pal, a huge and witty black man named Darryl.
Another funny white guy, skinny, named John. We'd stop and buy our tokens.
This station, I think.

I took my boy and took the passageway. Low ceiling, those cold thick walls with
rivets, dampness and old pee air.

Go back the other way.

The inverse of memory, where you climb down in, don't find what you thought
you could dig up, and climb back out, facing westbound.

Briyanna Hymms

Mirror

Today
I donned a cape of strength
I didn't know what for
I just knew I had to be brave

Something was tickling the air around me
As if to say
Something's coming
Something's coming

Water rushed around my feet
Bare in the cold
Toes turning blue black
But I couldn't feel the freeze

Eyes open
Looking up
The sun was setting
All around me were eyes
Upturned and glowing
Glowering in their hollows
Waiting for something

Was it the same something
That was coming for me?
Or were they waiting to see everything unfold
Watchers in the trees

Nothing looked more alive
Than the eyes
I felt the need to hide
But I knew I had to face something

Looking down
The water was at my navel
And my feet were no longer visible
Or feeling—
Were they ever?

Across the water
Angry ripples made their way towards me
This is it
The thing I had to face

I pictured scales and thick hide
Fins sharp and jagged
Eyes depthless
Rows of thin puncturing teeth
Sinewed torpedo style for accuracy
Twenty-five feet in length at least
All 365 pounds rushing at me

But all that momentum
All that buildup
Just to stop before me
Splash me in the face
And say from beneath the surface:

Face me when you wake up

William Roman

Brindlebass

Four little rods, a pretty pink princess harpoon rod (with sparkles, of course), and one crummy plastic water bottle with dental floss wrapped around it are held in our hands.

It is 7AM, and we wait together, at the curbside, for the brindlebass.

Six little hooks gleam, offering prizes: four worms, a marshmallow, and one lousy piece of corn, because my Dad says that's what really attracts the big ones.

I stare at the woodlice scurrying in and out of the cracks between the pavement. The seconds waiting for the bass' arrival feel like hours.

Six little bobbers dangle against our rods. Guess whose is a plain old piece of Styrofoam threaded through floss?

It's running late. Someone wonders if maybe the 'bass has finally croaked it. Another argues we would have gotten a sign. The girl with the harpoon rod sniffles and tells them to stop fighting. I check my watch, pretending to ignore them.

A low bellow shakes the ground, six tiny heads turn upward, and the brindlebass descends from the clouds like a zeppelin.

Mouth open, eyes vacant, mottled brown scales, the heads of kids peeking out like gophers where teeth should be: there is no mistaking it.

Together we cast our rods, six bobbers lifting six lines up into the air. The brindlebass accepts our offerings. It inhales, six hooks now lodged into its lower lip. We reel ourselves inside.

Moist. Cold. Salty. Full of plaque, too. That is the inside of the brindlebass mouth. The moment we're in, we get to work, cleaning out the lobsters, tires, potato chip bags that have wedged themselves into the gums. By the time we finish, the bass has descended, and we spill out of the mouth, right in front of the school.

The bass has something in its eyes: gratitude? Indifference? Love? Apathy? I can't tell as it swims back into the clouds.

Sometimes I wonder if it actually notices when we clean its mouth, or if it just travels the same routes out of instinct.

But for now, I have to head to school.

Carol McCullough

Othello: The More I Know

William Shakespeare is truly worthy of all the hype he has gotten throughout the ages. It is striking how deeply themes explored in *Othello*, written in 1622, resonate today. I appreciated the pace of our reading and the many opportunities for examination and discussion. We had time to reflect without the rapid-fire, racing-through-one-play-to-get-on-to-the-next style I encountered as an undergrad eons ago. To tackle the complex Elizabethan language and come away with solid understanding takes time, often in short supply with an already loaded full-time schedule. During this class I was able to read closely and spend time reflecting and gathering my thoughts. Concentrating on one play enabled the class to dig deeply, to mine the gold and then set it out to sparkle and illuminate the times. Comments from seasoned citizens who have lived through the chaos within our community and in our country helped highlight the timelessness of themes Shakespeare explored, while the scholarly depth of the honors students enhanced our understanding.

I enjoyed the side-by-side format, as I see great value in having two ends of the generational spectrum meet each other at a midpoint, to talk about literature, to talk about life, and to learn from each other's perspectives.

I remember being in a 400 level class the summer before my senior year and having two older women in class with me. At the time it seemed odd, and they looked slightly out of place amidst a roomful of college kids. This was years and years ago, as my antiquated observation attests. They were probably working on a Master's degree, or completing graduate hours to maintain teaching certification. Perhaps after their children grew up and moved out and their husbands died or moved on they finally had the chance to take a breath and pursue the degree of their dreams. I don't know. I just remember thinking it seemed odd to see them there. But the Side-By Side format welcomes the sage voices of community "seniors" who can often add insight to local history however it might pertain to the subject matter. I can imagine, however, the few honors students who might protest about community members hijacking or monopolizing the discussion, vowing to never take that type of class again. I, myself, like the format for its benefit of intergenerational exchange of ideas. Plus, it brings together people, often from different walks of life, who might not ever have had the chance to move beyond the preconceived stereotypes and misbeliefs that were at the very heart of Othello's troubles and Shakespeare's examination.

Othello was a good selection. I give it two thumbs up. Its themes of racism, sexism, militarism, jealousy, insecurity, and injured merit are timeless. People are still prejudiced. They still make snap judgments about one another colored by implicit biases they often don't even know exist. Men (some men) are still trash; women (most women) are still expected to maintain virginity while men whore around them like flies to sweet sugar.

Nothing is new under the sun...

Was that the Bible? Or Shakespeare?

Faculty
Writing

Introduction

Faculty writing reflects current, published work by professors in the College of Arts and Sciences. These texts have previously appeared in academic and scholarly journals, books, conferences, magazines, and websites. Some are poignant, some are funny, all are thought-provoking, and they serve to demonstrate the many forms that writing can take. *The 33rd* is enriched by the interests and passions of these writers.

— The Editors

Tim Fitts

Grasshoppers

There is the image of grasshoppers and two sound tracks. One track is the high whine of bug noise, the racket of grasshoppers going mad in the wilderness. The other track is the sound of angels singing with heavy reverberation – Enya meets the Mormon Tabernacle Choir. My mother holds her screen in front of me, and I can feel her waiting for me to comment. This is the moment where we reconnect, I know she is thinking. She raised me and guided my sensibilities, and now I will see the wonder of these insects singing sweet songs to one another.

The answer is clear to me. Forget about analysis, forget telling her that the sound track is probably fake, *definitely* fake. Forget asking her why this is so amazing, even if it were real, and just pause for a moment and tell her it is amazing, thrilling really. Just play the game. Just do the thing that is desired and allow happiness to wash through the household. A small token of appreciation.

"Hmm," I say.

"Let me guess," she says. "You don't think it's fantastic, do you?"

"I never said that," I say.

"I know you don't."

"I might. I might think it's amazing. I might think it is out of this world."

"You'll find a way. You'll say it's fake, or nothing is credible these days. You'll say nothing is true, and that the Internet is only interested in selling you something or stealing your identity. You'll tell me truth is dead."

"Well," I say.

"This is true, though" she says. "The sound of the singing *is* the grasshoppers. The sound has been slowed down so much that it sounds like angels."

"Okay, then. So what?"

"It sounds like they're in love. Doesn't it?"

"Alright," I said.

"Well, I think it is sad, to tell you the truth. I think it is very sad. I think it says something that you cannot just sit back and watch, or listen to something, and be inspired, or awestruck, or say, 'that's *fantastic!*' I think it speaks volumes."

"What does that mean, when people say that, *speaks volumes?*"

"It means it says a lot. It means that there is more to what you say than what you say."

"Then why don't people just say that? Why don't they say the thing that they mean?"

"Because this way everybody knows the meaning."

It is a curse, I know. How difficult is it to just fly over the weather? How difficult is it to let the blood flow to your face for ten seconds and let your eyes brighten with wonder? Is it that difficult? All you have to do is say *"goddamn, goddamn* the world is a special place, play that thing over again. Play those goddamn grasshoppers one more time." How difficult is it to let the soundwaves sink into all of those calcified capillaries and break them down one by one?

The truth is, it *used* to happen all the time. My eyes did once widen, and my heartbeat often wound itself up with amazement, and I just had to know. I think for a minute about a Sunday school teacher who once told me that scientists had located the approximate position of Heaven. He told us that scientists had counted the days backwards to the moment that God forced the Earth to stand still while the Israelites laid waste to the Amorites. Our teacher told us the scientists just kept counting backwards until the days doubled up. I had to know how these things worked. So, I asked. I asked, and inquired, at church and at school, at soccer practice and Boy Scouts, visits to the dentist and doctor. I asked about every, single thing.

Tim Fitts

Zero

In the ninth grade, a friend and I walked to the bus stop one morning when a meteor cut the cobalt sky in half, one horizon to the next, the white line sustaining the entire streak, the underside of a cosmic razor, slicing the sky from one side to the other. Of course, none of the other students waiting believed us. "There would have been a flash," one said. "A sonic boom," said another. One kid said it was just a plane or the space shuttle.

Twelve years later, a similar phenomenon occurred to me while walking home from work one morning in Seoul, Korea. The sound of a jet roared low, only several thousand feet above the ground. When I looked up, it was not a jet at all, but a missile. My heart started, and I began to shout and notify the people around me.

In fact, I never found out what it was. Truth be told, I had just fallen in love. There is a tradition in Korea where, when a woman has reached her critical point of devotion, she spontaneously presents you with song. Sure, we were only in the beginning phase of this affair, but I was on the verge. I could feel it, and I was eager to get home.

Valerie Fox

Andy Warhol Sightings

It's Andy Warhol, wearing a black, woolen cape, in a hamburger joint in California and chatting up a college kid. He's being personable and seems to expect the student to pay his tab. Not that Andy Warhol isn't good for the cash, but he isn't sure how to go about settling the check. Should he wait for the waitress? Should he approach the counter? Hm. Up until this point no one has asked him for money. Is it because they want to give him his Coke and hamburger for free, like he has a special coupon?

Andy Warhol cocks his head. He sticks up for a local indigent vet, also in the hamburger joint, who has forgotten his money. He gets his new friend the college kid to pay for the vet's meal. Andy Warhol has a lot of compassion for those returning from the war, or even for those who were stationed up in Alaska. Up there it's so cold people can rarely go outdoors in the morning and enjoy cappuccino and talk with friends. He and the vet take a picture together. Andy Warhol's regular entourage is unable to film the encounter because they are at the Amish market taking part in cheese-making.

Andy Warhol takes his stuffed lion out for a walk. No one stops him to make dumb cracks about Pittsburgh, his hometown. He rests in the town park on a bench near a vintage statue of Theodore Roosevelt. He takes over the local newspaper, known as *The Daily Trout,* one hand tied behind his back, and goes fishing. Andy Warhol visits the elementary school and talks to the children about what life used to be like before we all had electricity.

Meanwhile, back in the city, when Andy Warhol is shot, there is this sudden absence. Somebody has to temporarily take Andy Warhol's place in the lively diorama lodged in the minds of art lovers all over the world, next to other lions.

The mercury-colored cloudlike balloons Andy Warhol favors wander mote-style across his closed eyes, hidden by dark sunglasses. These are the same sunglasses donned by Andy Warhol that time he was going down the Mississippi in an old riverboat. This is the tie Andy Warhol wore when he was having lunch with Andy Griffith, who was not wearing a tie. Andy is giving Andy some sound advice about a quandary in his love life. Just ask Elvis with his cowboy gun. Time, Andy, fleeting, etcetera, etcetera.

Theodoros Katerinakis

"Philotimo": Concept and Semantics of a Unique Greek Term in an Era of Crisis

0. Introduction

Language is so tightly embedded to human experience since when people meet they are most likely that they start exchanging words or symbols [1]. In Greece people consider themselves a "brotherless" nation that maintained their diachronic identity by cultivating network bonds on spatial, cultural, and communal dimensions. Greek language enriches such bonding with signifiers which are definitive of Greek identity; philotimo encapsulates the expressive power of several attributes of Greek identity, has evolved as a floating signifier used from various agents in diverse contexts, during the years of economic crisis. The words and signals we use capture the most "human and humanizing" activity that people execute "[when] talking to each other" [2]. All these elements of our interaction using language determine the mode with which we act toward people and things: the basis is the meaning we assign to people or things [3].

Furthermore, meanings are in people –not in words only- and meaning is negotiated through the use of language, while people interact. Thus, you hardly understand Greece without referring to social relations embedded in the local, regional or national collective selves that provides the medium for concrete ties of diaspora Greeks with their homeland. Greeks as individuals live in a collectivistic culture, belong to their extended families and are enculturated in their peer-group called *parea*[1]. *Parea* is constructed in layers, from personal life to school days and professional activities. Society is organized in a set of relationships that are endemic in Greek identity. Communication materializes any type of relationship in the Greek tradition. The modern *homo communicans* seems to prefer to be connected to and stay in contact with their surrounding world. Mutuality matches philotimo with social cohesion as a security mechanism in the current era of turbulence and is projected in ethical virtues explicit in the use of language and terminology.

This paper argues that the semantics of philotimo cover multiple layers of Greek culture and behavior and are reinforced during the crisis years, and are perceived as identifiers in the network structure of establishing and functioning in the base of cooperation. Every national culture possesses and reflects a core value that is at the centre of its collective self and shared mindset. The USA is devoted to 'freedom' (e.g., [4]) and Canada to the concept of "social justice" [5]. In Hellenic culture, this central value is *philotimo*, which is an untranslatable and unique cultural virtue of honor and pride idiosyncratic to Hellenes [6], [7], [8], [9], [10], [11], [12].

Culture consists of relatively specialized lifestyles, values, beliefs, artifacts, forms of behavior, and patterns of communication. Culture includes anything that a group has produced and developed—i.e., language, religion, laws, ways of thinking, art, communication patterns, rituals, styles, and attitudes [13]. Hofstede [14] provides an operational definition of culture: "*A collective programming of the mind which distinguishes one group from another... [a type of] mental programming... [with] patterns of thinking and feeling and potential acting*". Culture defines a moral frame with standards about how to belong to, and be an upstanding of a group.

When people interact and exchange verbal transactions they may disclose different aspects of their private, public, collective, and inner 'self'; cultural, societal, institutional, and deeper value factors interfere with, and organize their perception of their actions. If virtues are ethical messages, then culture is the propagation channel of these virtues. In the case of the social networks that people identify with, the constituent elements of individuals and their relationships promote reciprocity in ethical behaviour and facilitate the supplier-customer interaction. Such an interaction communicates

1. The Hellenic Mindset of *Philotimo*

Since antiquity, Hellenes have considered economics (governing the *oikos*) as part of their inquiry into ethics, politics, and social organization [16]. Traditionally Hellenic economic thought is placed within the Mediterranean tradition that perceives the economy as embedded in a web of social and political institutions that are regulated by religious and ethical norms [17], [18]. Therefore, the economy contributes to developing interpersonal relationships based on the mutual respect of oral commitments, pride, and honouring the virtue of *philotimo* that generates bonds of trust [19]. Emphasis on integrity (*akeraiotita*), the primary layer of current *philotimo*, has been a constant value for centuries [20]. Integrity originally reflected public pressure to behave uprightly, a norm of the responsible citizen (*politis*). In this sense, while profit making can be considered legitimate and part of the atomistic system, profiteering is punished [21]. It would be unthinkable that someone without integrity—in terms of honesty, justice, and truthfulness—is admired. Philotimo seems to have earned the status of a collective conscience in modern Hellas, where people no longer philosophize about it or try to impose it on others, but rather take it for granted and assume its widespread existence.

Philotimo is defined as an innate faculty that may motivate people to do more than what is expected, without expecting anything in return. Hence, philotimo is a life principle for Hellenes; it is interpreted as love for honor—honor 'to show' for others and honour 'to receive' from others—and is a characteristic that is intense in small communities on the Hellenic periphery. It is a case of an ideal occurrence where participants generally accept a norm based on the foundation of that normative society, as defined by Habermas [22]. This type of normative ethics transcends the deontology of duties and rules, as well as consequentialism. In this sense, philotimo closely corresponds to the virtues and moral character that define virtue ethics. Furthermore, in its various manifestations, the three central concepts of virtue ethics—virtue, practical wisdom, and eudaimonia—are comprehensible, objective, and empirically truthful [23]. Philotimo is a virtue that corresponds with credibility, with the tendency to cooperate, and with the ritual of keeping your word (face and commitments) without writing a contract;[2] it is a way of life with *ethos*, consistent with the teleological approach of Aristotle.

This attribute of personal integrity, maintaining face, and trust is essential for all banking practices and acquires institutional support through community networks that form cooperative banks with elements of collective rationality. It is a script of a collective programming of mind for Hellenes [25], a determinant of the foundation of cooperative and credit-related institutions in European Mediterranean culture and the Hellenic tradition. In monetary transactions and intimate relationships, trust is mutually cogenerated and goes beyond the *homo oeconomicus* of 'rationality', 'calculation', and 'efficiency' as impersonal economic imperatives.

2. Moral Aspects of *Philotimo* in Routine Language

The community of members in the Greek periphery live by the notion of philanthropia as the gist of philotimo in several respects. In social enterprises and community-based markets, corporate governance issues are manifested as compatible with the concepts of accountability, reliability, and transparency. This widespread reference to philanthropia reflects the primary issue of philotimo: the collective self is explicitly related to approaches of trust. Trust can be described as reflex [26], as a fixed expectation of culture, sometimes as being learned and situational. Trust is also considered as a resource of social capital, power, and social support. Salem [26] suggests that trust emerges from communicative interaction; trust and communication are interdependent and lead to 'a probability of structural coupling' between humans.

Therefore, individuals achieve a sense of 'betweenness' that has its roots in ethical ties of well-informed citizens. Throughout Hellenic society, the premise of moral equality interacts with strategies to gain advantage among widely separated class or professional interests [27]. As Campbell [28] describes it, there is a nuance in philotimo, a dependability of moral respect and social asymmetry. Moral respect is simultaneously a mask and a condition of mutual dependence (and exchange) of shepherds, merchants, and politicians. On the other hand, others like Lyberaki and Paraskevopoulos [29] are skeptical of the 'elusive boundaries between social trust and its [Hellenic] substitutive notion of philotimo', especially when small communities are examined. It is a type of critique that supports the fusion of trust with philotimo at a group level beyond the criteria of the individual; this argument could be interpreted as a notion of institutional philotimo.

In rural areas, honour and the lack of it takes dimensions that embrace the whole family, whereas in the cities it becomes more confounding and individualized. The only social class that does not consider honour of such primary importance is the urban middle class. This is consistent with Herzfeld's idea that names are semiotic markers for moral boundaries (in non-urban settings), since those boundaries are themselves highly flexible: what is considered evidence of socially acceptable morality (*philotimo*) in one individual may be treated as its very opposite in another. This morality contagion is a projection of an implicit culture to an explicit identity [30].

Tracing the roots of community-based moral contagion in contemporary Hellas, there are several junctures that created an amalgam of Hellas with its 'oriental' self in the post-antiquity period. The pre-Islamic Arabs were proud of their pastoral way of life that gave birth to *murū'a* [31], the Arab concept of *virtus*, which embodies courage in war, hospitality in peace, independence of spirit, and love of liberty. A similar connotation is found in Turkish for 'honour': *seref, izzet, haysiyet and onur*. The most common word denoting pride is *gurur* whereas *onur* is connected with *philotimo*, respectively [32]. In decentralized Hellenic society, such effects in moral values are reinforced in local communities, and the value of *philotimo* is relayed through the social networks that shape people's lives [33]:

- Hellenes prefer self-organization in commons where they recognize common attributes forming networks of affiliation.

- Love thy neighbour: The Hellenic state is organized in geographically dispersed local communities, starting from the 'neighbourhood'. Thus, a solid fabric of connected members is typical in the Hellenic periphery.

- Communal protection cultivates bonding in Hellas.

- Hellenes are social—so inevitably connected—animals following Aristotle's principles.

Again, it is important to distinguish an honour of position, which is an ascribed category related to possessions, and a discrete moral category that devolves from achieving reputation among social peers. In egalitarian contexts, male competitions subsumed by honour may be expressed in terms of 'seniority', or 'respect' and 'honor' [34]. In recent years, philotimo has become an ideal; it is the consciousness of superiority of mental achievements against material interests in life, a subconscious voice of authentic humanism with its own rationale. Personal dignity is the consciousness of ultimate sacredness of the corporeal human, but for the Hellenes it is the axiom that directs life [35]. Philotimo is one of the ideals that traditional nuclear Hellenic families aim to implant in the generations that follow, and it is frequently invoked when asking someone to 'come to one's senses' or to correct an undesirable attitude. Similarly, the urge—conscious or not— to prove worthy of the nationally praised characterization of philotimos (as an adjective) might function as a self-fulfilling prophecy. It involves a collective sense of belonging [36], and the positive experience of this identity was the efficiency by, and dithyrambic recognition of Hellenic volunteers during the Athens Olympic Games of 2004. [3]

In economic terms and banking, philotimo filters relationship-based transactions to implement the 'know your customer' (KYC)[4] policy which involves constant communication with depositors and borrowers to increase awareness. This process is not routinely implemented by mainstream banks but by cooperative banks in a solidarity economy during the crisis. The lack of a credit record, fully documented revenues, and sufficient collateral is compensated by operational sources of repayment that connects the individual borrower-member of the bank with their collective relations and individual ethical traits of philotimo.

3. Philotimo as the Ethical Core Observed in Banking Transactions

One of the primary consequences of living in crisis years in Greece is the changes observed in transactional behavior. The island of Crete is a popular destination for tourism, employment mobility, military personnel, student population with diversified economy. Its island dynamics offer a nice example for the use of language and nissology culture. It could be the best of times for cooperative banking, as the current crisis provided arguments against the dominant theory of perfect information and the capacities of self-regulating markets. The crisis has also provoked widespread rethinking about the potential contributions of credit in local development and the behavior of the local towards their transactions. Finally, it has highlighted the pressing need for local societies to work towards exerting control on the global and its self-organized governance.

Along these lines, philotimo is a value of personal honor and pride that massages empathy for the "other", as expressed through acts of generosity and sacrifice. Greeks since antiquity put emphasis on integrity (*akeraiotita*), the primary layer of the modern philotimo. Integrity originally reflected the public pressure to behave uprightly, a norm of the citizen. It would be unthinkable that someone without integrity - in terms of honesty, justice, truthfulness- is admired. Emphasis on goodness is encapsulated in the ancient inscription *"kalos k' agathos"*[5] on numerous Greek artifacts; it means, literally, "good and purely good" in person and good as a social being. One is esoteric for personal improvement, the other extrovert to the quality of social relations. Integrity as a purpose and criterion of good life survived in modern times in Greece as the proverbial philotimo, with a teleological perspective but a deontological rootage.

Philotimo seems to gain the status of a collective conscience in modern Greece, where people no longer philosophize about it, or try to impose it on the masses, but take it for granted and assume its widespread existence[6]. That is the case of Crete, as an insular community constructed by scattered individual households with prowess to defend themselves against enemies. It is a society with a radical shame culture with a *"what we are and what we stand for"* lifeworld practice that also is represented in its ethical approach to banking[7]. The primary sanction that matters is *"what people in the community will say"*.

At a community level when living in affinitive local societies, transactions in local banks during the crisis transform their cultural values to ethical – originally meaning *daily-expected* – traits when they decide to start doing business after assuming the membership experience[8]. This is an Aristotelian ideal that *"we are what we repeatedly do"*; ethos is a way of life diffused through the cooperative network fabric. The core value of Greek *"philotimo"* safeguards integrity and performance in Cretan society, as an enthymeme of a social added-value. Greekness as identity[9], manifested in Crete with philotimo, enriches transactional ethos with a social dimension that makes local banking ethical and a benefit dimension that makes it sustainable.

Local cooperative banks, in such a context, adopted the definition of the International Cooperative Alliance (ICA) : *"[a cooperative is] an autonomous association of persons united voluntarily to meet their common economic, social and cultural needs and aspirations through a jointly owned and democratically controlled enterprise."* Socially organized business finds an exemplary application in cooperative banking and institutionalizes philotimo in daily life terms. The cooperative doctrine with seven internationally recognized principles that ICA[10] labels as *cooperative identity:* (i) voluntary and open membership, (ii) democratic control by members, (iii) member economic participation, (iv) education, training and information,

(v) cooperation among cooperatives, and concern for the community. These principles materialize the use of philotimo at an operational level.

It is a typical example of an amalgam of social and value capital supported by a banking network with connected members in the local community. Market share is not a goal but an inevitable evolution of togetherness between locals in Crete. Most importantly, by encouraging people's input into the ongoing development of cooperative banks' ethical policy, *Homo Communicans* forwards *Homo Economicus* to *Homo Dictyous (a connected member)*.

4. Globalized Use of Philotimo Terminology

The conceptualization of philotimo has become a story-telling narrative in major announcements, speeches, and occasions with international appeal when speaking about Greece. In this part, several examples of these uses articulate the advancement of term an entity synonymous to identity perception, formation, and sustainability.

In the event of 2010 White House ceremony for the Greek Independence day US President Barak Obama chose to analyze philotimo as a virtue, cultural identifier and roadmap in collective life. That reception's significance extends beyond the remembrance of Greek Independence Day, as Obama remarks on the enduring bond of USA and Greece forged by the shared history, common values, and the united obligation to build a better future [*emphasis added to highlight key points*][11]:

> *"There's a concept that captures it, and it doesn't translate easily; it* **doesn't really have an equivalent in English.** *But it's a virtue that all of you know well, because it's the* **very essence of being Greek** *-- and you will forgive if my pronunciation is just so-so -- philotimo. Right? Philotimo. Literally, it translates as "love of honor."* **I love that concept -- love of honor.** *But, of course, it means much more than that. It's a sense of love, to family, and to community, and to country --* **the notion that what we're here on this Earth to do is to be all in this together.** *We all have obligations to each other and to work together. And so it was that the democratic example of a small group of city states more than 2,000 years ago could inspire the founding generation of this country, that led one early American to imagine that* **"the days of Greece may be revived in the woods of America."**

Philotimo's semantics in the Presidential address show the essential attribute of being recognized as Greek, its connection with family structure, community building, togetherness, and the sense of respect.

One of the most prominent younger members of Greek- American business community, George Logothetis[12], Chairman and CEO of Libra Group, outlined how the financial crisis in Greece is currently dominating the agenda and overlooks the problems people face in their everyday lives."*We keep hearing about the financial crisis but not the social one. We do not hear about the massive jump in suicides, the rise in homelessness, the practical unwinding of the social fabric of society,*" he explained. In several og his talks and presentations, He identified how philotimo as a value is part of the Greek character and one he has seen over the years in every corner of his family's business:

> "*To me, the undercurrent of Hellenism, the commonest and starkest theme that unites us all as Greeks, is philotimo... duty, loyalty, integrity, honor, love, trust, faith and, perhaps most important of all, the pride in being decent. The fabric of what we have built as a family and a group has been underwritten by philotimo.*"

Logothetis adds the dimension of corporate values and the expansion of philotimo in the professional world, as a determinant of a Greek professional with the creativity and care for entrepreneurial good beyond the individual.

The Washington "Oxi Day Foundation" [13] is a nonprofit initiative founded in the US to promote the Greek resistance during WWII. On 2014 a whole campaign started with a video titled "The Greek Secret"; the video suggests that the secret to extraordinary Hellenic excellence – personally and as a people – may spring from the uniquely Greek word philotimo. Arianna Huffington, George Stephanopoulos, Bob Costas and Greek Orthodox Archbishop of America Demetrios, and key business figures are among the nationally-known Greek-Americans who appear in this video. This video features interviews with 29 leading Hellenes who each share their definition of philotimo, as they understand it in the Greek language. Those interviewed defined philotimo as:

> "*not only the "love of honor but also as finding pleasure in sacrificing for the good of others; doing the right thing; improving themselves and their families; and seeking to achieve respect and love from others... Philotimo may in great part explain the Greeks' spectacular achievements throughout history, as well as their close family and community relationships*".

The Foundation underlines that the video highlights such Hellenic achievements as: the miraculous leap forward that the ancient Greeks brought to humankind's standard of living and freedom; Greece being identified by America, Great Britain and Russia as the only other country essential to the defeat of Hitler; the Greeks' unsurpassed response to the Holocaust; and Hellenes alone in America's 20th century rising from universal, uneducated poverty to ranking among the top in education and income.

In this case, philotimo acquires a transformational function for the community and may help the Greek brand may be coming true[14].

On 2014 the "Stavros Niarchos Foundation" established the Annual Philotimo Award to recognize extraordinary acts of "philotimo" performed by everyday Greek citizens who, despite the economic crisis, have rallied around others working to maintain social cohesion. In the case of Stavros Niarchos Foundation philotimo reflects back to society, as a collective voluntary duty for a common good. In the Foundation's documentation:

> "the Greek word "philotimo" literally means 'friend of honor', however its definition encompasses multiple virtues such as decency, dignity, personal sacrifice, honesty, truthfulness, honor, courage, sense of duty, pride, love of family, country and humanity".

Philotimo in this case has been recognized as a desired attribute, a goal empowered by explicit motivation promoted by this award on an annual basis. Acts of philotimo, activities and campaigns, voluntary contributions to a collective "self", common efforts and incentives are, among others, aspects of the semantic load of the original term. The emergence of a prize in the nominal value of "philotimo" term forwards the use of the term in the additional dimension of an ideal situation.

The last but not least in importance example is the so-called Philotimo foundation[15]. It is an undertaking following the realization of the systematic epistemological gap in current international bibliography around the "complex and central to the Greek cultural identity, concept of philotimo", as noted in the Foundation's declaration. The Foundation's claim is that philotimo has its position in international in international dictionaries right under the word "philosophy". The first crucial step of this project involved the "opinion crowdsourcing", namely the international open invitation to provide contemporary definitions and stories on philotimo towards its universal understanding by Greeks and non-Greeks alike which was launched on 21 December 2014. The Foundation describes the theoretical socio-anthropological significance of investigating the term as follows (emphasis added on aspects of philotimo):

*"The specific case of esteem and importance attribute partakers of Greek language and culture where land is particularly valuable object of study since the **oxymoron** and identify complex traits such as gentleness, or condescension, selflessness even naivety on the one, and stubbornness, pride, or irritability or even eterodosolipsia other. Worthy of study and the evolutionary trend and plasticity concept pride seemed to show, when investing the period 1960-1970, where populations are rural areas of the country entered in the urban centers of the time by adopting, inter alia, **more personalized and mature existential beliefs esteem, personal freedom and dignity** in just a few months. Worth mentioning is the specificity of the term to negotiate **uniquely pairing personal virtues** such as honor integrity even pride – with more **social values** such as friendship, honesty in trade, and humanity. Besides their academic value, the above estimates of esteem exhibit specific innate behavior tendencies, thinking and feeling that are distinguished for their unique ability to enable and empower the person as to the **optimal individual functionality and development.**"*

The Philotimo's Foundation initiative is based on a key policy shift of the humanities do employ systematic research and specific interventions in order to understand and serve people as integrated entities specified by pursuing their welfare, excellence and prosperity.

In a recent book coming from the German world Andreas Deffner, a German Health Ministry executive, reviews current Greek reality with the "adventure, routine, and crisis" of philotimo. He goes one step further to provide a recipe metaphor for the multiple meanings and connotations of philotimo: *"two or three positive thoughts, a litre of joy of life, 500 grams of hospitality, a whole ripe friendship, ten drops of helpfulness, a little pride, dignity and sense of duty."* [37]

5. Discussion and Communication for "Philotimo" and Greeks

The traditional language relativity (known as Sapir-Whorf) hypothesis claims that language we speak influences the thoughts we have; people speaking widely different languages will see the world differently and will think differently "dividing areas of experience in a variety of ways" [38]. Philotimo terminology and documentation seems to be compatible with the relative differentiation of the Greek spirit. It is a case of language liaison with persuasion (for the uniqueness of philotimo traits in Greek language and culture) and is measured with the following criteria [39]:

• Intentionality: language focus is cautious and purposeful distinguished from social influence; it serves certain goals.

- Effect: persuasion does not take place if no one is persuaded (the process continues).

- Free will and conscious awareness: language cultivates good practices and not coercive acts

- Symbolic action: persuasion begins and ends with symbolic expression; i.e. language and meaningful acts.

- Interpersonal and intrapersonal: the dyad is indispensible; language imposes self-persuasion, rationalization and discipline, as the usual first step of perception.

- Language as a system of words, sounds, drawings and gestures in a standardized form incorporating four dimensions [40]:

- Pragmatics: social context, assumptions, expectations and beliefs for all interlocutors.

- Semantics: the meaning and knowledge of the signs. How do recipients connect signs with the interpretation of these signs?

- Syntactics: the logic and grammar used for the construction and transmission of signs.

- Empirics: the codes and the physical characteristics of signs and the various media of communication (e.g. pronunciation, legible gestures, proper wording).

In Greek language philotimo has pragmatic, semantic and empirical dimensions depending on the syntax used. The dominant role of philotimo in encapsulating the perception of the Greek spirit connects terminology with story-telling with some basic framing inquiries: (i) what does philotimo mean to you? (ii) what are some extraordinary examples of philotimo that you have seen? (iii) what are the things you can do in your daily life to exhibit philotimo? (iv) how can philotimo improve your life?

Lastly, taking into account the argument of nation branding theory [41] that he only "remaining superpower is the international public opinion" philotimo may become a viable "export product" . Comparing the ingredients of philotimo with prevailing international concepts such as kindness, fairness, honesty, gratitude, courage and other, offers a field that could be exploited by helping to rebuild the international image of Greece.

The last word comes from Nicholas J. and Anna K. Bouras Foundation Trustee, the Honorable Judge B. Theodore Bozonelis, who received the scholarship for Aristaia and Daria Pappas of La Habra, California. The 7th and 12th grade sisters spent most of their lives in a Russian orphanage. In their thanking note the text reads [emphasis on philotimo added][16]:

> "We are not Greek by blood...**but we are Greek by philotimo**...our parents came into our lives when we were lost and alone. They bestowed upon us all the things that meant the most to them: **their culture; their traditions; their morals and their values, their philotimo.** Now we know the meaning of the word philotimo and we can feel it too!"

Philotimo is now elevated as equivalent to the value system of the Greek national character, as a word that you can feel and a semiotic identifier of Greekness [42]. Further work, especially in the branches of psychology and sociology, would reposition the focus of study to create positive development experiences and relationships, starting from the individual and going up to the collective and including the institutional state.

Bibliography

[1]. Pinker, S. (1995/2000), "The Language Instict- The new Science of Language and Mind" (To Glossiko Enstikto) Greek Translation for Katoptro Publications.

[2]. Griffin E. A. (2006),. A First Look at Communication Theory, Sixth Edition, McGraw-Hill, USA (.Griffin for Mead, 2006, p. 56)

[3]. Griffin E. A. (2006),. A First Look at Communication Theory, Sixth Edition, McGraw-Hill, USA (.Griffin for Blumer, 2006, p. 56)

[4]. Kengor, P. (2004). *God and Ronald Reagan: a spiritual life*, New York: HarperCollins.

[5]. Kernaghan K. (1995). *Public administration in Canada: a text*, 3rd edn, Toronto: Nelson Canada.

[6]. Kourvetaris, G. A.(1971). Professional Self-Images and Political Perspectives in the Greek Military, American Sociological Review, Vol. 36, No. 6 , pp. 1043-1057.

[7]. Vassiliou, G, & Vassiliou, V. (1966). Social values as psychodynamic vanables. Preliminary explorations of the semantics of philotimo, Acta Neurologica el Psychologica Hellemka, 5, pp. 121-135.

[8]. Mavreas, V., Bebbington P., and Der, G. (1989). 'The structure and validity of acculturation: analysis of an acculturation scale', Social Psychiatry and Psychiatric

Epidemiology, 24(5): 233–40.

[9]. Triandis Harry C. (2000). Culture and Conflict, International Journal of Psychology, Vol. 35, No 2, pp. 145-152.

[10]. Hoban, S. and Hoban, G. (2004) 'Self-esteem, self-efficacy and self-directed learning: attempting to undo the confusion', *International Journal of Self-Directed Learning*, 1(2): 7-25.

[11]. Koutsantoni, D. (2004). Relations of power and solidarity in scientific communities: A cross-cultural comparison of politeness strategies in the writing of native English speaking and Greek engineers, Multilingua 23 (2004), pp.111-143

[12]. Obama, B. (2010) 'Remarks by the President Honoring Greek Independence Day', White House Archives, 9 March 2010. Online. Available HTTP: <http://www.whitehouse.gov/photos-and-video/video/honoring-greek-independence-day#transcript> (accessed 20 August 2011).

[13]. Devito, J. (2006),"Human Communication The Basic course" (10thed), Pearson, USA.

[14]. Hofstede, G. (1997) 'Riding the waves: a rejoinder', *International Journal of Intercultural Relations*, 21(2): 287–90.

[15]. Shannon, C.E. (1948) 'A mathematical theory of communication,' *Bell System Technical Journal*, vol. 27: 379–423 and 623–56.

[16]. Petrochilos, G.A. (1999) 'The Hellenic contribution to economic thought', *Global Business and Economics Review*, 1(2): 215 –46.

[17]. Baeck, L. (1994). The Mediterranean Tradition in Economic Thought, London: Routledge

[18]. Constantelos, D.J. (2005). Christian Faith and Cultural Heritage: essays from a Greek Orthodox perspective, Boston: Somerset Hall Press.

[19]. Ioannou, C.A. (2009). *Managing Employment Relations in Greece: a guide for foreign managers*, Athens: Kerkyra Publications.

[20]. Psaropoulos, J.(2009) 'From Homer to co-ops, Business File Quarterly Review no.74:49-50.

[21]. Doukas, P. (2007) *Oikonomikes Theories, Arches Dioikisis & Arhaia Elliniki Skepsi* [Economic theories, governance values, and ancient Greek thought], Athens: Livanis Publications.

[22]. Habermas, J. (1996) 'Discourse Ethics, from Moral Consciousness and Communicative Action' in W. Outhwaite (ed.) *The Habermas Reader*, Cambridge: Polity Press, pp. 180–192.

[23]. Held, D. (1980) *Introduction to Critical Theory: Horkheimer to Habermas*, Berkeley: University of California Press.

[24]. Clogg, R. (2002). A Concise History of Greece, 2nd edn, (Clogg 2002, 4-5). Cambridge: Cambridge University Press.

[25]. Hofstede, G. and Hofstede, G.J. (2005). *Culture and Organizations: software of the mind*, 2nd edn, New York: McGraw-Hill.

26]. Salem, P. (2009). *The Complexity of Human Communication*. New York: Hampton Press.

[27]. Herzfeld, M. (1991). *A Place in History: social and monumental time in a Cretan town*, Princeton, NJ: Princeton University Press.

[28]. Campbell, J.K. (1964.) *Honour, Family and Patronage. a study of institutions and moral values in a Hellenic Mountain community*, Oxford: Oxford University Press.

[29]. Lyberaki, A. and Paraskevopoulos, C. J. (2002). 'Social Capital Measurement in Greece', paper prepared for the OECD-ONS International Conference on Social Capital Measurement, London, 25–27 September. Online. Available HTTP: <http://www.oecd.org/dataoecd/22/15/2381649.pdf> (accessed 29 September 2011).

[30]. Hofstede, G.J. (2009). 'Research on cultures: how to use it in training?', *European Journal of Cross-Cultural Competence and Management*, 1(1): 14–21.

[31]. Shahîd, I. (2009). *Byzantium and the Arabs in the Sixth Century: economic, social, and cultural history*, Vol. 2, Part 2, Cambridge, MA: Harvard University Press.

[32]. Van Eck, C. (2003). *Purified by Blood: honour killings amongst Turks in the Netherlands*, Amsterdam: Amsterdam University Press.

[33]. Christakis, N.A. and Fowler, J.H. (2009). *Connected: the surprising power of our socialnetworks and how they shape our lives*, New York: Little, Brown.

[34]. Gilmore, D.D. (1982). 'Anthropology of the Mediterranean area', *Annual Review of Anthropology, vol. 11:175-205.*

[35]. Vakalopoulos, A. E. and Vakalopoulos, K.A (eds) (2003). 'O Haraktiras ton Ellinon: Anihneyontas tin Ethniki mas Taytotita. Ereyna, Porismata, Didagmata [The Character of Greeks: tracing our national identity—investigation, lessons, and

findings]', Thessaloniki, Greece: Ant. Stamoulis Publications.

[36]. Social Issues Research Centre (2007) 'Belonging', Oxford: SIRC. Online. Available HTTP:< http://www.sirc.org/publik/Belonging.pdf#search="belonging" > (accessed 18 August 2011).

[37]. Deffner A. (2012). Filotimo - Abenteuer, Alltag und Krise in Griechenland. Grössenwahn Verlag, Frankfurt, Germany.

[38]. Whorf, B. L. (1956)."Language, Thought and Reality" (ed.J. B.Carroll). Cambridge, MA:MIT Press, USA

[39]. Gass R.H., Seiter J. S. (2007) "Persuasion Social Influence and Compliance Gaining", Third Edition, Pearson Education, USA

[40]. Avgerou C., Cornford T. (1993): "Developing Information Systems", MacMillan Press, London, UK

[41]. Anholt, S. (2009). Places: Identity, Image and Reputation, Palgrave Macmillan

[42]. Adamopoulos, J., (1977).The dimensions of the Greek concept of philotimo. The Journal of Social Psychology, Vol 102(2), 313-314.

---

[1] Gregory Nagy (http://chs.harvard.edu/CHS/article/display/1234), Director at Harvard University's Center for Hellenic Studies, supports the spirit of "parea" as a unique Greek phenomenon. Moreover, he connects the Greek Spirit of parea with camaraderie described in the TV Series "Friends" (see the Greek Embassy's newsletter at http://us5.campaign-archive1.com/?u=6cb2d297ff616984b41ff4ba e&id=672e064336, Jan 2014). The connection between friendship and the Greek collective self is analyzed from Gregory Jusdanis in his book "A Tremendous Thing: Friendship from the "Iliad" to the Internet, Cornell University Press (2015)."

[2] It is also a direct response to *rouspheti*—the reciprocal dispensation of favours [24]—as practiced and enforced during the post-Byzantine Turkish rule of Hellas; it remains as a major obstacle to modernization.

[3] Jacques Rogge, President of International Olympic Committee, was quoted as saying: 'These Games were unforgettable, dream Games,' in his speech at the Closing Ceremony. He also thanked the 'marvellous volunteers who have charmed us with their confidence and kindness' (Associated Press 2004).HTTP: <http:// sports.espn.go.com/oly/summer04/gen/news/story?id=1870458>).

[4] Basel Committee on Banking Supervision (2004) 'Consolidated KYC risk management', Basel: Bank of International Settlements. Online HTTP: <http://www.bis.org/publ/bcbs110.pdf> (accessed 15 June 2012).

[5] A full explanation is offered in Petrochilos, G. A. (2002), *Kalokagathia: The Ethical Basis of Hellenic Political Economy and Its Influence from Plato to Ruskin and Sen,* History of Political Economy, Vol 34, No 3, Duke University Press.

[6] Several researchers document why, traditionally, in Greece philotimo is "taken for granted": see [6], [7], [9], [10], [11]. Also: Kostoulas G. (2008), *Philotimo and the Greek Manager* at http://www.capital.gr/news.asp?Details=502016 (accessed on 9/ 2009). Mavreas V., Bebbington P., Der Geoff (1989), *The Structure and Validity of Acculturation Analysis of an Acculturation Scale,* Social Psychiatry and Psychiatric Epidemiology, No 24, pp. 233-240.

[7] Brian Harvey (1995), *Ethical Banking: The case of the Co-operative Bank,* Journal of Business Ethics, p. 1005-1013.

[8] Geert Hofstede provides a well- documented analysis of cultural aspects in business in several publications and in his site at http://www.geert-hofstede.com/ (accessed on October 2013).

[9] Managerial and behavioral aspects of philotimo are explained in: Bourantas D. and Papadakis V. (1996), *Greek Management,* International Studies of Management and Organization, Vol. 26, Issue 3, pp: 13-32. Skiftou V. (2005), *Within Social and Cultural Practices of Greek Society Subjects Negotiate a Series of Issues that are Related to Family and the Complexities of It,* LSE Doctoral Conference. Vassiliou V. G. & Vassiliou G. (1973), *The Implicative Meaning of the Greek Concept of Philotimo,* Journal of Cross-Cultural Psychology, 4(3).

[10] ICA definitions and principles are described in http://www.ica.coop/coop/principles.html (2013).

[11] It is noteworthy that Presidential staff has used data from the author's paper cited as "Katerinakis T., From Kalokagathia to Philotimo: Connected Ethics in Modern Greek Cooperatives (at It is notworthy that http://www.afglc.org/katerinakis_ppt_AFGLC_2010.pdf). 15th Annual AFGLC-ICHS Forum/Conference 2010, *"Hellenic Values in a Global Civilization: Engaging the Colleges, Universities and Citizens"* USF, Tampa, February 18-20, 2010.And that paper received 50,000 downloads according to AFGLC's web administrator (at the time) Dr. Ulysses Ballis.

[12] Logothetis G. (2012). "What We Have Built Has Been Underwritten by Philotimo". Libra Group presentation for Greece, 2012 National Innovation Conference in NYC. Available at http://www.greekamerica.org/nic/nic-talks/talks-2012/ (or

http://www.youtube.com/watch?v=pBEXkmNGgDE) - See more at: http://usa.
greekreporter.com/2012/05/28/george-logothetis-what-we-have-built-has-been-
underwritten-by-philotimo/#sthash.td5IJBo4.dpuf. Logothetis data in Libra
Group is available at http://www.libra.com/en/people/executive-team/george-m-
logothetis.

[13] The Washington Oxi Day Foundation (at http://www.oxidayfoundation.org/
mission/#sthash.LKEE2fvU.dpuf) is a nonprofit, 501c3 organization dedicated to
informing American policymakers and the public about the profound role Greece
played in bringing about the outcome of World War II and celebrating modern day
heroes who exhibit the same courage as the Greeks did in continuing to fight to
preserve and promote freedom and democracy around the world - The so-called "
philotimo" video is available at http://www.oxidayfoundation.org/philotimo-the-
greek-secret-video/.

[14] See more at http://www.oxidayfoundation.org/philotimo-the-greek-secret-
video/#sthash.xrTBMeXc.dpuf from Oxi Day Foundation Founder and President,
Andrew Manatos.

[15] The story behind the philotimo initiative begins in London in 2011. Since that very
first research idea of exploring or rediscovering the "lost philotimo", as it's often
referred to by Greeks, begins an eventful path favored by illumined encounters and
improbable coincidences that lead to the incorporation of the non-profit center for
social innovation in September 2014. Details at: http://philotimo.org/?lang=en

[16] Former Presidents of the United States and Israel Bill Clinton and Shimon
Peres joined the growing number of world leaders and other opinion leaders in
recognizing the Oxi Day story — the David vs. Goliath courage of the Greek people
in WWII. - See more at: http://usa.greekreporter.com/2014/10/29/former-u-s-and-
israel-presidents-help-resurrect-greek-oxi-day/.

Miriam Kotzin

Lists

From the sun-bearing sea,
restless, issues its complaint.

Nothing specific, you understand,
but a general kvetch about

this and that: the burden of sun,
moon, all those boats, and,

of course, the fish, intrusive,
making themselves quite at home.

Ridiculous, you say, with a flourish
of your hand. Well then, no wonder

I smile and say, "Fine, fine. Never
better," when you ask how I'm doing.

I dare say nothing that matters: all
night the windows like tambourines,

the long white envelope I will not open,
the willow branches dripping with rain.

Miriam Kotzin

The Red Tiger

1. The Red Tiger

Davis lay awake listening. He listened to the jungle night birds, and thought about how different they were from the rhythmic thuk-thuk-thuk-thuk-thuk of the copters the men called birds, too. He wondered if all the calls were really birds, or signals. They did that, he'd heard.

The men were sleeping, and in the two hours since they'd sacked out their breathing had synchronized. Only Harris' snoring was off, and now and then he'd talk in his sleep. Clark was on guard duty. Davis did not have to be awake.

When he got home, he thought, it would be a long time before he'd want to walk in the rain or go camping again.

He opened his eyes and stared up towards the leaves. Without the moon he could see neither sky nor leaves. Canopy, he thought, remembering the layers of bright green that he could not see in the dark. He would have liked the luxury of looking at the patterns of leaves, or listening to the sounds without thinking about what they might be, without listening for a twig cracking or a burst of fire.

He did not want to desire anything. To have desire, he recalled, it was necessary to experience a sense of deprivation. He could not afford the luxury of desire.

Davis could empty himself of all earthly desires. For weeks Harris had been talking about it, saying he was "empty of all earthly desires." The men had laughed at him because Harris talked in his sleep. He had not rid himself of desires, they told him, quoting his sleep-talking at length. Harris had turned red, then shrugged. Davis told the men to knock it off.

Canopy, he whispered, thinking of a red-and-white-striped awning in his in-laws' back yard, of white flowers in vases and tall tropical trees imported for the day in pots that men carted away at the end of the party.

His little sister Carrie had read him a poem about a red tiger. It had nothing to do with the wedding, but she had read it to him anyway. It was a poem she said she'd written for school.

He'd said there were no red tigers, and if there were, what color would their stripes be?

"Red tigers don't have stripes," she'd answered "Then how do you know they're tigers?" he asked.

"You just know," she'd said as though it were something important, something he should remember. "They're very dangerous, and they pounce just as you're falling asleep."

"How do you know?" he'd asked again. He was annoyed with himself for being so aggressive, but he kept pushing her anyway.

"You know. You look into their eyes just before you die," she kicked a clump of grass. "Everyone they pounce on dies."

"Then how do you know they exist if no one is left to describe them?"

"You just know," she said again. She kicked at the lawn again. "You ask too many questions. Didn't you ever hear about poetic license?"

"So red tigers are poetic license?" He was beginning to feel like a bully, but he kept on, "They're not real after all?"

Julie walked over, carrying two mugs of coffee. She was still wearing shorts and a tee shirt. The ceremony wouldn't be for hours. She handed him a mug of coffee.

"I thought it was bad luck to see you before the wedding?" he said.

"Silly," Julie put her arm around his waist. "I want to see you all I can."

"Julie," Carrie said, "Make him believe me. He doesn't believe me about the red tigers."

Julie smiled. "I don't like the red tigers, Carrie. They scare me."

"You should be scared. They're very dangerous." Carrie turned towards the house. "I'm going to get more breakfast, she said, over her shoulder. "Their eyes glow in the dark. You can see their eyes coming towards you even when it's too dark to see anything else. When they pounce, their eyes are the last thing you see."

Davis lay still, awake, listening to the birds in the trees he could not see. It was too dark to see anything really. He lay awake watching.

2. Sister

At the end of the wooden dock, Jewel sat in last year's faded blue bathing suit, a blue plaid shirt beside her. She dangled her legs, scissoring the air above the lake. From time to time she'd lean forward to look for the little fish that swam among the pilings and bit if you held still but didn't if you kept moving.

From way out on the lake Jewel heard the wail of a loon and just caught sight of its checkered back before it dived. She wondered why it was hiding, how long it would stay under. It was the sort of thing Lane knew and would tell her if he were still here.

Jewel spread Lane's soft shirt across her lap. He'd let her have it, as a loan, he'd said, before he left for boot camp.

The edge of the dock cut into her legs, and when she stood up there'd be a red line across the back of her thighs that itched and burned at the same time.

She'd wait and watch for the loon to come back, to see its black head break the surface of the lake. She knew if she waited long enough and looked hard enough she'd find the loon. She was sure of it. The loon would resurface somewhere. It would, she was sure.

3. Jewel

My little sister Carrie thinks she's so special. Everyone in the family tells her that she's going to grow up and be a famous writer. She writes poems about things she imagines, like red tigers, and she makes you listen to them.

My name is Jewel, and I am not a writer. But I like to look at things and think about them. And I write down what I see and think.

My brother went to war right after he got married to Julie. Our names are almost alike, Jewel and Julie. Isn't that funny? Julie's nice, and sometimes when we're together she gives me a big hug for no reason at all, and then I know she's thinking about my brother and missing him.

The War is on television every night. The reporters are over in Vietnam taking picture of lots of what's going on. My dad said that in World War II there were newsreels that showed at the movies along with the features. One theater in Philadelphia, which is the biggest city near here, showed nothing but these newsreels. They weren't even in color. That's a part of history, too.

We try not to be having dinner at the same time we watch the news. My little sister has to leave the room because she's not supposed to be watching the news. She did one night, and she asked Dad about the body count.

Our brother Lane sends us letters, all of them addressed exactly alike: The Davis Family, and then our names. One of them asked me if I was taking good care of his shirt. I have to give it back when he comes home. Carrie got one, too.

Most nights I sleep with the shirt. When I was even younger than Carrie, I had blanket that I liked. This shirt isn't anything like that.

Once I came into my room and Julie was sitting on my bed. She was smelling the shirt. I looked at her and said, "Mom washed it by mistake. She didn't know that I didn't want her to." Julie held the blue plaid shirt in her lap, her fingers wound up in the soft flannel. Sometimes she cries when she thinks that no one is looking, but she wasn't then. Although her name is on the letters to the Davis family, she always gets her own letter, too.

Last summer while we were in Maine, there were riots in Chicago. Some people called them demonstrations. We learned about the Bill of Rights in school. Still, I wish they wouldn't. Lane asked in his letters about what was going on in Philadelphia in the anti-war movement.

Four years ago there was an anti-war demonstration in Rittenhouse Square. I was really young then, but I remember it because it was the first one and Dad and Lane talked about it a couple of nights in a row.

In my letters I didn't tell Lane how angry some of the kids in school are about the war. They say that if they have to go to Vietnam they won't go, but they'll run away to Canada, and some of them say that their parents have promised to buy them the ticket.

Dad says that when these people grow up they'll be nostalgic about protests and marches. He asked if I knew what nostalgia was. Sure. It was one of our vocabulary words in English.

I wonder if Lane has time to be nostalgic about our summers in Maine. We go to the lake every day. Our house has a long lawn and then there's a path down to the lake.

Loons are on the lake, and we like to watch them. Carrie and I try to guess where the loon will come up after it dives. We make it into a game to see who'll be right. We even keep score. Lane used to play that game with us, and he'd tell us Nature Facts. He wants to teach biology in a college when he gets home. He'll be good at that.

My brother Lane is a target. Today kids at school were talking about something they called fragging. I couldn't listen long because I'm worried about Lane. I think fragging is murder.

In a way it's funny to think about murder happening during a war. Where is the line? Killing someone on your own side is wrong. I would have trouble killing anybody, and I hope Lane doesn't. But he might have to.

4. Carrie

Everything is political: the personal is political. When my big brother Lane went to Vietnam, even though I was too young to realize it at the time, I was politicized. I realized that by the time I grew up, the war would be history, so I decided that I would teach history. I wanted people to understand how things were. I still do.

Lane left for Nam right after he married Julie. He'd signed up for R.O.T.C. and pretty much knew that he'd be going there. And then again there was the draft lottery anyway.

He gave one of his flannel shirts to Jewel and another favorite shirt to me. I liked to carry it around, and I slept with it. Once when Jewel wasn't looking, I took the shirt he'd given her to see if I liked it better than mine, but I put it back before she knew it was gone.

New York is not Chicago, and the demonstrations in New York last summer were nothing like the demonstrations in Chicago in 1968. I didn't go to either. I was too young to go to Chicago, and too cynical to go to New York.

Even though I didn't go to New York, I did vote. My husband Rob and I take our daughter, Lily, to the polls so she sees that it's important. Rob and I also have a son we named Lane after my brother. Lane didn't go with us this year—he's in the Army, Iraq.

Our son grew up hearing about his Uncle's blue shirt, and before he left he gave Lily one of his shirts—lent her his blue shirt. You wouldn't think he'd be sentimental like that, but he's a good kid.

Our family has voting traditions. After we vote Rob and I meet up with my family, and we all have dinner together and watch TV until about midnight. Then on Wednesday we have dinner again and go over the whole thing, listen to the talking heads on cable. We switch around from channel to channel. Each year the production values change, but, basically, it's the slow grind of the electoral college on the vote.

In 2000 I thought we'd be having dinner together the whole year because of the Florida debacle. That was an unnecessary circus. And depending on what your politics are you decide who's the clown.

Rob and I read the *New York Times* on Sunday, and we watch C-Span. We think of ourselves as independent.

I asked Lane what he thought about the Swift Boat Vets and Kerry. He put his hands over his ears, then over both eyes, then over his mouth—the three monkeys, See No Evil, Hear No Evil, Speak No Evil. Then he winked and reminded me that the three advisors were monkeys.

I'm glad I have those photos of myself in mini-skirts. It keeps me from freaking out entirely when Lily takes swatches of fabric off the rack and says that's the skirt she's been looking for.

When she wears her brother's shirt with her skirts, the shirt is as long as the skirt. Oh well, most of the time she wears jeans. The jeans she chooses aren't the ones that show her belly button, though some of her friends wear those low-rise jeans with little tee shirts that bare their midriffs, even in winter.

I try to remember that we wore miniskirts, hip huggers, bras optional, and we weren't all sluts. I try to stay non-judgmental about this fashion thing, but I'm glad that the fad is over for those tee shirts that said things like "slut" or "easy" or "candy." So far Lily hasn't mentioned tattoos or piercing anything other than her ears.

When she turns fourteen in June, I'll take her to get her ears pierced and she can pick out some earrings for a birthday present. But no nose ring, eyebrow ring, navel ring, etc. I can be such a prude!

This year we'll take one of her friends up with us when we go to the lake in Maine. Our family still has the house there, and we all go up in the summer. When I see Lily sitting on the end of the dock, it brings back the memories I have of sitting there, guessing about where a diving loon would resurface. Sometimes I sit there with Lily, and we talk about what she'd call "stuff."

She spent a lot of time with Rob and me in the den while we watched the war news when the embedded journalists were still sending their reports. Lane is there now, and I know something about what she must be feeling. I try to give her the opportunity to talk about it by talking about how I felt when her Uncle was in Nam.

She really looks up to him. And now I understand how tough it must have been for Mom not to let me know how worried she was when he was in Nam.

"Mom," Lily said, "please tell me again about the red tiger." She looked up from her spiral-bound notebook that lay open on the kitchen table.

She likes to start her homework essays in handwriting before she uses the computer. She has an assignment to write about some aspect of family mythology.

"I'm not sure the red tiger fits the assignment," I said. Immediately I was sorry. My words couldn't have been better chosen to annoy a teenager. I apologized while she was still wailing, "Mom."

"I have to write about family stories and myths. 'Specially a significant one." She dropped the pencil eraser straight down so it bounced on the Formica tabletop. She caught it and dropped it again. Each time she held the pencil up higher, and it bounced higher.

This would be a fine physics experiment; I shuddered thinking about the upcoming Science Fair. I hoped this year's experiment wouldn't involve rotting fruit. Or gerbils.

"The red tiger is very significant in our family, Mom. Uncle Lane talks about it all the time." She paused. "Well, not all the time, but lots, anyway."

She was right, and I wasn't actually positive what Mrs. Ellis means when she talks about family mythology, anyway. One year the classes worked on a joint project, history and English, using documents and artifacts as an indication of family history. She'd probably like a poem being significant in a family story.

"I need to know about the how the red tiger affected the wedding. I'm going to talk to Aunt Julie and Uncle Lane tonight. I'm supposed to bring together "different narratives." She took a deep breath, then added, "To reconcile inconsistencies."

She held out a piece of paper so I could read it. Yup. That's what it said.

"You get to go first," she said.

"There's not much to tell, Lily." I said, "Uncle Lane and Aunt Julie were getting married at her parents' house. On the back lawn. It was early in the day before any of the guests had arrived, but preparations were in full swing A big tent with folding chairs, and so on."

"Where was the tiger?"

"The tiger was in a poem I wrote in school, that's all. There was no real tiger."

"I know," she said, "it was a red tiger." Her voice changed, "Where was the red tiger at the wedding?   What was so dangerous?"

"I imagined the tiger," I said, "The tiger itself was dangerous." I paused. "I think I must have been upset about Lane leaving to go to the war."

"And getting married,"

"Oh, probably not,"

"Probably yes," she said. "I want my brother to be happy, but I know that when he gets married, it will change everything."

"I was in the wedding," I said, surprised at the petulance in my voice. "I had a frilly pink lace dress and a big satin bow."

Lily wrinkled her nose, "You liked that?"

I laughed. I never wear frilly clothes now. A warning voice whispered to me. "I wasn't the frilly type, but I liked Julie."

"Julie's cool," Lily said.

"It was just a poem I wrote. The tiger would pounce. Its eyes were the last thing you saw before you died."

"Creepy," she said, "and a little weird for a wedding day— especially before Uncle Lane goes to war."

"It was weird," I admitted. Lane said he'd thought about the red tiger the whole time he was at war.

He'd mention it even now when something bad was happening. "Is that a tiger's breath I smell?" he'd say.

I guess it was a myth, kind of. "They're quiet and sneaky, these red tigers," I added.

"Oh, when did 'the' red tiger become 'they'?"

"I don't know," I said, although I did, in fact, know, to the day. "If you want me to, I'll look to see if I can find the poem."

"Awesome," Lily said. "I don't know why I didn't think of that." She bent over her notebook and started writing.

I went, but I knew already what I would find, four corner holders and a pale space in the scrapbook where the paper had been. I had torn it up myself.

When Lane said he'd got his orders to go to Iraq I'd found my scrapbook and turned to the page where the poem had been pasted by my parents. I re-read the poem, and I can visualize the page still, wide blue lines and dark pencil with careful printing on yellowing brittle paper.

I pulled it out and tore it into tiny pieces, put them in a big plate and burned them. The volume was surprisingly small. I mixed the ashes into a meatloaf and served it up for dinner. I didn't tell Lily or Rob what I had done. I thought I'd understood the concept of devouring your enemy's heart.

What I hadn't considered was that by eating the tiger I had made it a part of myself. And although they didn't know it, now Lily and Rob had the red tiger within them, too.

I went back into the kitchen. Lily looked up from her work and frowned. "No luck?"

"It wasn't there," I said, conscious of the deception. "But you have everything, don't you?"

"I'll be fine," she said.

I knew that she would. Tonight her Uncle and Aunt would tell her their stories. Lane might tell her about his nights in the jungle in Nam, while my son is making his way across another alien landscape.

On the evening news we see dark smoke rising from a metal carcass, victim of an I.E.D. I look at my husband and daughter, serious, intent, watching. I am restless. The red tiger paces. These days I avoid mirrors, afraid I will recognize, reflected, what I still fear most to find, the red tiger's wide gold eyes.

Harriet Levin Millan

Bumming a Cigarette

I pretend to read as if the words on the page (Carl Andre's *Cuts*) are more important than the voices in my husband's studio. I hear one of his fellow students—a girl with shiny otter hair all spun around—ask him for a cigarette, when the girl could have asked others, those sitting beside me, making letters out of smoke. Not a smoker myself, I can't read the curlicues before they dissolve, don't know their language, their languid gauge. *A girl reached him, her hipbones were sharp*...that is how their story is going to begin. He rips open the cellophane on a new pack, peels it off like the shirt over his head, the jeans on his legs and inserts a cigarette in the crook of the girl's fingers. They align and produce a current. They're glowing, the two of them, they're so attracted. I'm standing on their periphery. They feel me opposing them, trying to poke through. The silver face of a dime sparkles on the floor. High cheekbones and upturned nose look too valuable to leave behind. I think about picking it up before anyone else grabs it. Should spend it, mark the outline on a patch of prairie, set fire to it. Resting my hand on one of the power saws until I see how close to the blade I've placed it, I sashay toward him, pull a cigarette from his pack and snap it in half.

Harriet Levin Millan

Crush

Choose One—Then—close the Valves...

He kept his eyes on me as if collapsing
the space between us, bringing the ceiling down
to its foundation, flattening the dimensions
of my thinking. The slow and deliberate way
he pulled back the plastic sheeting covering the marble
only an inch or two while he continued
holding my gaze, then abruptly turned his head
to stare at something else instead—some garbage cans
filled with refuse from his studio, curious
about the garbage and what it held.
He could turn it into art. It could become
part of his process, using it for his art.
Instead of working just one project,
he surrounded himself with another,
marble and refuse. The one still wrapped in plastic
ready to be moved and the one that's been
removed from floor, chair and bed—
my dusky voice, my half-smile—swept up, crushed.

Harriet Levin Millan

My Oceanography

A strand of algae leaves its rubbery
translucent swatch on my skin. My first impulse
is to peel it off lest a horror
movie version of contagion unfold
and my skin turn zombie green--telltale alien,
more slime than flesh, attracting gnats, pin head skitters
moving so rapidly all is flux.

My second impulse is to keep it as a totem
of subterranean life, a scrap chiseled
from things that are meant to sink. Deep is form,
like a snail that burrows into silt, shell
growing out of sludgy cravings.
A life-in-death feel. The croaks frogs make
drowning in natural desire. Believe me,
diving into this mosh pit, I do not
float softly through water.

Pond life is too shallow. No flotsam or jetsam,
sneakers, ice-hockey gloves, Chinese message
in a bottle. Even the dam's stopped up,
no bigger than an oversized sink filled
nightly with dishes. No reputable
oceanographer will chart its depth —
another thing I'll never know
about myself. Territorial and fiercely defensive,
rock bottom will not be reached.

To be essential something must be both deep
and wide. Eyes with skies in them. Upswept
lashes and brows. A western monsoon.
Dreams that stretch over many nights to mimic
the feel of sea-foam on ankles,
down to the cellular properties of summer.

Harriet Levin Millan

Waterfall

Swirling round stones regardless the roaring,
edged sideways, your knees—can you bend them?

Can you hold the angle without becoming cramped?
Can you continually step down, fingers pushing back

hair in strands, a cascading, hurtling continuity
over basalt rock slopes? Imagine the fall, wheels in your heels,

birds, lilacs, laughter, your wings, your talons your arms spread
to embrace the landscape's plowed fields,

cars swooshing past on the Interstate. Fall over stones
slip down to a trickle in a pool my body fills with

yours drop-by-drop icy cold at first then lukewarm
then aflame, ferns on the lower story, lilacs in the canopy

ringing rind and leaves. Such dampness seeps
from the edge of your boots, unless you remove them.

When I stand here I feel my limbs expand
like poses in yoga. The thunderous current

lifts my arms and knees.
I rise like a flock of starlings

scattering rhapsodies—the rigor, the truss,
the rib cage bursting through.

Lynn Levin

Insecurity Questions

In order to provide your account with an extra layer of protection, we may ask you to verify your identity by answering a security question when you sign in. Please select three security questions from those below.

1. What street did your best friend in high school live on?

Janie Watkins lived on Pin Oak Drive, but I think she liked Beth Bishop more than me. I mean, I wanted to call Janie my best friend. Not sure I should type in Pin Oak Drive.

2. Where was your wedding reception held?

I had a deposit (non-refundable) at Golden Rings, but my fiancé called off the engagement. So, never been a bride. Thanks for rubbing it in.

3. Who was the best man at your wedding?

See above.

4. What is your spouse's hobby?

You mean my ex-fiancé's hobby? That's hard to say. He was in a secret men's club. He called it a lodge. Several times a week he'd say, "I'm going to the lodge."

5. What was the name of your first boss?

Mrs. Hartman. She was a single mom. I babysat for her kid, Dougie. She had a ton of makeup. It was so cool to go through her stuff. They didn't have nanny cams then. I never took anything, but I still feel guilty about the snooping.

6. Who was your date to your high school senior prom?

Do you think that everyone goes to the prom? I wanted to go, but I didn't have a date. Janie Watkins went. She double-dated with Beth Bishop and Ralph Beale. Later she told me that Ralph had asked for my phone number, but she didn't give it to him because she didn't think I liked him. I would have gone to the prom with Ralph. I liked him enough. I stayed home, and all night my mom was saying, "Isn't this prom night? Aren't all the kids going to the prom?" I was going to give Janie a piece of my mind, but then I thought why? It's all over and done with.

7. In what hospital were you born?

I was born in a Honda Civic. My mom was in labor, but my dad wanted to finish watching an important football game.

8. What was the name of your first pet?

My dog's name was Candy, but he ran away when I let him chase a rabbit. He really wanted to get that rabbit. I thought he'd come back. I feel so terrible about losing Candy.

9. What color was your first car?

I don't drive. Too nervous. That's why I live in Boston. You don't have to drive there.

10. If you had a super power, what would it be?

Teleportation. I'd save a lot on Ubers and the MBTA. No wait, shapeshifting. Then I could look like Kate Beckinsale or Amy Adams. No wait, invisibility. For sure, invisibility.

Lynn Levin

Six Riddles

I
Flat as the old world, white as bone
nearly as dated as a public phone
two-faced in a nice way yet burdensome.

II
Your legions shape the self and crowd the soul.
Some of you are grim. Some of you are gold.
Like leaves you fall away as one grows old.

III
It is zero degrees but very hot.
Crossing it should feel odd but does not.
Above it, cyclones spin against the clock.

IV
It's a film through which your secrets break
like restless imps from a frozen lake
and act their worst until you wake.

V
Your master dictates right and wrong
and that's a comfort for those who long
for only one way forward, one way down.

VI
We will stop, but you'll go far.
Fickleness itself you are—
in love with change yet constant as a star.

Suggested answers to "Six Riddles: I paper II memories III the equator
IV the subconscious V a crossword puzzle VI evolution

Lynn Levin

To My Teens

My potato years, my toad years, my years in the dreamy wood
in you I shrank from *Seventeen's* apotheosis
of the cute high-school girl yet missed
the hippie bus of good times. You had me slogging
through the swamps of dejection, reading a lot
of Plath and Sexton. Like that helped.

In you I never learned to drive but marched
against the war in Vietnam, pollution, the bomb.
I was against practically everything.
I discovered that life was absurd but chose to live anyway.
I had sex for the first time with a boy named_____.
Everyone else was doing it. Those were liberal times.
Too bad that_____ regaled the guys
with all the details. I was slut shamed.
Not such liberal times after all.

Teens, after a while your agony withers
like everything else. Since you, I have known nearly
five decades of loss and good harvest. Yet still you sit
in the attic examining old scrapbooks.
O unwise underage parent of my current self
if I could tell you what to do over, I would say:
live as you did, correct none of your errors.

Jonson Miller

Samuel Spangler's Handmade Table

Dark, smooth, glossy plank-wood
buffed one hundred thousand times
by dishrags after every meal,
after each of two hundred Thanksgiving dinners.

Buffed by carelessly tossed mail,
by elbows of wool, then cotton, then polyester,
and then, once again, cotton.
And buffed by morning papers
bringing anguish

and then relief
as they revealed the latest casualty lists.
From Ramadi and Kandahar.
From Khe Sanh.
From Iwo and Normandy.
From Meuse-Argonne.
From Gettysburg
and Monterrey.

Dark, smooth, glossy plank-wood
scrubbed smooth by the history of a people,
by the intimate and ordinary gestures
of nine generations of Spanglers.

Steaming tea – drunk too soon
Shared by an internet-age Buddhist professor
wearing "Made-in-Vietnam"
and a wagon-age Mennonite farmer
wearing homespun.

Don Riggs

Review of *Heavy Metal, l'autre Métal Hurlant* by Nicolas Labarre

Nicolas Labarre's study of *Heavy Metal* as an American version of the French comics magazine *Métal Hurlant* is both a chronicle of transatlantic cross-pollination in the realm of comics and a record of influences, misunderstandings, personal and professional relations, and the ultimate parting of ways between the two groups—neither of which was cohesive on their own. In addition, it is a record of a complex network of artists, writers, publishers, and film makers in the last three decades of the twentieth century in the United States and France, but also to a much smaller degree Spain, Italy, Germany, the Netherlands, and Great Britain. Labarre cites one of the French founders, writer Jean-Pierre Dionnet, frequently in terms of that participant's assessment of the aesthetic value of the American magazine—despite his initial vision of revolutionary avant-garde comics artists like Art Spiegelman dominating *Heavy Metal,* H.M. soon went in the direction of scantily clad pin-up girls (12). By the time the text reaches its *"Conclusion générale,"* it becomes obvious that Labarre also finds the American magazine to be a poor adaptation of the French original (205). *Métal Hurlant* lasted for twelve years, from 1975 to 1987, while *Heavy Metal* is still in publication today, forty years later.

This book is very rich in references to specific comics artists, and if one is familiar with Moebius—a.k.a. Jean Giraud—Druillet, Bilal, and writers like Dionnet and Jodorowsky, it is very meaningful, or if one can do online searches for examples of these creators' art and collaborations. Although at the outset Labarre gives a sweeping general overview, over the course of the body of the text the reader is immersed in a flood of specifics. At times there is a sample page of a given comic, with a very close analysis of it in the text, but this doesn't happen often. In one case, where Labarre is making a point about the influence of *Métal Hurlant* on the cover art of other similar magazines in Germany—*Metall Menschen, Star Fantasy, and Schwermetall*—and *Heavy Metal,* there is a plate with five such covers, in color, but unfortunately in this reviewer's copy the colors were for the most part too dark for one to see significant details of the images (141).

The friendships and subsequent influences, often mutual, between various individuals are fascinating in terms of the development of comics and their extension into other arts, like film. Labarre reveals that René Goscinny, the writer of the Astérix comics later in his career, knew Harvey Kurtzman, later cartoonist and editor of *MAD* magazine, in the late 'forties, and that the two of them produced a series of children's books (42). Similarly, Moebius and

Dan O'Bannon, brought together by Jodorowsky to create the *Dune* movie that never materialized, collaborated to produce a comic strip story, "The Long Tomorrow," with Moebius' illustration of O'Bannon's story influencing the look of Ridley Scott's *Blade Runner* (146) as well as Moebius and Jodorowsky's graphic series about the *Incal* (both of these were initially published in *Métal Hurlant*). If for no other reason, Labarre's study is invaluable for its chronicling of fortuitous interpersonal contacts and subsequent inspired art works.

The study is meticulously researched, with a seven-page small-print bibliography, interviews with twenty-five people involved in various aspects of the two "Metal" magazines and others, and most of the quotations from Americans are in French translation in the body of the text and the original English in a corresponding footnote. This is of particular interest to those with a good reading knowledge of both languages, as the American interviewees often use colorful colloquial expressions which are translated expressively in the French text. Translation theorists know that there is no such thing as a "strictly literal" translation, but there are translations that can either get the essence of the original or miss it. Ted White, the editor of *Heavy Metal* in 1979-80, is quoted as saying, "I do have gripes with the issue on a whole, though" which is translated as, "J'ai des reproches a faire au numéro [d'octobre 1979] dans son ensemble, malgré tout" (102). To "have gripes" and "avoir des reproches" do mean the same thing, but there is something more physical, and more Anglo-Saxon, about having a gripe than reproaching someone for something.

An aspect of the *Heavy Metal* illustration practices that is addressed is that of sexism, which takes the form of depictions of naked, or scantily clothed, female bodies. Labarre gives us a chart enumerating the occurrences of "femmes nues" and "hommes nus" subdivided as to decorative function or narrative function, number of occurrences and number of pages—unfortunately, it is not clear how many issues this analysis covers, or whether it is a representative analysis of one issue. Labarre points out that the magazine's strategy for dealing with the complaints about the unequal representation of male and female nudes was to have the highest-ranking woman staff member, Julie Simmons (later Simmons-Lynch), one of the founding members of the editorial staff and ultimately editor-in-chief, write an editorial, "Billy Likes Naked Girls" [*Heavy Metal* vol. 6/11 February 1983, p.6] (85) pointing out that 95% of the readership of the magazine was male, hence the matter was primarily economic. Near the end of Labarre's study, his interview with Julie Simmons-Lynch in 2015 touches on this topic as well, though more in relation to whether criticisms of her editorial choices resulted from her being a woman (201).

Overall, *Heavy Metal, l'autre Métal Hurlant* is an excellent compendium of specific facts and connections concerning the American popular magazine and comic book world of the years leading to the formation of *Heavy Metal*, the analogous but not identical world of French parodical magazines and vehicles for comics at the time, the various attempts to publish a French *National Lampoon* and an English-language *Métal Hurlant*—which was what *Heavy Metal* was initially, at least to a certain extent—and the breakdown in communications between the two publications. There are several graphs and charts showing the relative frequency with which French originals were published in the American magazine—though with translation of the text that was at times in large part guesswork (79, 81)—as well as indicating the number of adult science-fiction comics for adults in the United States, arranged showing the duration of the periods when they were published (130). Finally, there is a graph showing the relative distribution of *Heavy Metal* from 1977 through 2012—the material context in which commercial publications necessarily exist.

Despite this last awareness of the bottom line in publishing, the general conclusion denigrating the American publication in relation to the dashed hopes of the French initial movers and shakers leaves the reader with the inescapable conclusion that either one publishes a comics-oriented magazine of high quality and radical innovations or one publishes a sleazier version of such a magazine that sells, and that stays on the stands for decades.

Jack Santucci

Why Adopting Proportional Voting May Bring Back The Big-Tent Political Party

Not in about 70 years have we seen so much interest in proportional voting. Otherwise known as multi-winner ranked-choice, its basic idea is to shake up the two party system. A majority of votes would mean a majority of seats — unlike what we may get in this week's election. Meanwhile, parties would be more diverse on the inside, instead of being so ideologically rigid.

Lost in the story is how all this works. The key is a constructive tension. Parties still will want to win their majorities. The difference is that, with multi-winner ranked-choice, they'll have to cater to protest voters. I'll explain what I mean based on recent research.

Multi-winner ranked-choice voting: what it is and how it works

In this type of voting, the voter ranks candidates in order of preference. Winning a seat requires a quota. If your vote doesn't help some candidate get a quota — either because that candidate is hopeless or because they have enough votes already — your ballot flows to your next-ranked pick.

The size of the quota is the critical difference between two kinds of ranked-choice voting. In a one-seat district, it's a majority, and that's the system in San Francisco or Maine.

In an earlier time, though, many US cities had multi-seat districts — Cleveland, New York City, Cincinnati, Worcester (Mass), and 20 more. The larger the district, the lower the quota — typically about 10 percent of the vote.

Contrast ranked voting with the current system, where the most votes in a district determine the winner. That makes it rational for all sorts of people — money, the media, and party hacks — to winnow a candidate field. In the words of the late Kenneth Arrow, the "plurality system chokes off free entry."

Ranked-choice voting doesn't kill parties

When any politician can win a seat with 10 percent of the vote, you might expect parties to evaporate. Or you might expect legislatures to be filled with third parties. Not so.

In any democracy, there needs to be a legislative majority. That can be issue-by-issue, or the same group of people can just stick together. Humans are lazy, so they prefer the latter. This is why, even in countries with more than two parties, we tend to see the same parties working together. Sometimes they even announce such deals before an election begins.

One irony in this country's history with multi-winner ranked voting was a tendency toward two-party competition. In Cincinnati, for example, the Republican Party squared off against the Charter Party in 16 elections, from 1925 to 1957. Charter was a coalition of Progressive Republicans and institutional Democrats. Other parties came and went — Progressive Democrats for two elections, Roosevelt Democrats in one of them. But of 144 winners over 32 years, only four weren't from one of the two major parties — three in the late 1930s, at the height of the Great Depression.

And in Massachusetts cities, seven of which had multi-winner ranked systems, parties like the Cambridge Civic Association or Citizens' Plan E Association were common fare. In 1932, in fact, the national group behind this reform also recommended forming "good government" parties.

The ranked-choice system itself gave people reasons to form political parties. Say you've decided to form a majority. The next step is to get it elected. Parties would do this by asking voters to use their rankings just for its candidates. That way, ballots wouldn't flow "accidentally" to the opposing party or independents.

Big-tent dynamics

If parties can "game" ranked-choice voting, how is it better than what we have now? Weren't they just choking off free entry?

Remember that parties want to win a majority. Sometimes, those coalition deals would close out key constituencies. Government might ignore important issues like civil-service desegregation or what ethnic neighborhood a new highway would run through. Property taxes were another concern.

Sometimes, issues unrelated to current policies would make their way into public debate. Examples included air pollution, a woman's role in politics, and what to do about the Depression.

Independent candidates were common in periods when people didn't feel that government was responsive. This is when the magic of ranked-choice kicked in.

The minority party in city council would see the ferment in election returns. To it, independent candidates would represent an untapped market for votes. In the extreme, independents might get a seat of their own, depriving some party of a majority. So, when the next election came around, the minority party would recruit independents, putting them onto a major-party slate. Getting back to a majority meant being responsive.

Responsiveness was visible in council business. One way to see this is to track party unity on city council votes. As newcomers challenged status quo policies, fights would ensue between them and the old guard. These fights turn up in data as party-unity dips, typically after some party or faction had returned to majority status. Then, as the party worked out its new disagreements, party-line voting would recover.

Over the long haul, the interplay of party strategy, independent challengers, and issue-based politics was constantly remaking parties. In the language of business, this is constructive tension.

Beyond extreme claims

I don't want to oversell ranked-choice voting and the constructive tension it may lead to. I have no measure of whether such dynamics exist in just-pick-one voting systems. They sound like they should, but do they?

Multi-winner ranked voting does not blow up the two-party system. It does not open the third-party floodgates, nor lead automatically to policy change. On all of these metrics, it may disappoint.

But, over several elections, constructive tension with independents makes parties work harder to win their majorities.

This article is based on the paper, "Evidence of a winning-cohesion tradeoff under multi-winner ranked-choice voting" in Electoral Studies

David Seltzer

Taking Back Philosophy – Through Reform, Not Revolution

Taking Back Philosophy is a popularly-written but seriously-intentioned book by noted Chinese philosophy scholar Bryan Van Norden. The book is interesting because of its combination of radicalism and conservatism. On the one hand, Van Norden suggests making two radical changes to academic philosophy as it is commonly practiced in America: (1) vastly expanding the canon to include Chinese, Indian, and other non-mainstream forms of philosophy, and (2) changing the main focus of philosophical inquiry from specialist debates in metaphysics and epistemology to the practical question of how to live one's life. On the other hand, Van Norden argues for these changes on the grounds that they are demanded by a consistent application of the standards of mainstream Western philosophy, and have precedent in the past of mainstream Western philosophy. This mix of radicalism and conservatism allows Van Norden to keep the best of both worlds. He moves beyond the exclusivism of mainstream philosophy without sacrificing its intellectual rigor.

The book arose out of two circumstances. The idea for the book started with a half-joking suggestion by Jay Garfield that mainstream philosophy departments should rename themselves "department of Anglo-European Philosophy." Van Norden liked the idea, and Garfield and Van Norden developed it into a short online piece for *The Stone*. That piece ignited an online firestorm, which threatened to leave the realm of academia and enter the popular consciousness, and convinced Van Norden (Garfield had other obligations) to develop it into a book advocating for the place of Asian philosophy and other less commonly taught philosophies (LCTP) within the mainstream philosophical canon.[i] This topic would eventually become the focus of chapters 1 and 2. Chapter 1 looks at the arguments made against including LCTP in philosophy and shows that none of them hold. Chapter 2 then shows the benefit of expanding the canon by providing examples of Chinese-Western comparative work and the developments it leads to.

While Van Norden was at work on the book, a second major event took place: the election of President Trump. This made it important for intellectuals to enter the public sphere and engage with ethnocentrism in the wider world, and to defend the importance of the liberal arts in what figured to be, and has been, a hostile political climate. At the same time, it also showed the need for soul-searching on the part of the progressive left. These became the topics of chapters 3 through 5. Chapter 3 draws the analogy between intellectual wall-building within the philosophical profession and physical wall-building in the wider world, from Trump's wall to China's Great Wall. Chapter 4 then defends the relevance of philosophy for practical economic gain, civic engagement, and against scientism. Chapter 5, finally, develops a conception of philosophy that will allow it to best address the world at large

In chapter 1 Van Norden lays out the arguments made against including LCTP in the canon. These arguments generally fall into two main strands. The first is quality: critics hold that LCTP doesn't measure up to the standards of mainstream Western philosophy. They generally support this claim by citing a few out of context examples of apparently nonsensical Asian thought, and sometimes also by maintaining that Western philosophy uses logical argumentation to address carefully defined problems in core subdisciplines while Asian philosophy consists of sages sitting on mountaintops dispensing obscure and quasi-mystical pearls of wisdom for their followers to meditate upon.[ii] Van Norden takes evident delight in showing that canonical Western figures like Heraclitus and Parmenides can be made to look nonsensical when taken out of context (3, 45); that Chinese philosophy sometimes proceeds in rigid syllogistic form while major Western philosophers such as Plato often rely on poetic suggestion to make their point (144-7); and that the ancient Chinese engaged in highly technical discussions about topics in logic and the philosophy of language that Western philosophy has only recently begun to address (6-7). Mainstream philosophers who doubt the merit of LCTP either haven't read any at all, or have looked briefly at a few of the less approachable texts (Van Norden mentions the *Analects*, *Daodejing*, and *Changes*, but the *Upanishads* are equally puzzling at first) and then given up without bothering to consult commentaries or secondary sources, as we would do with any major Western philosopher we didn't understand. Those who do put in the effort to understand LCTP invariably find much of value (16, 28-9).

The second argument is definitional: "philosophy" is a Greek word which refers to a particular intellectual tradition beginning in ancient Greece.[iii] To counter this argument, Van Norden looks back into the history of ideas, to show that what we think of as the established philosophical canon is actually a quite recent invention. In the Enlightenment, philosophy was generally understood to begin in either Egypt or India and to include Chinese Confucianism (19-21). I would add that the Enlightenment canon also included women like Margaret Cavendish and Anne Conway, whose views Leibniz described as close to his own,[iv] that Moses Mendelssohn associated with the leading figures of the German Enlightenment,[v] and that Ibn Tufayl's *Hayy ibn Yaqzan* was translated into English in 1708 as a forerunner of Enlightenment natural religion.[vi] The exclusion of African and Asian thought from the canon began in the 1800's due to a combination of factors. Outside the academy, as Europe shifted from trading with other cultures to colonizing them, it became less important to understand these cultures on their own terms and more important to justify colonialism by showing the superiority of Western culture. Within the academy, a group of Kant scholars realized they could increase the value of their intellectual capital by rewriting the canon to make Kant the culmination of Enlightenment thought. Over time this new canon ossified to the point that philosophers now take it for granted and no longer recognize it as the product of deliberate choices made on philosophically irrelevant grounds (21).

This history helps to explain the vitriolic and sometimes silly nature of the responses to Garfield and Van Norden's editorial, such as the person who argued that they wouldn't fly in a plane made with non-Western math, not realizing that our numbering system comes from India via Arabia (11-12). Actual differences of interpretation can be resolved through calmly reasoned academic debate; when debate becomes shrill, it is often a sign that something else is really at stake. Garfield and Van Norden's editorial challenged established power structures both within academia and in the wider world. It was this, rather than the actual call for the inclusion of LCTP, that provoked the response. The history of the canon also helps to explain why Garfield and Van Norden got such a huge reaction to a partially tongue-in-cheek editorial. Institutional resistance – which Van Norden (150), following Lyotard, calls a form of terror – can always overcome rational arguments, but is far more vulnerable to humor. The idea that philosophy departments should rename themselves makes Van Norden's point in a clever way that sticks in the mind as a reasoned argument would not. Thus the popular and often "cheeky" (xxiii) tone of *Taking Back Philosophy* does serious work: it helps to dislodge us from our habitual and nearly invisible assumptions. It's important to note, however, that Van Norden uses humor fairly. He answers serious arguments with serious counter-arguments, and only mocks statements that are obviously false or stupid.

Having rejected the objections to studying LCTP, Van Norden can talk about the benefits it would bring. In the wider world, China and India are increasingly becoming powers that can influence our daily lives (as the threat of a trade war with China has shown), and one way to better understand these societies is to understand their philosophical underpinnings. Van Norden shows that Confucianism, Buddhism, and Daoism still exert a significant influence on modern China (3-4). The same may be true in India: I've had international students tell me the caste system is far from dead in practice. The study of Islamic philosophy helps to counter the image of Islam as a religion of fundamentalism and terror, and the narrative of a clash of civilizations falls apart when we realize medieval Islamic philosophy is in fact a branch of Western philosophy. In the classroom, students are increasingly diverse, and they connect with writers like Beauvoir and Fanon in a way they don't with white male writers. In my own survey classes, I've often seen Beauvoir and Fanon generate the most class discussion, and I've had multiple students thank me for teaching them. At the faculty level, teaching LCTP will encourage more women and minorities to enter the field, which is particularly important given that so much of philosophy depends upon thought experiments designed to clarify our basic intuitions, and a diverse field will help to ensure that those intuitions are broadly held, and not just the unquestioned background assumptions of a particular group.

The main benefit, however, is that studying LCTP opens possibilities for interesting comparative work. In chapter 2, Van Norden gives several examples of comparative philosophy using his specialization, Chinese philosophy. The key for this kind of comparative work is to find two traditions that "are similar enough for comparisons to be legitimate, but different enough for both traditions to learn from each other" (5). Some of Van Norden's examples work better than others. There is really no need to appeal to Buddhism to critique Descartes' conception of substance and the soul when Hume's criticisms will work equally well. It would be much more interesting to see a discussion of Buddhism and Hume, or Hinduism and Descartes. Similarly, it would seem to make more sense to compare Hobbes with Xunzi, Han Feizi, or Mozi than with Mencius, and any Anglo-European communitarian could make a relatively similar critique of Hobbes coming out of Aristotle. The most interesting parts of chapter 2 are the sections on ethics and weakness of will, in which Van Norden runs Aristotle and the communitarians against Mencius and the Neo-Confucians. In these sections, because the philosophers' views are suitably close, we are forced to see differences of nuance, and comparative philosophers have invented new concepts in order to describe these differences, such as the distinction between development, discovery, and re-formation models of ethical cultivation (66). The key point is that these concepts can then be turned around and used to understand Aristotle. Thus comparative philosophy also helps to improve our understanding of Western thought.

It's worthwhile to think about the benefits of reading LCTP within the canon in more detail. LCTP is a catch-all category, and different branches of LCTP have different relations to mainstream (MCTP?) philosophy, which means that they will have different effects when added to the canon. At one extreme, Van Norden discusses Chinese philosophy, which has, as far as we know, no significant historical connection to mainstream Western philosophy. The same is true of the indigenous philosophies of the Americas, Australia, and the Pacific islands before contact with the West, and of African philosophy before the introduction of Christianity and Islam. In these cases, because there is no historical connection, comparative work must necessarily be organized around some problem, to which historical figures from various traditions reply. This is how Van Norden organizes chapter 2, with sections on metaphysics, political philosophy, ethics, and weakness of will. He also suggests the same comparative approach when talking about African philosophies and the philosophies of the Indigenous peoples of the Americas (83, 149). On the one hand, this kind of comparative work should produce many new concepts, because of the juxtapositions it creates. On the other hand, it does not contribute to our understanding of the development of the history of philosophy. The same is true in the classroom: these types of philosophy could be integrated into a problems-based course, but because they are not part of the same story, they are hard to fit into a chronologically-ordered historical survey course.

At the other extreme are works that fit seamlessly into the mainstream canon but were excluded for reasons that had nothing to do with merit. A good example is Beauvoir's mid-1940's ethical writings. These were explicitly intended as philosophical works along the same lines pursued by contemporaries like Sartre and Merleau-Ponty. They are clearly works of the first order: *The Ethics of Ambiguity* stands as the main statement of 1940's French existentialist ethics. They engage with canonical figures like Kant, Hegel, Marx, Husserl, and Heidegger, and address central issues in philosophy like ethics, political philosophy, phenomenology, and ontology. Including these works in the canon would give us a more accurate picture of the history of Continental philosophy. They also fit easily into survey courses on ethics or the history of philosophy (I've taught *The Ethics of Ambiguity* many times and "Moral Idealism and Political Realism" once, generally to favorable reviews.) Finally, we might get a better translation of *The Ethics of Ambiguity.* Having said that, while there are important differences between Beauvoir's ontology and Sartre's, they are so closely related that reading Beauvoir as well as Sartre will not create the same type of juxtapositions as cross-traditional work, and thus will not lead to the same conceptual advances. The same could be said, in a previous generation, for Cavendish and Conway – their work fits nicely into the Enlightenment canon as two alternative replies to the mind-body problem. [vii]

Contemporary Africana, feminist, and LGBTQ philosophies are historically grounded in mainstream Western philosophy, although it's worth noting that they are often grounded in Western Continental philosophy, and that many of the schools Van Norden (163n8) mentions as teaching Africana philosophy have Continental or at least pluralistic departments. Reading these works as philosophy clearly enriches our understanding of them, because it allows us to see the connections to the Western tradition. It also highlights the need for philosophically competent translations: the Parshley translation of *The Second Sex* was notoriously bad. At the same time, these works not only respond to the Western tradition but also help to advance it. For instance, the early Continental tradition tends to conceptualize self-other relations in abstract and thus symmetrical terms, whether we look at Hegel (the reconciliation of consciousnesses), Sartre (an endless oscillation between subject and object), Merleau-Ponty (all consciousness is embodied), or even Levinas' account of politics. The best statements of an asymmetrical notion of the Other really do come from Beauvoir and Fanon. Both recognize that, beneath the abstract symmetry between all people, there are concrete asymmetries, which prevent symmetrical relations from developing in practice.

In chapter 3 Van Norden moves from exclusion within academia to exclusion in the wider world. The chapter is synthetic in character: Van Norden sees the resistance to including Asian philosophy within the canon as reproducing, in microcosm, the resistance to globalization in the wider world. Van Norden starts with Trump's promise to build a wall along the Mexican border. He easily shows that the wall has no rational justification and is instead a cynical attempt to appeal to racist and nationalist sentiment. In this sense, Trump is not an outlier within the Republican party, but rather the logical outcome of the "southern strategy" which the Republican party has used, in a far less overt form, since Nixon in 1968 (85-9). I would add that Trump's success is actually part of a much larger phenomenon, on all sides of the political spectrum, which also includes the Brexit vote, the election of far-right nationalists in Hungary and Poland, the near-success of the Scottish independence referendum and the subsequent overwhelming victory of the SNP in parliamentary elections, and the failed Catalan independence movement, among others. Van Norden cleverly juxtaposes this Western nationalist turn with a discussion of a similar phenomenon in China. China is rapidly expanding, it is ethnically diverse, and cracks are forming in the social fabric. To hold his country together, newly-appointed dictator-for-life Xi Jinping cynically uses the *Chinese* canon to appeal to nationalistic sentiment (91-7). Van Norden's discussion of China forces us to see wall-building from the other side: not only are we building walls against the world, but the world is building walls against us.

Conservatives from Edmund Burke to Allan Bloom defend this kind of wall-building because it promotes adherence to the norms of one's own society and culture. Van Norden, however, responds that the most vibrant cultures are constantly evolving. They hold strong communal norms, but they constantly question, evaluate, and refine those norms (99-105). They are also outward-directed. The early Ming dynasty mounted massive maritime expeditions, Rome was cosmopolitan, America was built by immigrants. Societies only build walls when they have started to decline and want to hold on to what they already have. This attempt to hold on to the past only serves to accelerate the decline: the Ming dynasty was successfully overthrown shortly after constructing the iconic sections of the Great Wall,[viii] and Trump's attacks on immigrants will deprive America of cultural exchanges and the innovations that arise from them. Instead, Van Norden claims, history shows that societies which do not make gradual and intelligently guided adaptations eventually change cataclysmically and disastrously. This is what happened in the French Revolution, the Russian Revolution, and Mao's Cultural Revolution (102). As in the macrocosm so in the microcosm. *Taking Back Philosophy* repeats the warning from *The Stone* editorial that the philosophical field must voluntarily change before change is forced upon it. In this sense, *Taking Back Philosophy* is not really a call for change: the change will happen regardless. Instead, Taking Back Philosophy is a call for the professoriate to intelligently integrate LCTP into the philosophical canon, using the standards and methods learned from mainstream philosophy, before this change is forced on them by poorly-informed student agitators and money-hungry administrators.[ix]

Chapter 4 seeks to defend the value of philosophy and the liberal arts generally. Philosophy has come under attack from right-wing anti-intellectuals, but also from scientists who don't see the value of the liberal arts given that science seemingly furnishes a better tool for understanding the world, and most concerningly from students (or, more likely, parents) who don't see why they should spend God-knows-what on tuition only to leave college with a major that appears to have no practical value. Some of the attacks are easily dealt with. Marco Rubio's claim that welders make more than philosophers is simply an alternative fact (1-2, 110-11). The idea that philosophy has no practical value is also mistaken. Philosophy may have almost no direct practical value, except to the few people who go to graduate school, but it is particularly effective at developing a set of general skills – reading, writing, and reasoning – that are essential for advancement in almost any career (113-4). At a deeper level, the liberal arts are necessary for democratic citizenship. Democracy places substantial power in the hands of the people; it is therefore necessary for the people to be able to think critically and independently and to be used to encountering views beyond their own. This observation has its darker side. Van Norden, like John Dewey and Plato's right-wing Straussian interpreters, recognizes that the liberal arts can serve as a tool for manipulation. If the study of the liberal arts becomes a luxury confined to the elite, they could use it to control the masses, who would be given the technical training to serve the elite but not the critical thinking skills to question the status quo. At the extreme level, the anti-intellectual rejection of the liberal arts produces blind faith, conformism, and intolerance: it is consistent with, and leads to, fascism (127-30). As for the critique that science renders philosophy obsolete, Van Norden's strongest response is that philosophy is a form of what Thomas Kuhn[x] would call pre-paradigm science. That is, we do philosophy when we haven't yet developed a method for investigating a particular question. Over time, as various fields of inquiry become more systematized, they break off from philosophy and become their own disciplines. The discipline of philosophy, as we define it today, is simply what is left over (133-4, 142-3). Thus "philosophy is like a glacier: it moves so slowly that it appears to be going nowhere, but in the long run it radically transforms the world you live in" (143).

Van Norden also, however, thinks that some of the problems of philosophy, and the liberal arts, are self-inflicted, and he discusses these in chapter 5. In the first place, Van Norden thinks that philosophy has become overly technical and remote from daily life. Analytic philosophy, at its worst, can become an exercise in solving abstract thought-puzzles; Continental philosophy, at its worst, can become an exercise in using complex jargon (151-153). Van Norden doesn't exactly say so, but this is probably connected to the rise of the academy and the subsequent cloistering of philosophy within academia. This created a situation where academics write to impress other academics; they are positively rewarded for displays of intellectual virtuosity while the topic they display it about is unimportant. The anti-intellectualism Van Norden (119) notes in American culture might be a reaction to this tendency. It's important to remember that, until the rise of the modern research university (which took place in the late 1800's in America), most philosophers worked outside the academy and wrote for an educated but non-academic audience. Philosophers like Locke, Mill, Marx, and Sartre wrote not to impress their fellow academics but to persuade people to change the world. Even professional academics like Dewey and (when he wasn't being fired) Russell devoted a considerable amount of their work to influencing public opinion.

To address the problem of relevance Van Norden suggests that philosophy should focus on the question "What way should one live?" This does not mean that we should entirely neglect philosophical thought-puzzles, but rather that we can never allow these thought-puzzles to become ends in themselves, apart from the practical concerns which motivated them. It is important to note that this suggestion is not particularly new. Van Norden correctly traces it back to Socrates (151-3), but it motivates much of Ancient and Hellenistic philosophy down to Augustine and Boethius. Philosophers of that time saw philosophy primarily as describing a way of life, and sometimes even withdrew from society in order to live an alternate, philosophical way of life. The same approach can be found in the Existentialists, as well as in Chinese and Indian philosophy. Van Norden also, importantly, shows that the question of how to live our lives motivates some of the most seemingly abstract and technical thinkers of recent times. Bertrand Russell was motivated by a kind of mystical experience; Rawls' conception of justice was motivated in part by seeing the aftermath of the atomic bombs; Hare's prescriptivism was motivated by his experience as a Japanese prisoner-of-war in World War II (153-6). Thus, by focusing on how to live our lives, Van Norden does not seek to change philosophy so much as to restore its original meaning.

Van Norden also thinks the liberal arts have become intellectually lazy. Based on his experience, Van Norden thinks that most fields in the liberal arts have been colonized by some combination of the hermeneutic of suspicion and relativism. The hermeneutic of suspicion attempts to find the interests – economic, psychological, or otherwise – that are served by the text. The hermeneutic of suspicion can be a valuable tool when used in conjunction with other methods, but when used exclusively, it spares us any need to critically evaluate what the text actually says (139-40). Relativism – from the medieval "two truths" doctrine of Siger of Brabant to contemporary individual or cultural relativism – goes even further by holding that every person or group is entitled to its own opinion, and thus eliminates the need to think at all (18, 140-2). To address the problem of intellectual laziness, Van Norden suggests that philosophy is distinguished by a hermeneutic of faith, or more simply by the principle of charitable reading. In other words, we start with the assumption that the author may actually be right, and that it is therefore worthwhile to figure out what the author actually said. Of course, different authors take different positions, so we also need to understand and evaluate the reasons that various authors give for their own positions and against rival positions (159). The hermeneutic of faith explains the practical usefulness of philosophy: philosophy is particularly good at teaching general critical reasoning skills because the hermeneutic of faith holds philosophers to high standards of critical reasoning.

Philosophy as Van Norden conceives it also has a canon: a more or less defined (but never fixed) set of texts from its history that are acknowledged to be of the highest merit. The evaluative character of the canon – a canon implies that some works are better than others – is justified by the hermeneutic of faith; its historical character is justified by the pre-paradigm nature of philosophy. Of course the canon Van Norden suggests is much broader because it includes LCTP, but the LCTP supplements the mainstream canon rather than replacing it. In contrast to "Manicheans" who insist that we should entirely eliminate dead white men from the curriculum, Van Norden (2017, 159) holds that we should study all works of the highest quality, including both those written by (now-)dead white men and those that were not. Van Norden's (124, 195n40) expansive canon includes theists, both from the history of philosophy (Descartes, Berkeley, Leibniz, Kant) and from more contemporary times (Anscombe, MacIntyre, Charles Taylor). It also includes thoughtful conservatives. Thinkers like Burke, Matt Lewis, and Allan Bloom play by the rules of the hermeneutic of faith and advance serious arguments for their positions, so they deserve the same consideration from us. Of course taking an argument seriously, and teaching it, is very different from agreeing with it (82). The inclusion of thoughtful theists and conservatives, at the very least, prevents the pronounced left-leaning tendency of the liberal arts profession from hardening into what Mill[xi] calls dead dogma. At the most, they may sometimes be right. Transferred from philosophy to the wider world, Van Norden's position implies that we should take seriously qualified candidates like Bush 41, Dole, and McCain (again, taking a candidate seriously is very different from voting for him), although it does allow us to reject out of hand politicians like Trump, Bush 43, Reagan, and Palin (119-21, 125-6).

I find Van Norden's position appealing because it allows for change without falling into the pitfalls of some of the more naïve attempts at reforming the curriculum. Van Norden doesn't exactly say so, but it is possible to construct a kind of history of the liberal arts from his remarks. In the past, most fields in the liberal arts had canons that were as limited as the philosophy canon still is. Literature meant American and European literature; religion meant Catholicism, Protestantism, and perhaps Judaism; women's studies and Africana studies didn't exist; and so on.[xii] The reasons motivating this limitation were, again, probably a combination of cultural imperialism and battles over intellectual capital. Then at some point these fields underwent the kind of sudden, undirected change Van Norden warned about in chapter 3. Because excluded voices couldn't gain a fair hearing according to the old standards, the most obvious solution was simply to get rid of the standards. The liberal arts shifted from being reflexively and uncritically Eurocentric to being reflexively and uncritically left-wing. Relativism and the hermeneutic of suspicion replaced the hermeneutic of faith. Van Norden refers to the excesses of this period in his book: he was a graduate student at Stanford when the undergraduates agitated to eliminate the Western tradition from the curriculum (102-3). Philosophy is the last holdout. Thus philosophy, the most intolerant of the liberal arts, is also the most academically rigorous.[xiii] Allan Bloom would feel vindicated.

Only afterwards did the problems of this revolution become apparent. With no point from which to gain a critical purchase, postmodernism proved easy to subvert. If everything is discourse, then why shouldn't Russian bots make up an alternative discourse? If science is defined by its institutional practices, then why not eliminate global warming by firing the scientists? If men and women have different values, then what is wrong about excluding women from cutthroat boardrooms? Or, to take an example a bit closer to home, if we should all avoid offending one another in the name of tolerance, then why shouldn't a Christian claim to be offended by an art installation of a crucified frog, and demand that it be taken down in the name of tolerance? The student agitators of the 1960's can hardly have wanted Trump to become President, but they may have inadvertently helped to create an intellectual environment which made the Trump presidency possible.

Van Norden points to a third way. Rather than sudden, undirected change coming from below, we could have intelligently directed gradual reform led by the professoriate. This gradual, Deweyan reform would give us the best of both worlds: it would both expand the canon and preserve the standards of the philosophical field. Because it preserves the high standards of the field, Van Norden's conception of philosophy would be able to teach general thinking skills and develop informed citizens. Because it insists on arguments, Van Norden's conception of philosophy provides a critical purchase. The bare assertion that we should adopt multiculturalism can easily be countered by the bare assertion that we should not. The argument that we should adopt multiculturalism because it leads to innovation and critical self-reflection is much harder to refute. (It also leads to a much richer notion of multiculturalism as cultural interchange instead of bare coexistence). And, because Van Norden's conception of philosophy is oriented toward questions that affect everyone, not just philosophers, it should be relatively easy to communicate these arguments to a general audience.

The only question is whether Van Norden's reform can come about. At a purely logical level, there is no reason why it could not. In fact, as Van Norden shows, if we consistently applied the standards of the philosophical field, we would have to make these changes. But the philosophical profession runs on institutional logic rather than philosophical logic. Van Norden writes mostly about top-50 philosophy departments (as determined by Brian Leiter) or sometimes just doctoral programs (2-3, 162-3n3-8). At this level, the prospects for change appear relatively bleak. Because these departments judge themselves mostly in terms of their academic prestige in the eyes of other researchers, they are relatively insulated from the external forces which Van Norden thinks will drive change, such as student demographics and the rise of China and India. At the same time, because these departments already occupy the top positions in the field, they have the most incentive to preserve the status quo. Thus most top programs will probably continue to emphasize Analytic metaphysics and epistemology for some considerable time.

At lower levels, however, the equation changes. Prestige is less important; meeting the needs of students becomes more important. Thus the change Van Norden refers to may already have happened. My department head at La Salle University works in all three medieval traditions with a focus on Islamic Philosophy. My catch-all program head at Penn State Abington specializes in the history of Buddhist medicine. I previously taught at Rowan University, which includes an Asian philosophy specialist in a permanent faculty of seven. The rise of untenured teaching faculty and adjuncts, problematic as it is, also creates space for exploration. If a tenure-track faculty member researches in LCTP it costs the department prestige. The faculty member could always, as Van Norden (34) suggests, work to develop an AOC in an LCTP, but even this takes away from the time they could be writing. In contrast, if a teaching professor or adjunct with no research expectations offers a class and it attracts enough students to run, the class can be considered a success, regardless of the topic. In my own experience as an adjunct, I've never encountered obstacles to offering LCTP courses. Penn State Abington allowed me to offer a course in Asian Philosophy, simply because the course description was on the books, and it turned into a regularly-offered course. My program director at Drexel University hired me to teach Critical Reasoning, but regarded my AOC in Asian philosophy as an advantage, and supported my efforts to offer special-topics courses in Arabic Philosophy and Jewish Philosophy. Of course, all of these opportunities could also be viewed as a sad reflection on the state of higher education: as the institution of the university itself breaks down, the institutional resistance to LCTP is breaking down with it.

Notes

1. Bryan Van Norden, Taking Back Philosophy: A Multicultural Manifesto (New York: Columbia University Press, 2017), xxiii-xxiv, 8-11.

2. Nicholas Tampio, "Not All Things Wise and Good Are Philosophy." Aeon September 13, 2016, https://aeon.co/ideas/not-all-things-wise-and-good-are-philosophy; Jay Garfield, Foreword to Taking Back Philosophy, xvi; Van Norden, Taking Back Philosophy, 12-3.

3. Tampio; Garfield xiv-xv; Van Norden 19.

4. Margaret Atherton, ed. Women Philosophers of the Early Modern Period (Indianapolis: Hackett Publishing Company, 1994), 2-3, 47

5. See, for instance, Alexander Altmann, Introduction to Jerusalem, by Moses Mendelssohn, trans. Allan Arkush (Hanover, NH: University Press of New England, 1983), 26-7.

6. Ibn Tufayl, Abu Bakr Muhammad. The Improvement of the Human Reason, Exhibited in the Life of Hai Ebn Yokdhan: in which is demonstrated, by what Methods one may, by the Meer Light of Nature, attain the Knowledg of things Natural and Supernatural; more particularly the Knowledge of God, and the Affairs of another Life. Trans. Simon Ockley, 1708, www.gutenberg.org/ebooks/16831

7. Atherton 5.

8. Arthur Waldron, The Great Wall of China: From History to Myth (Cambridge: Cambridge University Press, 1990), 160, 164.

9. Jay Garfield and Bryan Van Norden, "If Philosophy Won't Diversify, Let's Call It What It Really Is," The Stone May 11, 2016, www.nytimes.com/2016/05/11/opinion/if-philosophy-wont-diversify-lets-call-it-what-it-really-is.html; Van Norden 36.

10. Thomas Kuhn, The Structure of Scientific Revolutions (Chicago: University of Chicago Press, 1962), ch. 2.

11. John Stuart Mill, On Liberty, 1859.

12. Garfield xx.

13. Garfield xx; Van Norden 139.

Scott Stein

Excerpt from *The Great American Deception* (Chapter 1)

Our second case was a real humdinger, which everyone knows is the most challenging variety of dinger. Maybe I'll tell you about it some time, if you have the required security clearance. Right now, however, I'm telling you the story of our first case. It might not have been a humdinger, but it more than made up for that by being quite a doozy.

* * *

The clocks didn't strike 13.

There were no clocks. That took a little getting used to. Out there, time mattered. In here, you could lose time completely if you didn't watch yourself. And in Frank Harken's business, minutes counted.

There were no clocks. Not in here.

The famous detective checked his wrist. 13:01.

His prospective client was late.

* * *

Or so I'm told. I wasn't there. At that precise moment I was in a compression carton rocketing at three times the speed of sound through a long-distance vacuum tube far beneath the Great American. Don't worry! I was securely ensconced in styrofoam and rather enjoyed the ride.

* * *

Harken checked his wrist.

13:04.

It was a fine afternoon at the food court, but all afternoons were fine at the food court as long as you weren't the one on trial. Serving french fries and justice in the same place was very convenient. Of that there was no doubt. Sunlight filtered through atrium windows, harmful radiation removed, beneficial vitamin D enhanced. Eighty-six eateries encircled 3,504 tables. There were an appropriate corresponding number of chairs, but I won't bore you with specifics.[1] Approximately 12,478 people were eating lunch and observing the legal proceedings.

Harken sat alone at a round table for two near sushi, diet pizza, and burger stands. A man in a meatball costume held a platter of mini-meatball samples for passing shoppers. The costume was made from protein-emulation and had the texture and aroma of a traditional Italian meatball. Steam emanated from its surface. Were his legs and arms not visible, were he not handing out samples on toothpicks to people walking by, were he not yelling, you would have had no reason to suspect he was anything but the largest meatball[2] you'd ever encountered. He was a born pitchman, and shouted with gusto, "Free meatballs! Get your free meatballs here! They're fat-free! They're meat-free! They're free-free! They're balls!" His booming voice seduced most browsing diners into grabbing a ball or two as they passed.

At 13:07, Harken's prospective client arrived.

Her name was Pretty Lovely, and she was neither. Her legs were longer than legs should be.[3] Her nose was a kind of straight that nature never intended. Her eyes were a shade of purple that could only be purchased in the best stores. Her black hair flashed with an audacious, rare weave of blinking lights. Her ears, however, were original equipment, and they were gorgeous. If you were into ears. Harken wasn't.

"Frank Harken, I presume?"

It was presumptuous of her, but correct.

"I'm Frank Harken. You're late."

"I would have been here sooner, but there was a shoe riot[4] in Blue Neighborhood 254."

"A shoe riot?"

"More of a skirmish, really. They ran out of size sevens and someone caught the business end of a stiletto."

Harken shook his head in disapproval. "Molk."[5]

She corrected him. "*Meople.*"

"*Meople?*"

"*Molk* is officially pejorative."

"Since when?"

"Since Wednesday. There was a poll. *Meople* is the preferred term in my demographic." Clearly, there was more to Pretty Lovely than her looks. Or less.

She extended her hand, not far enough for Harken to shake, then withdrew it with a flourish. "I'm Pretty Lovely.[6] But you can call me Pretty."

"What can I do for you, Ms. Lovely?" Harken motioned for her to sit.

Pretty Lovely sat, an operation that required minor legstension adjustments. When she had made herself comfortable and had managed to cross her legs, she swept her blinking bangs to one side. "I wish to hire you for a case. Case is the right word, isn't it? I've never hired a private detective before, but I'm desperate." She was definitely nervous.

"*Case* is fine. Why me?"

"Your reputation precedes you, Frank Harken."

"I've asked it to stop doing that. Damn thing never listens."

"A joke? At a time like this?"

"I would have made it seven minutes earlier, but you were late."

She let that pass. "Is it true that you've been out there?"

Harken nodded. "It's true. Lived my whole life out there till a couple years ago."

"Is it as bad as they say?"

"I don't know who *they* are or how bad they say it is. But yes, it's exactly as bad as they say. Probably worse. You think I'm in here because I prefer the ambience?" Harken gestured broadly at the people crowded all around.

In the center of the food court, a man stood accused of counterfeiting counterfeit pocketbooks. A leading producer of knockoff goods had charged the defendant with producing counterfeits of such poor quality, they undermined the value of the genuine fakes made by reputable counterfeiters. It was a serious offense. The dining jury of thousands listened to testimony by industry experts and carefully considered how they would vote on the matter as they dunked nuggets in sweet sauce.

Boos punctuated the closing remarks of the counterfeiter's defense. The attorney attributed her client's crimes to a traumatic upbringing that included being repeatedly beaten by fashionable parents who used high-end brand-name pocketbooks as disciplinary tools. Anyone who'd experienced such horrors could hardly be blamed if, years later, the pocketbooks he counterfeited failed to closely resemble the real thing. If he'd been fortunate enough to have parents who only beat him with low-end merchandise, he wouldn't have developed his painful aversion to quality luxury goods and would have made counterfeit pocketbooks indistinguishable from the real thing. The uproarious crowd, largely unconvinced, briefly eclipsed the pumping bass and grinding metal of a chainsaw song piping from speakers in the ceiling.

Harken glanced at the floor, muttered something about needing coffee, then looked at Pretty Lovely. "Enough about me. You didn't ask to meet so I could sign autographs."

"It's my little sister. She's missing..." Her voice trailed off.

"Missing what?"

"Missing, as in I don't know where she is."

"I thought you paused, that you were going to say another word."

Pretty Lovely adjusted her legstensions again as she uncrossed her legs. "I didn't, and I wasn't."

"It sounded like you did, and you were."

"Are you always this easy to talk to?"

"No. Sometimes I'm downright difficult."

"It's a wonder you get hired at all." The lights in her hair had started blinking more rapidly. She swept her bangs from her eyes.

Harken said, "That's the problem with having a reputation that goes around preceding you all the time. It's a curse, really. People want to hire you no matter how much you try to dissuade them."

"I'm not dissuaded. What about my sister?"

"What about her?" Harken almost sounded annoyed.

"She's missing."

"Right. That. Ms. Lovely, how old is your sister?"

"Twenty-two."

"What makes you think she's missing?"

"I don't know where she is."

"You said that already. There are a lot of people whose location is unknown to you. They aren't all missing."

"Is everything a joke to you? Do you take anything seriously?"

Harken shrugged. "I take serious things seriously."

"This is serious. My sister is missing."

"How do you know she's missing?"

"She disconnected. I haven't heard from her since yesterday."

"So?" Harken was unconcerned.

"So? So?"

"That's what I'm asking you," Harken said.

"So? So, she's never disconnected."

"Maybe she disconnected to get a little peace and quiet. Some people do that. You can't declare a person missing just because she disconnects for a while, not without evidence of a crime."

Pretty Lovely jumped to her feet and raised her voice. "My sister isn't some people! She's never disconnected! Never! As in, not ever! Something is wrong!"

Harken waited a moment and motioned for her to sit back down. After she adjusted her legstensions and sat, he asked, "Have you filed a missing person report with GAS?"

She was calmer. "I went to GAS.[7] They were no help."

"What did they say?"

"They said maybe she disconnected to get a little peace and quiet. They said some people do that. And they said without evidence of a crime, there was no basis for declaring a person missing just because she disconnected."

"And that's when you called me?"

"That's when I called you."

"Ms. Lovely, it's only been one day. She's probably just taking a break. There's no law against disconnecting in here. Another couple of days, she'll reconnect. Most people do. Why not wait?"

Pretty Lovely considered him with her purplish eyes. "You're not connected, are you?"

"No, I'm not."

"Why?"

"I don't want to be in touch with everyone all the time, don't know how you people manage to think with the constant stream of updates."

"You don't even wear lenses?"

Harken laughed. "You know how easy those are to hack?"

"Frank—may I call you *Frank*?"

"Let's stick with *Detective Harken* for now. If that goes well, we can consider working up to *Mister*."

Harken couldn't tell if he'd insulted Pretty Lovely—her sculpted face betrayed no emotion. "Detective Harken, because you're not connected, you can't possibly understand. My sister never goes five seconds without checking in."

"Five seconds?"

"Or maybe 10 minutes. I'm not good with time. The point is, if she's disconnected, something bad has happened."

"You don't know that."

"I do know that. But even if you think I'm mistaken, how could it hurt to take my case? If nothing's wrong, you'll find her right away. This should be easy money for a man with your reputation and all the preceding you it does."

"That reputation causes me nothing but trouble. I should probably trade it in for a smaller one that knows how to keep its mouth shut."

She was quiet for a long moment. Finally, she said, "Joke all you want. You're supposed to be the best, and I need your help. Please, I just want to find out where she is, that she's safe. I can pay whatever your rate is."

Even though easy money was some of the best there was, taking on Pretty Lovely as a client went against Frank Harken's better judgment. But, as he sometimes told me, if he didn't do things against his better judgment once in a while, he'd never get out of bed in the morning. At least for *this* lousy decision, he'd be getting paid.

* * *

Frank Harken tried unsuccessfully to get a cup of coffee on the way back from his meeting with Pretty Lovely. The lines at the food court were too long and the jury of thousands had become even more boisterous once a new trial had started, involving a woman accused of stealing her friend's digital contacts and going on a shopping spree under false lenses. Harken left the food court with all due haste, knowing that heading home would take him past Beans and Nothing Less, a gourmet coffee kiosk with suspiciously existential decor. Its beverages were on the exotic side for his tastes, but there wouldn't be much of a line since many of its regular customers were rarely awake that early in the afternoon.

He was inconvenienced, though not entirely shocked, when he discovered that his access to coffee was blocked. GAS officers had cordoned off the area. They were forever cordoning off one thing or another, and often both. Yellow tape imprinted with *Great American Security* separated Harken from the coffee kiosk, which was near Feet the People, whose clerks were being questioned about who'd wielded the red stiletto. The store manager was being chastised for not keeping a proper stock of size sevens. She could face a stiff fine. A career in shoes was not for the faint of heart.

Neither was a career as a famous detective, especially without coffee. Don't worry! Frank Harken would have a superb cup when he got home. I'd make sure of that.

Notes

1. 14,715

2. Unless you were among the lucky few to have visited the recently opened Spherical-Food exhibit at the Great American Culinary Museum in Orange Neighborhood 423, which had on permanent display the largest meatball ever made (1,503.8 pounds, after cooking).

3. By 3.4 inches; Legstensions peaked in popularity in 2075. (Not to be confused with Legspanders, an inferior product that came to market first but was discontinued after explosive parts failure left eight customers legless.)

4. The deadliest shoe riot in Great American history was the Sandal Brawl of 2064, in which there were 71 fatalities. The tragedy was blamed on a combination of supply negligence and deep discounts.

5. Mall Folk were people who had spent their entire lives in the Great American, or who had lived there long enough to have embraced its customs and culture.

6. Self-naming and name changing started as a Great American fad in 2068 before becoming common practice by 2073. While frequent changes were not typical, some practitioners were known to change names daily. Extreme types changed names several times per day. Name Deafness was not recognized as an official disorder until 2084, though there were documented cases of people unable to respond to any name as early as 2079.

7. Great American Security.

Kathleen Volk Miller

At Harleigh Cemetery

It's been 200 years since Whitman's birth and 15 years since my husband's death and the two are not connected, other than the fact that Walt's self-made crypt is down the lane from my husband's grave.

My husband's grave. It's 15 years later and I still don't know if I did the right thing. We didn't talk about what we wanted to do with our bodies when we died because we didn't think we'd die.

Even when he was diagnosed with cancer, even when he lost so much weight, even when each chemo embolism made him lose his gorgeous thick black hair. This period of our lives seemed like it would be a blip on the screen one day, a stage of our lives we'd remember with a shudder.

So when he died I had no idea what he'd want. I had no choice but to do what I thought made the most sense: If I buried him, the kids would have a place to go. If I bought two plots next to each other, the kids could see us both at the same time sometime far far down the road. Don was an environmental technician, a camper, hiked most of the Appalachian trail, Montana, Washington state—fly fishing was his passion.

My brothers-in-law said there'd be nothing available, that Harleigh Cemetery had been "sold out" for at least 50 years. If my husband needed to be buried, he had to be there. Like everything else, my concern was the kids; if they wanted to go there, they should be able to go and Harleigh is a 5-minute car ride or a 25-minute walk. It felt like truly the least I could do to keep him close.

Stubborn as Whitman, I called anyway. Not only was there one grave available, there were two, side-by-side, close to Whitman's crypt and also less than 100 feet away from the poet Nick Virgilio, under a huge oak tree, on a gentle slope facing a pond—it was almost too much to bear.

What do Whitman and I have in common? Maybe we live the same way: my brother's death, my first gut-punch of a death, didn't make me cower in a corner, but instead makes me want to squeeze every second out of every day until the day becomes as breathless as me.

Whitman focused on the construction of the mausoleum, with one of his concerns being that the iron gate at the front swing smoothly through the decades. In contrast, Don had no input on the style of his burial, and I regretted the coffin immediately after I bought it—too ostentatious—not my husband. Yes, it was made of natural oak, but—the brass! The lining!!!

Later, I tried to make up for the coffin by buying a huge boulder for the headstone. I explained what I envisioned to one of his fly-fishing friends and he found a place and one of his fly-fishing friends found a place that would smooth and glaze one side. I'm still happy with the words I chose: *Son, Brother, Husband, Father, Friend,* and his name. Simple.

Whitman's grave has thousands of visitors a year. We don't go to Don's often enough, though I don't even know what "often enough" means, exactly. The kids and I are still always stuttering around, bumbling about with ways to mark his death anniversary, his birthday, Father's Day—is it good or bad that all three of those markers are within a week of each other or is that just another question I'll never be able to answer?

Meanwhile, we've had toasts, thrown things in fires, gotten tattoos, and sometimes even had the nerve to pretend it wasn't happening.

On the fifth anniversary, a family friend who barely left our sides in those early years and my new partner came out on the back steps of our home with helium balloons for us to take to the cemetery. These men were awkward and lovely, stopping us in the driveway with this surprise as we got in the car to go, alone, to the cemetery on a brilliant blue-sky day.

We were meant to each hold a balloon, then say or think of messages for Don—and let go.

Somehow, as we moved to take the balloons, two floated free. We had all been talking at once, my beautiful generous children assuring these men, who had tried so hard to make it okay, that their idea was so great. We all fell silent and watched the balloons drift further and further away.

I remember the hot tears I willed away, my rigid smile, when I remember this moment. I remember looking at everyone's face, the loves of my life and all in a complicated pain. Someone, I don't remember who but it was surely one of the kids, said: "Let another one go, too. It will be better if we all hold on to just one."

All of us always trying to fix things, all of us always trying to make sure the rest were okay. All of us always trying to ease the other, to still make something of this beautiful day.

Whitman would go on to have his father, mother and siblings exhumed from their graves in New York and moved to his Harleigh Cemetery tomb. But now, I'm not sure I still want to be buried there. Maybe I could have half of me buried there, and the rest cremated—the other half in the ocean, to join my mother, sister and brother.

Is that OK? Should I even make this decision now? If the kids need a marker, I think I'd like just a big freaking rock with no engraving. Wouldn't that be something—to be silent after all these years of trying to make sense of myself through words? People tell me that I am strong and I don't tell them that I am devastated; I let them believe their truths; it's best for all of us.

I always loved "Song of Myself," but wasn't a huge devotee of Whitman and never really studied him intensively, though I can sing the "Fame" song all the way through. But these years of always acknowledging Whitman when I go to Harleigh, has made me feel closer somehow, like I have more of a right to him, if that makes any sense. I visit my husband's site; I blow a kiss toward Walt.

What Whitman and I have in common: I am often obscene. I also had countless jobs. We both love champagne. We both believe in democracy and poetry that can be easily understood. We both believe in idealism, individuality, and divinity in the trees.

I know this. Don don't know he was going to die. I don't want to, ever. Walt tried to make the best of it.

Part of Verse 52 is inscribed on an onyx marker at the Whitman site:
I depart as air—I shake my white locks at the runaway sun;
I effuse my flesh in eddies, and drift it in lacy jags.
I bequeathe myself to the dirt, to grow from the grass I love;
If you want me again, look for me under your boot-soles.

I'd like to place these last three lines at my husband's site, though I know I won't, instead I'll just recite them in my heart:

Failing to fetch me at first, keep encouraged;
Missing me one place, search another;
I stop somewhere, waiting for you.

Scott Warnock

Can We, Should We, Introduce Adversity, Even Pain?

Each day that I head over to my job at Drexel, I think about how I get to be around amazing, motivated students. That's one of the main benefits of the career I chose.

I say that so you know that I'm on the students' side. I respect them, and I find I'm able to avoid the, ahem, generationism that I see exhibited by some of my friends who aren't around the 20-something set much. In other words, sure, these young kids have grown up a certain way and expect certain things, but they also have confronted bigger challenges, including financially, than most of the people my age had to deal with.

I think it's easy for older people to pile on, but I don't totally agree with it all. However, I do think many of these students, perhaps in contrast with the experiences of their peers in other parts of the world, have been protected from significant adversity. By us, their loving parents.

For the past few summers, I have conducted a workshop at my local library about writing the college admissions essay for rising seniors.

Using prompts from the Common Application, I show these students—who, by the way, are giving up two summer nights for this endeavor—that they have multiple paths to their essay. The hero motif, that grand tale of adversity overcome, has great appeal, so many students spend their workshop time brainstorming about a personal adversity story as their way "in."

I'm struck by the difficulty that most of them have had in defining such an event. They are aware of it too.

As I read many of these mechanically correct, tidy pieces about we-weren't-the-best-team-but-we-won-the-big-game or at-first-I-got-a-C+-but-with-hard-work-I-got-an-A, it strikes me this is exactly how we have raised them: Not to have to want, to need, to suffer.

Sometimes, in those many dark moments that you are inevitably going to have as a parent, it makes me wonder if I've done the right things.

I remember an experience I had many years ago as a high school wrestling coach. One of our guys had an aching shoulder. Mind you, this kid was tough as nails and went on to be one of the best wrestlers in the state. His dad was a specialist physician. Before an early-season, high-stakes match, he gave his son an injection. Our trainer expressed concern about this, and the dad simply replied: "Do you want my son to be in pain?"

At the time, I didn't get it.

Now I think I do. Where is the line between allowing your kids to face adversity/toughing it out and suffering? If we can take the pain away, won't we?

Yet, without adversity at a young age, how will they shape themselves as they get older? It's a question we must ask, but it is clouded by the over-involvement many of us have had in their lives, which means we have seen their every grimace and reaction. Every social media snub. Every missed goal. Every almost grade. How do we *not* step in?

I was talking to some of those smart Drexel students about this topic recently, but I struggled to voice what I wanted to say. Parents don't wish for adversity, and in most cases, we don't plant it in our kids' lives. In the past, we mostly didn't need to.

But we all know they will face plenty of difficulty at some point. And if you haven't experienced adversity, will you be ready later on? In the story of your life, what will you have to write about?

Contributors

Hasala Ariyaratne is a Business and Engineering major with minors in Finance and Analytics. His hobbies include sports photography, hiking, and travelling. He is currently an opinion writer for the *Triangle*.

Michael Bash is currently a Mechanical Engineering student at Drexel University. Prior to attending Drexel, he spent four years as shipboard engineer onboard a 270-foot United States Coast Guard cutter which was home-ported in Boston, MA. His primary purpose on board was to operate, maintain, and repair the electrical generation and propulsion systems of the ship, so that they could successfully carry out the mission, whether it be a simple vessel inspection, an adrenaline-driven chase with drug smugglers, or a direct trip into a storm for a search and rescue case.

Christopher Bream was raised on a family-owned apple orchard just outside historic Gettysburg, PA. He is majoring in International Business, and is minoring in both English and Spanish. Throughout his life, he has enjoyed creative writing as a means of expression and reflection. Christopher is currently completing his final Co-op as an Administrative Paralegal at Morgan Lewis.

Marisa Browne is a freshman, at Drexel University from Willow Grove, PA. She is a pitcher on the softball team and has spent many years on the highway traveling to softball games. Her work was inspired by Tumblr posts.

Amy Carson is currently a Music Industry student with a focus in Recording Arts and Music Production. In her free time, she enjoys knitting, sewing, and making music, and genuinely loves the process of presenting concepts and ideas in the form of essays.

Upoma Chakraborty is a second-year English major. She is interested in possibly pursuing a law degree specializing in immigration law and most definitely interested in documenting the experiences of first generation and second generation immigrants to America, as can be read in her stories and poems. She attributes her love for books and writing to her parents and while she has had other previous publications, it never gets old to see her name in a book.

Humna Chaudhry is currently an undergraduate student studying management information systems at Drexel University's LeBow College of Business. From a young age, she's loved to write, something she hopes to continue during her time at Drexel. Humna is also passionate about politics, photography, and traveling. In fact, she has competed in national debate tournaments, maintains a photography-focused Instagram account, and is preparing to go study abroad during her sophomore year.

Amanda Christian is a senior Graphic Design student minoring in Fine Arts and Art History. Her love for design and writing stem from her passion for mass communication and social reform. Outside of school, Amanda enjoys hiking, volunteering at local events, and exploring new Philly restaurants with friends.

Nishat Fariha is a Philadelphia native, who is currently studying Biology. You can often find her typing away at either Pearlstein or Korman while sipping on Dunkin iced coffee. Nishat is a self-proclaimed coffee and tea enthusiast and the proud owner of her own online shop, *Nishicake.*

Chris Faunce went to La Salle College High School in Cheltenham, PA. He now commutes to Drexel University as a freshman studying Civil Engineering. His work is previously unpublished.

Tim Fitts lives and works in Philadelphia. He is the author of two short story collections, *Hypothermia* and *Go Home and Cry for Yourselves*. His stories have been published by over thirty journals, including *Granta, The Gettysburg Review, Shenandoah,* and more.

Valerie Fox has published several books, including *The Real Sky*, which is a collaborative work with artist Jacklyn Niemiec, and *The Rorschach Factory*, a book of poems. She has published writing (poems, flash fiction) in *Hanging Loose, The Irreal Cafe, Philadelphia Stories, Across the Margin, Literary Orphans, Reflex Fiction*, and other journals.

Jordan Franklin is a Computer Engineer at Drexel University. When he was young, he loved taking pictures on his Father's old Canon. At 16 years old he got his first Nikon. From there he began shooting architecture, and abstract subjects.

Sophie Geagan is a freshman at Drexel University studying biomedical engineering with a minor in chemistry. She currently writes poetry for Maya Literary Magazine and sings soprano in the University Chorus. Before Drexel, she wrote and edited for *Facets*, her high school's literary magazine.

Natasha Hajo (Drexel '19) majored in English and minored in Writing and Philosophy. She has been involved with Writers Room since her sophomore year and was a writer-in-residence for the Canon TRIPOD project 2017-19. "Layers in Three Parts" appeared in *Anthology 5: Notes to Self* (from Writers Room).

Timothy Hanlon has been described by critics as "Two steps above average," "Rain Man with puns," "The pinnacle of Dad Fashion," and "The ultimate friend group Mom." Tim is currently in his sophomore year pursuing a major in biology with a minor in neuroscience and certificate in writing and publishing. In the future, Tim hopes to become a medical doctor with particular interest in surgery. At the old age of 20, Tim enjoys a nice, quiet night in with some ice cream and the rare movie that is as funny (looking) as him.

Heather N. Heim is currently working toward a Bachelor of Arts in English, a minor in French, and an accelerated Master of Science in Technical Communications. In addition to completing co-ops at The Philadelphia College of Osteopathic Medicine and Oracle, she has also worked as a peer reader at the Drexel Writer Center, a copy editor at *The Smart Set,* and a contributor at isportsweb.com. When she has time, Heather loves watching baseball and traveling.

Briyanna Hymms is a Drexel alum (BS Biology '18) and is exploring career choices. She is working as a lab tech, but is secretly a poet, painter, gardener and amateur banana bread baker. Her writing evokes feelings and her art creates connections. She shares her creativity with loved ones and leaves a trail of paper cranes wherever she goes. Her work included here previously appeared in *Anthology 5: Notes to Self* (from Writers Room).

Izzy Kaiser is a freshman nursing major from Sandy Hook Connecticut. In her free time she plays field hockey for the Drexel club team. She also loves to cook and spend the majority of her time outside. While Izzy has little professional writing experience, it has always been something she has excelled at.

Kevin Karnani is a Computer Science major in the Class of 2023. He is in the 5-year co-op cycle and wishes to participate in the BS/MS program as well as attain a dual minor in Spanish and Mathematics. Albeit he was never a fan of creative writing, academic research is one of his fortes. He has written various academic papers in both English and Spanish on ideas such as language acquisition, automation, and the influence of music on culture.

Theodoros Katerinakis combines industrial, military, and academic experience in information theory, banking, and critical environments. He holds a PhD in Organizational Behavior and an MSc in Communication Science focused on cooperative networks and negotiation management, both from Drexel. He serves as an Adjunct Faculty in Drexel COAS and LeBow College of Business, for which he had prepared master classes DVDs on business resilience. Currently a member of Drexel On-line Council and SCDC Coordinator for Greece. His latest Springer book *The Social Construction of Knowledge in Mission-Critical Environments* uses aviation cases to explain innovation and knowledge management.

Mary Kilgallon is a first-year student at Drexel University, studying Animation and Visual Effects. When she isn't doing CGI homework at her computer, she can be found reading, sketching, and writing whatever stories pop into her head. Although this is her first published piece, more of Mary's writing and artwork can be found on YouTube, Instagram, and ArtStation under her name.

Viktor Kim is an international student from Russia who is majoring in Biomedical engineering. Viktor is an aspiring physician/scientist.

Elizabeth Kimball is a member of Drexel's Department of English and Philosophy. Her research interests include college writing, public and community writing, and civic and engaged learning. She serves as co-chair of the executive board of the Philadelphia Area Council of Writing Program Administrators. Her work included in *The 33rd* previously appeared in *Anthology 5: Notes to Self* (from Writers Room).

Miriam Kotzin recently completed her 50th year as a creative writing and literature professor at Drexel University. Her collection of short fiction, *Country Music* (Spuyten Duyvil Press 2017), joins a novel, *The Real Deal* (Brick House Press 2012) and a collection of flash fiction, *Just Desserts* (Star Cloud Press 2010). She is the author of five collections of poetry with the most recent, *Debris Field* (David Robert Books 2017). Her fiction and poetry have been published or are forthcoming in *Shenandoah, Boulevard, Smoke Long Quarterly, Eclectica, Goliad Review, Mezzo Cammin, Offcourse,* and *Valparaiso Poetry Review,* among other periodicals, and in anthologies. She is a contributing editor of *Boulevard.*

Harriet Levin Millan is a prize-winning poet and novelist. She is the author of three books of poetry, *The Christmas Show, Girl in Cap and Gown,* and *My Oceanography.* She is also an author of the novel, *How Fast Can You Run.* She holds an MFA from the University of Iowa and teaches writing at Drexel and is the direct of the English Department's Certificate Program in Writing and Publishing.

Lynn Levin is a poet, writer, translator, and teacher. She is the author of seven books, including the poetry collection *Miss Plastique* (Ragged Sky Press, 2013); a translation from the Spanish, *Birds on the Kiswar Tree* by Odi Gonzales (2Leaf Press, 2014); and, with co-author Valerie Fox, *Poems for the Writing: Prompts for Poets* (Texture Press, 2019 second edition, 2013 first edition). Her poems have appeared in *The Hopkins Review, Artful Dodge, Mezzo Cammin,* and in several TV, and *The Bloomsbury Anthology of Contemporary Jewish American Poetry.* She teaches at Drexel University. Her website is www.lynnvinpoet.com.

Tracy Marcelis is an undergraduate student that is currently majoring in Biological Sciences in the College of Arts and Sciences. When she is not studying or in the lab, she likes to spend her time reading, writing, or painting. Previous writing experience includes writing for her high school's literary magazine and media outlets.

Carol McCullough writes to give life to her fantasies, dreaming out loud on paper, to capture things that might otherwise slip away—remembering, exploring, processing, recording, sharing, and celebrating—because the world is filled with wonders too fantastic to ignore. She is an Afrolachian poet and memoirist at heart, a native West Virginian now residing in Philly, re-writing her life's story. Her work included in *The 33rd* previously appeared in *Anthology 5: Notes to Self* (from Writers Room).

Jonson Miller grew up in Johnstown, Pennsylvania and now lives in Bucks County with his partner Jo. His poems have appeared in *Blue Collar Review, Schuylkill Valley Journal,* and *Ninnau.* These poems are part of a larger project about the history and meaning of Pennsylvania, especially as experienced by his ancestors and his experience of growing up in a working-class family in the context of the state's deindustrialization.

Karim Khaled Mohamed is a second-generation immigrant from a mixed ethnic background including North African and European countries. He found his passion for medicine at a young age and has been working towards his goal ever since. Through hard work and determination, he hopes to make strides in the fields of medical ethics and research in the field of oncology.

Tracy Ng, a first generation college student, is a freshman Chemistry major who aspires to become a veterinarian. In her free time, she enjoys improving her cooking, watching Asian dramas, and writing poetry. Often times, Tracy can be found browsing bookstores or exploring eateries.

Isabella Pappano is a biological sciences major whose passions include libraries, coffee, feminism, and brunch. During the summer, she works as a classroom assistant in a special needs elementary school. She hopes to study the brain and perhaps write on the side in the future.

Tori Popescu is an international student from Romania studying Marketing and Business Analytics with a Minor in Psychology at LeBow College of Business. Tori has a passion for writing since she started her first diary when she was seven years old. She is constantly writing about her college experiences on her personal blog, applying concepts of philosophy and psychology in her writings. She is currently the founder of Flow, a mindfulness club on Drexel's campus, and How to College, a project aimed to help.

Bibhav Pradhan is a music industry major. His focus is on music production and writing. He has written several poems and articles for newspapers in Nepal.

Kyle Prekeris is a BS/MS student in Chemical Engineering with a concentration in Biological Engineering and a minor in Philosophy graduating in June 2020. He enjoys reading fiction, science fiction, and fantasy novels.

Anh Minh Quach is an international student from Saigon, Vietnam. She is a first-year Biology major with an interest in research in pathobiology. She loves The Beatles, bacteriophage, and very long walks in which she can indulge in her passion for birdwatching and plant-spotting. She sings, plays the piano, and does photography in her free time and is still looking for the right moment to add photos of birds to her collection. She has written short pieces inspired by her upbringing in urban Vietnam; her poem on spring in her hometown, completed while she was in the shower, was published in her high school's literary magazine.

Sanjana Ramathan is an amateur writer from New Jersey. She is interested in creative media and screenwriting. She writes poetry and short stories in her spare time.

Don Riggs studied French from the fourth grade through his Ph.D. His reading of comic books dates from the same era and has evolved to graphic novels. He likes to write reviews for scholarly journals of the fantastic because he gets free books.

Nicole Robinson is a freshman English major trying to find her voice through writing. She is not new to receiving recognition for her writing, but this would be her first time winning a contest at Drexel University. In her spare time, she writes about local and national issues. Her interests include volunteering and filming.

William Roman is a person not much is known about, beyond his love for dinosaurs and the museums that house them. He started writing when he was ten, and continues to write on and off as he sees fit. With regards to writing, he advises aspiring authors to create the story only they can. Roman's work included in *The 33rd* previously appeared in *Anthology 5: Notes to Self* (from Writers Room).

Jack Santucci is an Assistant Teaching Processor of Political Science at Drexel University. His research covers both political parties and election reform episodes in the United States and on the local government level.

Ally Schneeman is a psychology major who loves writing, singing, playing guitar, and running cross country. Ally loves writing creatively and even writes some of her own songs in her free time. She is really looking forward to her sophomore year at Drexel!

David Seltzer is an adjunct professor of Philosophy at Drexel University. He has published in *International Studies on Philosophy, Philosophy Today, Listening, and Expositions*. His original research specializes in existentialism.

Scott Stein will publish his third novel *The Great American Deception* in 2020 (Tiny Fox Press). His short satirical fiction has been published in the *Oxford University Press Humor Reader, National Review, Art Times, Liberty, Reason, The G.W. Review*, and *Liberty*. He teaches at Drexel University.

Kate Stone is a second year student in the accelerated BA/JD program. She is majoring in English and enjoys all aspects of creative writing. She is involved with the Drexel Community Scholars, Honors College, and Drexel Autism support group.

Medina Talebi is a freshman political science major with an affinity for creative writing as well as journalism and photography, the latter of which she hopes to express as a writer for the *Triangle* and other student organizations in the future.

Kathleen Volk Miller is an essayist, a professor, and Director of the Graduate Program in Publishing at Drexel University. She has written for *O, The Oprah Magazine, Salon*, "Modern Love" in *The New York Times, Family Circle, Philadelphia Magazine* and other venues. "How We Want to Live," an essay, was chosen as the penultimate piece in *Oprah's Book of Starting Over* (Flat Iron Books, Hearst Publications, 2016). She is co-editor of the anthology, *Humor: A Reader for Writers* (Oxford University Press, 2014). She is co-editor of *Painted Bride Quarterly* and co-host of PBQ's podcast, Slush Pile. She has also published in literary magazines, such as *Drunken Boat, Opium*, and other venues. She consults on literary magazine start up, working with college students, and getting published in literary magazines.

Scott Warnock is a professor of English at Drexel and Director of the University Writing Program. He writes the bi-weekly blog/column "Virtual Children" for the website *When Falls the Coliseum*.

Alexis Washburn is a criminal; justice/ psychology major with a passion for issues relating to human rights. Among writing, her other joys lie in painting, music, and fashion. This is her first published piece and she is beyond humbled.

Jie Zhi is a recent 2019 BS/MS graduate from Drexel University's School of Biomedical Engineering. She is currently working as a Quality Engineer at DePuy Synthes. Her hobbies include obstacle course racing, CrossFit, cooking, and watching TV. She has several writing experiences, aside from Science and Engineering, in Honors courses such as Superheroes in America, Fashion as Material Culture, and Art and Creativity.